Repairing and Restoring Antique Furniture

John Rodd

VAN NOSTRAND REINHOLD COMPANY
NEW YORK   CINCINNATI   TORONTO   LONDON   MELBOURNE

© John Rodd 1976
Library of Congress Catalog Card Number 75-37898
ISBN 0-442-26970-6
Reprinted 1979

Printed in Great Britain

Published in 1976 by Van Nostrand Reinhold Company
A Division of Litton Educational Publishing, Inc.
450 West 33rd Street
New York, NY 10001

Van Nostrand Reinhold Limited
1410 Birchmount Road
Scarborough, Ontario M1P 2E7, Canada

16   15   14   13   12   11   10   9   8   7   6   5   4   3   2   1

Library of Congress Cataloging in Publication Data
Rodd, John
      Restoring and repairing antique furniture.
      Includes index.
1. Furniture—Repairing.   2. Furniture finishing.
3. Furniture—Collectors and collecting.   I. Title.
TT199.R62   684.1'044   75-37898
ISBN 0-442-26970-6

The author's workshop *(Roy Ettershank)*

Contents

Preface

'The lyf so short, the craft so long to lerne'. Those words were written by Geoffrey Chaucer in the fourteenth century but I first heard them from Frank Morriss who had served as ship's joiner aboard HMS *Condor,* a vessel equipped with both steam and sail.

He was typical of many craftsmen who have been so willing to share their knowledge and experience with others. For more than fifty years I have enjoyed the benefit of this exchange and would like to acknowledge my indebtedness and express my thanks.

I am grateful also to my customers who, for the most part, have been both a pleasure to serve and an important part of my education. People of culture are usually very well informed about their possessions and discussions with dealers are particularly helpful.

It is my hope that amateurs as well as professionals may receive some benefit from this work. In these days of high wages and greater leisure, it is perhaps they alone who are in a position to devote all the time desirable and their reward is both in the pleasure of the doing and in satisfaction with the result.

Lastly, regardless of the length of their hair or beard, I would like to dedicate this book to those young people who wish to live by doing their 'thing' with their hands; who are more interested in the quality of their environment than in joining the ranks of the big consumers and who value peace more than excitement.

1 The Role of the Restorer

When the restoration of a piece of antique furniture is contemplated, it is important that both the owner and the individual or firm which is to carry out the work come to an accord regarding exactly what is to be done.

Now it may be argued that any competent craftsman will know what to do. This may be true, but even well informed and experienced collectors and dealers will vary greatly in their instructions.

The first book which the author owned on antique furniture was called *The Present State of Old English Furniture* by R. W. Symonds (Duckworth 1921). Mr Symonds made much of the value of a good patina, and deplored the practice of French polishing. While perhaps he oversimplified the subject, his assertion that a French-polished antique is worth less than half as much as a similar piece with a good patina is often valid.

Now of what does this so desirable surface comprise? Perhaps it might be summarised under the following headings

A hand-made article
Restriction as to the original finish
Loving care in the home.

A hand-made article The foundation of the surface must have been made by hand. A planed surface is never quite flat although one is not normally conscious of the plane marks—they are there as almost invisible concavities caused by the rounded corners of the plane iron. Of course this effect is less marked in the more highly finished pieces, especially those made in the larger towns. In addition, all details such as turnings and mouldings reveal slight variations which, though not too obvious in themselves, produce that quality which might be called the human touch.

Restriction as to original finish Probably more nonsense has been written about this than about any other aspect of antique furniture, for one receives the impression that a good patina consists solely of linseed oil and beeswax. It is obvious, however, that any piece of furniture that has survived for more than a hundred years will have been subject to a great variety of polishes and creams containing various ingredients including stale beer, French polish, olive oil

7

and vinegar, all these being mentioned in old recipes.

It is generally conceded that linseed oil formed the foundation of practically all finishes until well into the twentieth century, when sprayed-on lacquers were introduced. Beeswax either hard or soft (dissolved in turpentine) certainly forms a major ingredient of most patinated surfaces of the oak and walnut periods and a small percentage of Georgian mahogany which has escaped the attentions of the French polisher.

There is evidence to support the belief that a varnish was used on walnut of the Queen Anne period but no varnish produced in modern times in the author's experience has failed to deteriorate in less than fifty years, unless protected from wear and light, and so he doubts the assertion that the polish on such pieces is indeed the original varnish.

In *The Cabinetmaker's Book of Prices* of 1824, seven shillings and sixpence was allowed for making a dining table of eight superficial feet, and for oiling and polishing the maker received nine pence extra or one tenth the construction price. Had this been French polish it would probably have been about a quarter. Ten years later it had become fairly well established as a separate trade and it soon became the standard polish in England and is still in use in spite of the introduction of spray finishes in the early thirties.

During that time its evolution went through many phases. As the materials used (mainly shellac) were imported at great expense in sailing ships from the Far East and labour was cheap, every effort was made to economise on material. Usually the thinner the coating, the better the job, both in regard to appearance and durability. Thus we may assume that early polishers did a very fine job quite different from the full bodied, shiny work common in the 1920s which Mr Symonds deplored in his book.

So popular was the new finish that the great houses had much of their furniture French polished and workmen from such firms as Gill & Reigate in London, or Marsh, Jones & Cribb in the North would spend a month or more carrying out the work in individual homes. People of less importance would be served in the same way by itinerant polishers who travelled the country. In many houses these visits became an annual service.

Towards the end of the nineteenth century, competition encouraged the use of short cuts mainly in the form of fillers such as cornflour or plaster of Paris. These substances fill the grain very well and when oiled become inconspicuous especially if colour (dragons' blood, tumeric and nigrosine were common) is added to the polish. Time and sun soon fade out the colour and the oil dries leaving a most unsightly substance in the grain which is very hard to remove, especially in veneer.

Later fillers using powdered silica coloured with pigment were better, but by that time shellac was cheap and labour dear, so the work was padded with a heavy coat to obtain a polish in the minimum time.

In the larger cities of North America, the finish followed the practices of the parent countries fairly closely until the last quarter of the nineteenth century when varnishing superseded the older methods. By this method a fairly thick layer was built up by repeated coats of a full-bodied oil varnish quite different from the early ones which were dissolved in alcohol. When sufficiently thick it was mechanically levelled by the use of abrasives and polished with rottenstone powder and water applied with the palm of the hand, hence the term 'hand polished' which was sometimes confused with French polished. After 1900 almost all North American factory-made furniture was finished in this way, until it too became supplanted by spray finishes which include a variety of formulae.

These finishes have been described in some detail because the author believes that a good patina is not possible on either a full-bodied French polish, a varnish or a spray finish.

Varnish is subject to checking—tiny cracks appear and gradually multiply until they completely obscure the grain; the film also becomes brittle and easily scratched with the fingernail, shattering into a yellow line. This normally takes place within twenty-five years.

Sprayed-on cellulose lacquer at first seemed to be the perfect finish as it did not check and withstood moderate heat, moisture and alcohol. Time however revealed that its bond with the wood was imperfect; first, small opaque patches appeared where it had started to separate and then it would not be long before it began to flake off. Improvements have been made but at its best it has an unwooden appearance; one has the impression of a piece of celluloid or some similar substance.

Loving care in the home   Most authorities refer to this as being of the greatest importance. Of course this treatment includes the use of an infinite variety of polish, waxes, oils, creams and cleaners. The most common ingredients in the past, however, were vegetable oils and wax. The oils had a tendency to form a paint in combination with dirt and soot and are responsible for a pleasing variation in tone at best, and just plain grubbiness at worst. The good feature of wax was that it wore off almost as fast as it was built up, remaining only in the pores of the wood.

The itinerant French polisher at his best added little more than a lustre to the effect and his materials became embodied with the other ingredients of the patina. Meanwhile, time was introducing two opposing effects—the wood beneath the surface and those areas in shadow were getting darker, while other surfaces exposed to much light were getting bleached. Thus the top of a dressing table which has been in front of a window may have faded to a pale yellow while its front remains a pleasing brown; if one were to remove a shaving from the surface, the wood beneath could be many shades darker.

Warping, shrinkage, wear, children, and pets each made their own contributions. Obviously when such a variety of factors are combined to produce a result, it is stupid to imagine that because a piece is old, it must be beautiful. An old piece is rarely in first class condition. Hopefully, a good application of wax with plenty of hard rubbing with cloth on flat areas and with a good shoe brush on carved and other irregular surfaces will suffice, but

if not, one or more of the following may be used:
  (a) Washing with soap and water
  (b) Washing with 'Bon Ami' or similar cleaner
  (c) Dressing with linseed oil and 6-0 finishing paper or fine steel wool and then waxing
  (d) Removing finish with solvents and starting a new foundation
  (e) Removing both finish and the surface of the wood by scraping and sanding and renewing the foundation.

The first three are simple enough and mainly a matter of trial, but the last two should be undertaken only if the uglification has got beyond a certain point. This point is of course a matter of opinion.

Assuming that removal of the finish has been decided, it will likely be the result of (a) fading, (b) wrong kind of finish having been applied, (c) large areas of the surface having been disturbed by repairs, stains, dirt, and abuse.

Sometimes the finish can be scraped off without much trouble, but usually a solvent will do a better job, especially in the carved or moulded parts. When this has been done the question will arise whether or not it will be worth while to remove the surface of the wood in order to uncover richness and figure beneath the bleached surface. This can be determined by trial in an inconspicuous place with alternate sandpapering and wiping with a rag moistened with raw linseed oil.

Assuming that the indication is positive, considerable skill and judgment will be needed if the character of the surface is to be retained. There are many kinds of power sanders which can be used, but the only satisfactory method is the use of a cabinet scraper followed by hand sandpapering with fine garnet paper. The reason for this is that a scraper removes an extremely thin shaving and the effect is immediately revealed. In carrying out this work, the object is to produce an even colour without removing all the blemishes, a surface that still looks used, but has beauty.

It now remains to consider laying a foundation on which a new patina may be built. This will vary with the character of the piece and whether or not colour matching will be involved, and it is perhaps the most difficult problem which a restorer faces.

Quoting from an old book we hear, 'the wood should first imbibe a little raw linseed oil'. This may be put on with a rag aided by a brush in the carvings and mouldings. It will result in the maximum darkness and richness, somewhat on the red side in some mahoganies. It is very possible that one's customer will find it too dark and rich and lacking the mellowness he likes, but since it is in the nature of things for it to become faded and monotonous in time, it might be better to err on the side of richness than to tone it down prematurely. More often than not the matching of colour is essential to a satisfactory job and staining and filling and other dodges have to be used.

The question of French polish as a further sealer and enricher before waxing now arises. A surface almost indistinguishable to the eye from a genuine patina may be achieved by the application of heated beeswax to which pigment may have been added. It is perfect for old oak except that it remains somewhat soft for tops or seats, but is lacking in lustre for more sophisticated woods. A thin application of French polish applied with a rubber which is kept as dry as possible and to which very great pressure is applied will fill the grain and bring out the lustre of the wood in a way that no other method can approach. During the process, toning and final colour matching is also carried out. The degree of finish to which it is brought will vary with the individual and also the wood. Rosewood and satinwood seem to call for the highest finish.

After thorough drying, a rubbing down with very fine steel wool will prepare it for the first waxing. From now on the owner must take over. A vigorous waxing with shoe brush and cloth once a week for a month, and once a month for a year is suggested. For table-tops and other areas of constant use the waxing is of course very much more frequent and simply as required.

Having disposed of the more esoteric part of the subject, let us now consider the following: loose joints, replacement of parts, veneers, drawers, backs, metalwork and mirrors.

Loose joints To quote again from Mr Symonds' book regarding tests for antiquity, 'Resilience in a piece is another simple test. A genuine old piece will invariably give a little under stress. A chair when sat in or a table when pressed down will give a little or rock slightly and then gather itself together as it were, and firmly resist further pressure. This is due to slight shrinkage of joints'. In 1921, when these words were published, it was less likely than now that reglueing had been carried out and also the average date of those pieces regarded as antiques would be a great deal earlier than would be the case today. It is true, however, that many pieces have resilience and one is instructed to 'tighten them up'. Normally, this is the correct procedure and once it is undertaken it is of the greatest importance that every loose joint be taken apart and properly reglued just as it was originally, even if it involves removing upholstery or steaming apart sound joints. If, for instance, the arm of a chair is glued leaving resilience in the other parts of the frame, on leaning back in that chair the arm joints will attempt to take the load which should be shared by seat rails and stretchers. Should the glue hold, it is more than likely that the wood will break.

On the other hand, if the piece is early and particularly if it is draw-bore pinned together, and the resilience is not excessive, reglueing should not be recommended. This would be particularly true if it were intended for a museum. To properly reglue an early gate-legged table for instance would involve the removal of about forty pins through its twenty-four tenons. Perhaps half of them could be marked and driven out, but many would have to be bored out and renewed. If the joints have been nailed, it is probable that the measures taken to dismantle it will result in still further damage.

Replacement of parts If a part is lost there is of course no alternative to

11

replacing it. A badly shattered or rotted part however may be either patched up or replaced and so the question arises as to which is preferable.

For use in a museum one should follow the basic rule and retain as much of the original as possible. Glueing a shattered piece is a somewhat tedious operation, for it often has to be done in a number of stages, each one being bound or cramped together and allowed to dry. Worm-eaten parts can be built up with sawdust and glue and treated with preservative to arrest further deterioration.

For domestic use there is no virtue in retaining a part which is either too weakened by decay, too badly broken or too poorly repaired to give satisfactory service. Replacing such components is part of the process of growing old with loving care and it should be carried out honestly with the most suitable materials available. This means if possible to match the original with a sound piece of the same kind of wood of the same age and colour. Failing this one should choose the most suitable. For instance when old beech is not available for seat rails of an upholstered chair, new beech or maple will serve because of their strength and tack-holding qualities. If part of the old rail was polished and showed, one would cut a ⅛ in veneer from it and glue it to the new rail.

The inlaying of patches to make good chipped corners, beads and other faults is a matter requiring patience, skill and some artistic judgment in making them harmonise with the original grain and figure. The smaller faults can be reduced with judicious rounding with sandpaper, particularly on chair legs where jagged edges may cause ladders in nylons. Other gaps may be filled with stick shellac but only if they are very small.

While a replacement should be honest and unashamed, there is no reason why it should not be matched to its mates even to the extent of rounding corners and beating it with a cat-o-five-tails made of chain. A perfectly smooth leg with square corners can look very unsightly on a well worn piece.

Although it has never been the author's practice, perhaps it would be useful if the restorer were to attach in an inconspicuous place on a piece on which he has worked a card listing any major replacements either made by him or by former restorers which he has noticed and any other details which he thinks might be interesting, and add his signature and date.

Veneers   Loose veneer is frequently the result of damage or movement due to shrinkage in the ground on which it is laid. No permanent repair can be made unless this is attended to first.

Having made sure that everything is sound beneath, all loose veneer should be glued down and missing pieces replaced. It is hardly necessary to say that they should match the surrounding veneer as well as possible regarding kind, age, colour and grain and a restorer should lose no opportunity to acquire old wood from which to make repairs and to cut veneers.

When for a number of reasons shattering has occurred extensively near the edges of, say, a desk fall or table-top, it is sometimes advantageous to remove a border all round and replace with cross banding. This has the advantage of providing ample veneer for other patches.

The outline of a patch should rarely be rectangular but cut to conform with the direction of the grain and be irregular in outline. Assuming that suitable veneer is available, patches in cross banding should always extend the full width.

Generally speaking, patches should be levelled and the finish matched, but an exception to this rule is the cross banding on walnut furniture of the William and Mary and Queen Anne periods and the following remarks also apply to the cross-banded mouldings.

This veneer was saw-cut by hand and is commonly about $\frac{3}{32}$ in thick. Age and shrinkage coupled with its extra strength usually result in its having taken up the form of a series of slightly cupped pieces. Each of these should be tested with a thin blade and those which are loose should be reglued but not levelled for it would destroy a characteristic of the period. If, however, very much is missing, then those places where new veneer dominates will have to be levelled.

Drawers The bottoms of drawers in which the grain runs from front to back (roughly before 1740 in England) are usually in a number of separate pieces or have become split. As this type of construction makes no provision for expansion and contraction with changes in humidity, it is not recommended that they be glued together with a strip added to make up for the shrinkage as is a common practice. If, however, the gaps are excessively wide, the boards loose and split, etc, they may have to be removed and any which are narrower than say, six inches, could be glued together and cleaned up before being replaced. It would be ideal if only hand-made wrought-iron nails could be used for securing them.

Drawers with bottoms grooved into the sides or slips and with grain running across should be rejointed where necessary, cleaned up and glued into the groove in the front; in this way they can swell and shrink beneath the drawer back. They should also be supported by screws placed as necessary into the lower edge of the back through slots in the bottom at right angles to the back edge.

Drawers of the walnut period which have a lip on ends and top of fronts (1715-35) are very vulnerable to having them damaged by being slammed in, especially when the front is twisted in such a way that one corner will take the shock. In order to reduce this danger, fit an additional stop behind the back of each side.

When the lower edges of the sides become worn they should be levelled off and refaced with strips glued in place to restore the original dimensions. Nothing is better for this purpose than hard maple from the point of view of smooth running, but American walnut may be chosen for its colour. The runners on which the drawers rest also often need refacing.

Another cause of unsatisfactory running is the top edges of the back dragging against the underside of the dust board above. When this occurs

13

there is usually room for a piece $\frac{3}{16}$ in × ½ in × 3in to be glued to the upper edge of the drawer sides at the back. After fitting, this will stop the drawer tilting.

Backs   The boards which form the backs of carcases are usually of such poor quality that many people assume that they are replacements made of old packing cases. Examination, however, will usually reveal some hand-wrought iron nails, although others may have been added when shrinkage etc has loosened them. Often, in fact, representative examples of the history of nails, including hand-wrought nails, cut nails, oval brads and modern finishing nails, are included.

Generally speaking there is little one can do without changing the character; however, strips of imitation leather may be glued over cracks to exclude dust and make a tidier job.

Occasionally, worm or rot have made replacement necessary of at least part. When this is the case, remove the back, cut out the rotted part, glue the remainder into 8-12 in boards, then replace them. New boards, perhaps from panelling from an old house, can then be added to make up the difference.

The correct way to make a back was to frame it up and panel it in the same way doors used to be made, and one finds this in pieces of the best quality. This would be the choice for a replacement if there were room for it. In many cases, however, it will be found that there is not sufficient clearance between the back of the drawers and the carcase back, in fact shrinkage of carcase sides sometimes prevents the drawers from coming flush with the front. In this event, a strong case can be made for using plywood which can be closely fitted and stiffen up the whole carcase. By reason of its thinness, it can also be packed out to give the extra clearance which may be necessary.

Metalwork   Dealers usually give instructions to remove any irons which have been fitted to reinforce old repairs. If they are old, made at the forge by a blacksmith, and especially if they are inlaid into the wood so that they are approximately flush, they should be left in place. If the joint is loose it should of course be reglued and made as strong as possible, but the irons should be retained.

The fact that they have been fitted and a certain amount of the wood cut away makes a weak repair without them almost inevitable unless a good deal of new wood is added.

Modern stamped brackets screwed on the surface should of course be removed and the repairs properly made.

It is always desirable to retain original handles, locks and any other metal parts even if some copies have to be made to complete the set. Replacements should be tolerated if they are reasonably appropriate and especially if they are old, but when, as so often happens, their style bears no resemblance to what might originally have been fitted, suitable reproductions should be chosen with spacing, if possible, matching the original holes. Modern copies are often rather poorly finished but they may be improved in the manner described on page 181.

Castors are commonly neglected when they are badly worn, to the detriment of floors and also, by reason of failing to roll easily, adding greatly to the strain on legs when the furniture is moved. They should be oiled and, if necessary, rebushed etc as described on page 178. Generally speaking the castor is beyond repair only when actually broken or when the pivot hole in the horn member is so worn that it has split down the side.

Should brass handles be polished or left alone? It is the author's opinion that brass should look like brass and that rules out the black or green patina some-times found. On the other hand, the brass mounts of a very fine old clock which had been pickled, buffed and lacquered certainly seemed out of harmony with the case. Between these two extremes there is a happy medium achieved by the occasional use of metal polish, giving the brasses a cared-for appearance.

If they have much modelling, such as the oval back plates of Sheraton handles or ormolu mounts of French furniture, they are usually lacquered and may be cleaned with a soft brush and soapy water immediately dried off to prevent damage to the surrounding woodwork. If badly tarnished it is possible to restore such brasses in such a way as to have certain areas burnished, others matt, and then lacquered with a dissolved mixture of shellac and other gums to give an old appearance.

Mirrors   Old mirrors were silvered by means of a deposit of tin and mercury and may be distinguished by the fact that the backs look like dull aluminium paint. The later processes using silver as a deposit are always painted on the back.

The consensus of opinion is that mercury mirrors should not be resilvered, and it is generally valid provided the backs have not become scratched as is often the case when the frames became unglued or broken. Of course, one would more readily tolerate a duller glass in an ornamental frame such as a girandole than in a toilet mirror.

As a rule, mirror people decline to resilver a mercury glass, but if one is willing to accept it regardless of the quality of the job, they can usually be persuaded to do it. It is usually quite a shock to find the number of faults and scratches which were unnoticed before; the silver may also be somewhat patchy.

Summary

A good patina is a great treasure and should be retained even if it means enduring faults such as warping, cracks and stains.

An ugly patina should be removed and the surface prepared in such a way as to provide the best possible foundation on which a new patina may eventually be built.

When this step is decided on, the correction of faults which would otherwise be overlooked may be attended to, but never to such an extent that it will destroy the human touch desirable in a hand-made piece.

The use of any form of varnish or lacquer applied with brush or spray should never be tolerated.

Joints   Resilience is acceptable if not excessive in any piece with pinned tenons. If reglueing is to be carried out it is important that all loose joints should be attended to.

Replacements   As much of the original fabric as possible should always be retained for museum use. For domestic use the replacement of parts which would be too weak if repaired is acceptable.

Veneers   All loose veneer or inlay should be glued down and missing parts replaced. While it is normal practice to level and polish such repairs, this part of the work should be omitted if it is liable to destroy the character or patina of the piece. This particularly refers to walnut of the Queen Anne period.

Drawers   While it is not important that drawers operate smoothly in a museum, for domestic use extremely worn surfaces should be faced.

Backs   There is often little one can do to repair a back without changing its character. If boards need replacing use sound old panelling and fit with care. Sometimes plywood can be effectively used to give strength with minimum material.

Metalwork   The use of metal braces for strengthening joints and repairs is not acceptable, but old metal braces made at the forge and set into the wood should be retained.

Mirrors   Mirrors silvered by the mercury process should be replaced only if they have become so marred that they are not only useless but ugly.

2 Inherent Causes of Failure

While it is usually quite obvious why a piece of work has been brought to the restorer and often the event which caused the damage is equally easily explained, yet more than half of his work is the repair of a condition that, as it were, just happened.

In order to understand the causes and deal adequately with these problems, the peculiar characteristics of wood must be thoroughly understood as well as the history of progress in the science of adapting construction to meet them. The cabinet-maker should think of wood as being in a continual state of movement as in fact is nearly all material; but whereas most substances expand and contract in all directions with changes in temperature, wood remains practically constant in length with the grain but varies in width with changes, not in temperature but in humidity.

The power with which this change in size takes place is very great; so much so that it has been used for centuries to split rock by driving pegs in rows of holes and pouring water on them. The constancy in length is such that clock-makers used to choose wood for their pendulum shafts in preference to metal for accurate timepieces.

A common form of coffer in the Middle Ages had end boards with vertical grain extending to form feet with front and back of single wide boards nailed in place. With variations in humidity they would swell and shrink against the static end ones bending the outer nails up and down until they finally broke off. In some cases the nails were heavy enough to hold and the board on shrinking would split and open up.

A cure for this was to have the grain of the ends horizontal with the result that the box simply varied in height with the humidity.

A very interesting form on this principle is the chest shown in Illus 1 which is peculiar to the West Coast North American Indian. The front, back and sides of these boxes are in one piece of cedar cleft from a large log. They have a groove to receive the bottom and three cleverly designed cross grooves which mark the corners and make possible, aided by heat and water, their bending at right angles. Just before closing the final corner, the bottom, also of cleft cedar, is inserted: in the earlier examples the unbent corner was laced with sinew or thong but later ones were nailed. The top was usually a very thick slab.

1 Box of Western red cedar by the Tsimshian Indians of Ksan, near Hazelton, British Columbia. Height 23½ in.

Because the front, back and ends not only have a matching direction of grain but are also one and the same board, this is an almost perfect example of construction which is in accord with the nature of the material.

A very important advance was the invention of panelling. By making frames of narrow material, the overall dimensions could be expected to remain stable enough for most purposes; the panels being free to expand and contract in their grooves. Its application was seen everywhere; in the majority of house doors, in wall panelling, oak chests, cupboard doors and carcase ends and backs. As long as it is in its true form, there is no problem but trouble may arise when other details of construction such as cross members (drawer runners maybe) are glued to the panel inside or similarly applied mouldings or ornaments outside restrict their freedom: or, when some misguided apprentice has glued the panel itself in its groove.

During the eighteenth and nineteenth centuries the craft of cabinet-making was developed to a very high degree of scientific construction designed to permit this motion without detriment to the article.

In spite of their best efforts, however, there were a number of problems which remained unsolved until new glues made the production of high quality plywood possible: the two most common being the lid of a box or enclosed dressing table top in the form of an inverted tray and the flush-panelled door with which is included the slope-fronted desk fall.

But the use of plywood, by enabling the manufacturer to ignore the traditional methods, has in many cases caused them to become ignored or unlearned. This is to be regretted for rarely is plywood the sole material used and, while it is possible with kiln-dried timber under ideal conditions of central heating to have such furniture give good service, a few months' storage in a damp warehouse will reveal the weaknesses.

Then there were practices which, though known to be unsound, were still used. For instance it was recognized that it is wrong to glue two pieces of wood at right angles to one another, yet the corner block in a common bracket foot usually is vertical in opposition to the horizontal grain of the outer part (see Illus 2A). Expansion and contraction will eventually break down the glue and, though it may remain attached at one end, a light blow will remove it. In a high quality piece one may find it in the form of a number of layers with horizontal grain alternately parallel to each side of the bracket and nicely rounded on the inside: this usually stands up well because the narrowness of each piece makes the movement negligible.

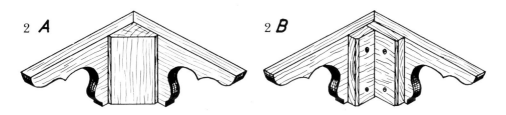

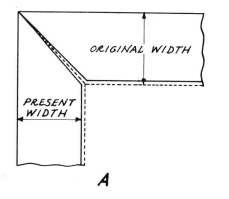

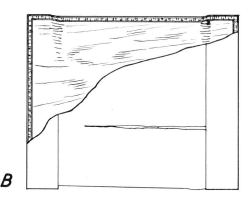

ORIGINAL WIDTH

PRESENT WIDTH

A   B

3

Illus 2B illustrates a third method using a dovetailed corner glued and screwed in place.

The Sheraton type of flush-panelled door (see Illus 3B) is another example. In spite of a careful choice of well seasoned wood and the practice of oiling and polishing inside as well as outside, shrinkage will almost always take place in centrally heated apartments. The drawing illustrates some of the resulting damage; edges out of line, veneer shattered where movement between panel and clamp has taken place, split in panel and most likely missing inlay and veneer.

The repair of this sort of damage entails much more work than is apparent to the average customer, who sees only the superficial fractures and does not realise that the loose joints and changes of dimensions in the ground on which

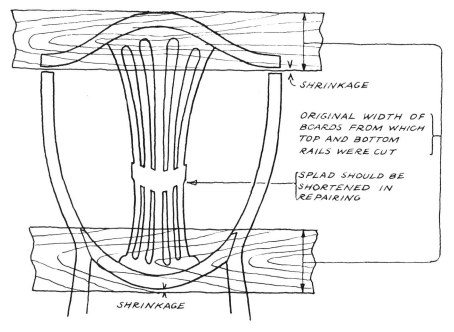

SHRINKAGE

ORIGINAL WIDTH OF BOARDS FROM WHICH TOP AND BOTTOM RAILS WERE CUT

SPLAD SHOULD BE SHORTENED IN REPAIRING

SHRINKAGE

4

the veneer was laid provide the major part of the repair man's problem.

Another effect of shrinkage is the change of form and consequently fit of components. For instance, an old-fashioned wide door-casing though perfectly fitted in the first place is often found open on the inside of the mitres. A glance at Illus 3A will explain this. A great number of similar examples might be mentioned, but one of the less obvious is the top rail of a Hepplewhite oval or, to a lesser degree, shield-back chair; Illus 4 explains this cause and effect. Of course, the repair man may glue these back as they were, leaving the poor fit or perhaps filling in with composition; then again, he may refit the joints, a process which may change the dimensions of the part, causing the necessity of further alterations to other parts which may have been in good condition.

The main thing for the novice is to consider the job from all angles, the cause of the damage and the various ways in which it may be made good, before he starts to work.

One of the peculiarities of the business is the variety of ways in which most jobs may be done. On the one hand, a loose chair leg may be fixed by putting in one screw and covering the head with composition, taking probably twenty minutes, while a conscientious workman might well spend a whole day removing upholstery, dismantling, cleaning and reglueing and replacing the upholstery. The apparent difference is very little and the screwed chair may give many years of service.

Similarly, the repair of the ground on which veneer is laid is often the major part of many jobs, and it may be entirely omitted, as the glueing down of the face veneer will hold it for a time.

For this reason a customer who takes the time to discuss the work with the repair man and to examine it when it has been dismantled will appreciate what he is paying for and get a better job. It is most annoying to get a job with inexplicit instructions from a wealthy customer and when he complains of the charge to find that he has only the vaguest idea of what was wrong with the piece in the first place. Such a person will probably get short-cut work at half the price of a good job and be paying for it two or three times what it is worth, and he will feel that he has had a bargain. The question of whether or not a first-class job is warranted will depend on the value of the article to the customer and the cost of the work.

It is all very well to say that nothing but the best work should be done. This would in many cases cost many times the value of the piece, while a short-cut job may put it into service for many more years.

The repair man should consider the customer's point of view; if he is a dealer, he will want the greatest improvement in appearance for the least cost consistent with reasonable freedom from complaints from his customer. If he is a genuine lover of old things, he will want the article put into the best possible condition so that posterity may continue to enjoy it but at the same time disturbing the patina and other characteristics that he admires as little as possible. Such customers are rare.

The more common point of view is expressed by, 'Is it worth mending or shall I get another one either new or second-hand?' The answer, of course, is the cost of repair compared with the cost of replacement.

There is very little excuse for shoddy work on a really fine piece. Far better to store it away, if prevented from having a good job done either by lack of funds or of a good craftsman, than to have it ruined by poor workmanship.

Before beginning the work it is well to consider that the customer expects to pay only for the damage which the piece had sustained before coming to the cabinet-maker. Every precaution should therefore be taken to ensure that no further damage is caused in the workshop. Careless handling can easily consume any profit that might have been made.

First provide a rug to form a pad when a piece has to rest on its polished surface, such as a chest resting on its end or a table turned upside down. All drawers should be removed and, indeed, if not damaged should be left at home, as they are liable to fall out when a piece is handled. Hinged table-leaves should be watched, as they are liable to fall open when the table is turned over and this may possibly cause the breaking of the rule joint or the splitting of the top. Upholstery should be covered with paper tied down with string.

Pieces of 2in × 2in about 24in long covered with carpet are handy as rests for polished table-tops, etc. They enable the fingers to get underneath to handle the pieces. Wooden jaws covered with ½in saddler's felt should be made for the vices for holding chair parts, etc, while shaping and sandpapering.

3 The Six Steps

Dismantling

This part of the work varies from the simplest child's-play to the most exasperating puzzle which could well be imagined.

Most of the difficulties are caused by previous repairs in which nails have been used, a practice which cannot be too greatly deplored, for, while it may stiffen joints for a while, it has the ultimate effect of breaking up the components both during the time the piece is in use and even more so when it is to be dismantled. It must be remembered that a nail holds only at one point, while glue, when properly applied, holds the two surfaces together wherever they should touch.

Before the actual work is started the decision should be made as to how much dismantling is necessary. If there is any possibility of confusion due to similarity of parts, or of putting back the other way round, these should be marked. A common way of doing this is by marking with a screwdriver, thus making a I. Similarly II, III or X may be made.

Screws made before 1825 are hand made and should be put into holes drilled in a board corresponding with their original positions so that they may be put back where they came from. If they are hard to start, a red hot iron applied to the head will often free them: also, after this treatment try turning to right as well as left alternately. On the other hand, if they are loose in their holes (particularly in the case of old screws in hinges) and therefore unlikely to hold when the time comes to put them back, thin glue should be put into each hole with a pointed matchstick; this will not only swell the fibres but harden the walls of the holes. This is only practical when there is time for thorough drying before re-assembly for otherwise the result will be that the screw threads will be full of powdered wood and glue.

Most of the knocking apart is carried out with a mallet; one with a rubber head is less liable to mark the furniture but seems less effective. Screwdriver, pry bar and wedges both of wood and steel are also used. A scrap of wood may be cramped in position to take the blows and protect the finished surface.

If the tenon though loose refuses to come apart, the following must be looked for:

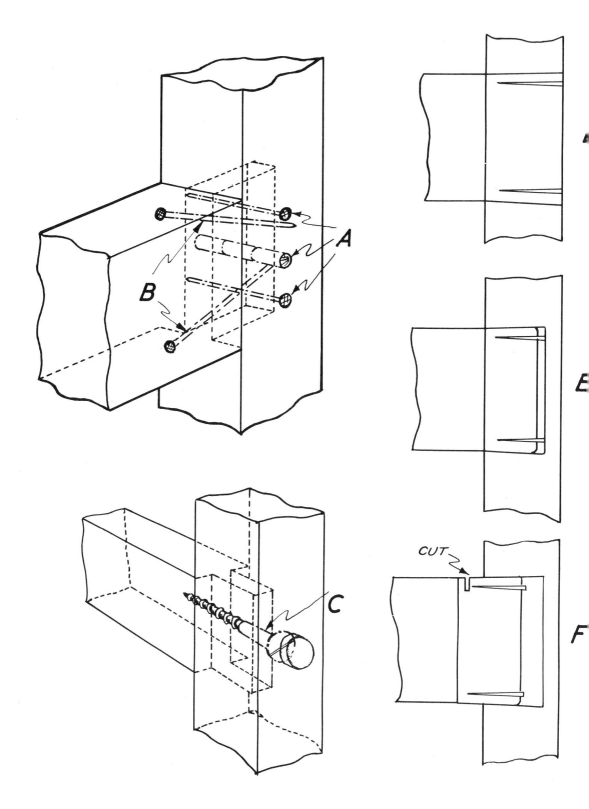

A

B

C

CUT

F

24

1 Nails or wooden pegs through the joint as in Illus 5A. The pegged tenons are nearly always found in antique oak. It was customary to bore the morticed member first, insert the tenon and mark the hole, withdraw it and bore the hole slightly nearer to the shoulder than the mark. When assembling, a tapered pin would draw the tenon home. This was called draw-bore pinning. The holes go right through, and the pointed ends of the pins usually project about ¼in to ½in. They can be easily driven out, but first mark each one on the lower edge and replace in their respective holes as soon as the tenon has been drawn.

2 Nails or screws inserted diagonally through rail into post as at Illus 5b, in effect toe-nailing rail to post. Quite often these nails go only into the tenon, thus having no effect at all.

3 Nails or screws through post into rail from the opposite side usually plugged as at Illus 5C.

4 Common or fox-wedged tenons as at D and E. Common wedged tenons are obvious as soon as the joint is examined, though people will sometimes pound the piece to destruction before even looking for a reason.

Fox wedges are less obvious; they are started as the joint is glued, and as the tenon is cramped up they are forced home against the bottom of the mortice. Should they be encountered and prove obstinate, withdraw as much as possible and then cut down to the top wedge as indicated at F; then break away the upper wedge with a screwdriver leaving it in the mortice.

If the tenons are found nailed as at A, as they very frequently are, especially in old chairs, it is likely that the work of dismantling will be both long and annoying, but one or other of the following expedients may be tried.

The obvious thing, of course, is to pull the nails out, and this can sometimes be done if they are neither too deeply embedded nor too much rusted in. It is worth while to grind a pair of pliers especially for this job. The idea is to form a more or less pointed corner that can be driven into the wood around the head of the nail. Illus 6A is the jaws of a pair of ordinary square-nose pliers; the dotted lines indicate how the corner may be pointed. B shows further grinding, so that the point is slightly spade-shaped and a place is thus made for striking with the hammer. C shows a small recess ground inside the points to make room for the nail-head.

It is sometimes practical to drive the nails right through with a small drift punch, first cramping up the joint in order to straighten the nails, which are likely to have been bent by the partial withdrawal of the tenon. The method giving the surest result is to drill round the nail with the aid of a specially made hollow drill.

This tool may be made of a piece of ¼in drill rod. This is placed in the chuck of the lathe, centered and a $\frac{7}{64}$in hole drilled about 1in deep, thus making a tube. Three cutting edges are then formed by grinding on the corner of a square-cornered emery wheel as shown in Illus 7. It may now be hardened and tempered.

It is first necessary to cut a slight depression ¼in in diameter with a gouge

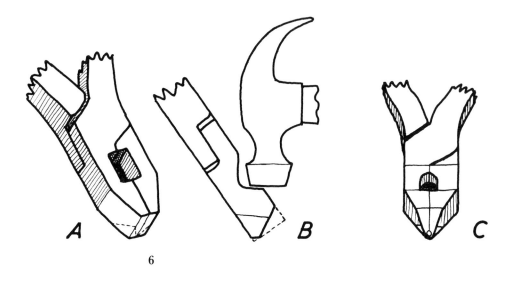

6

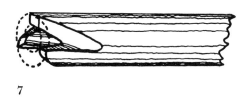

7

around the nail-head, as it is impossible to start it without this precaution. During the drilling operation it is well to withdraw and clear the drill frequently, continuing until the hole is ¾ in deep or until it is considered to be through the tenon, when an attempt may be made to withdraw the nail. If unsuccessful, the drilling is of course continued until the nail is finally removed. The holes thus formed serve to pin the tenons with wooden pins, and for this reason, as well as to straighten the nails, it is important to cramp up the joint first.

If the nails are very close to the shoulder of the tenon, it is better to force the joint by splitting a small piece off the side of the mortice, and this can be glued and tacked, with cigar-box nails, back in position. A ¼ in hole on the edge of the mortice will have a considerable weakening effect, especially if it is in the back leg of a chair.

Having disposed of the metalwork, the next consideration is to separate the joints. This is usually done by tapping with a small mallet. If not immediately effective, a piece of wood should be interposed between the mallet and the piece of furniture to prevent bruising, as fairly hard blows are sometimes necessary. It is sometimes worth while holding this in position with hand-screws.

If still more force is required, although the joint already moves a limited amount, it is well to check again for screws and nails. If these are not found present, wedges should be made use of. Old worn-out irons from a wooden plough (plane) are very good; they taper from $\frac{1}{4}$in to about $\frac{1}{16}$in and are $\frac{1}{2}$in or so wide. Wooden wedges are also effective, although they do not last very long. It is well to make a collection of wedge-shaped pieces of steel such as broken chisels, hatchet-blades, etc.

The practice is to insert them against the shoulders of the tenon, on each side, and follow up with another pair against them in the opposite direction.

If it is necessary to unglue a firmly glued joint it is advisable to make the following apparatus:

Take a tin, such as a syrup tin, with a close-fitting lid that can be prised off, and solder a short piece of tube through the lid. Attach a piece of $\frac{1}{4}$in rubber tube to this and at the other end an old oil-can spout for a nozzle; fit a wooden handle to it so that it can be handled without burning the fingers. Partly fill with water and put on to boil. Now bore a hole into the mortice at an inconspicuous place and try to get into that space between the end of the tenon and the bottom of the mortice. Put the nozzle loosely into the hole, allowing room around it for the steam to escape. After the steam has been hissing for about five minutes the joint can usually be easily broken.

In very obstinate cases the joint may be wrapped in wet cloths overnight and steamed again the next morning, but this is rarely necessary.

The foregoing has mostly dealt with mortice and tenon joints, as they are the ones which give most trouble; in fact, other joints rarely give any trouble except those secured by nails or screws.

Screws are often responsible for holding when there is no apparent reason for the joints not coming apart. Plugs of the same wood with the grain in the proper direction are quite hard to find, especially under a dirty finish; then again, dowel or double-pointed screws are quite often used and do not show at all. Tripod table-legs, or claws, as they used to be called, are often fitted with this type of screw, and a nail may have been added after they have been screwed up by turning the whole claw.

Dovetails which are fast should be soaked by placing wet cloths in contact with them for a few hours and then pouring boiling water into the inner angle, holding the piece over a bucket or sink.

In some cases it is a help to go round a joint with a razor-blade, mounted in a suitable handle, working it in as far as possible. For instance, the top back rail of a chair was broken off leaving a small piece firmly glued to the leg. The first time round the blade barely entered $\frac{1}{16}$in, but after the second or third attempt a knife-blade could be inserted and the piece prised off. In another

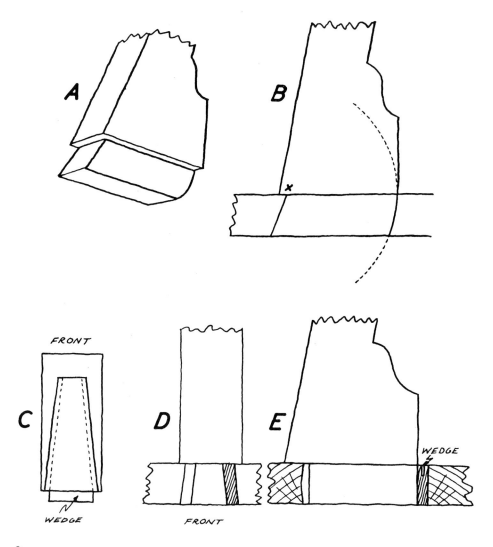

8

instance the top of a box had to be taken off due to shrinkage. In this case little more than the corner of the blade could be inserted, but it was enough to prevent the wood on each side from being torn away when it was finally lifted by prising up from the part that was loose.

Particular care should be taken not to jar rosewood, as it is very brittle and is apt to split when being knocked apart, the split sometimes occurring at some distance from the part being hammered. Old Spanish mahogany is occasionally found to be of a similar nature.

Unusual joints Sheraton mirrors consisting of a swing mirror mounted on a stand containing small drawers presented a problem to the craftsmen of old, due to the necessity for making a strong joint between the supports and the

½in top. Two of the less obvious methods are shown in Illus 8.

A and B show a hook type of joint which holds wonderfully well even after it has become slightly loose, the idea being that the weight of the mirror is tending to force the supports backwards, thus lifting the front edge. This is prevented by undercutting the mortice as shown and making the tenon to correspond, the back of the tenon being a radius with centre X.

If this is pulled straight up it will probably smash the top, whereas it will easily come out if pulled forward. A thin piece of veneer glued to the front face of the tenon is usually sufficient to take up the slack.

A rare dovetail type of joint is shown at Illus 8C, D and E. The tapered dovetail-shaped slot in the top was elongated behind sufficiently to permit the supporting dovetail to be inserted; when thrust forward it fitted perfectly, leaving a gap behind into which a wedge was fitted and glued.

Of course, this might be tightened by driving a thin wedge alongside the old one, but it should be remembered that this is putting a stress on the top tending to break out the piece between the post and the edge of the top. Any extra load, such as picking up the mirror by the post or a blow, may cause a fracture, while if the post is removed and reglued, the glue tends to hold the whole thing together.

Victorian mirror supports are more often attached by means of screws from underneath, and turned ones have a threaded wooden pin which enables the post to be taken out for packing, etc, by unscrewing. Some have wooden nuts underneath.

More modern supports are found with a metal nut about 1½in in diameter having slots all round so that they can be turned with a screwdriver; others have steel wedges, but these give little trouble to anyone who takes the trouble to examine the job before he starts using force.

Cleaning joints after dismantling

Having taken the article apart, the next step is to clean the parts: all old glue must be removed before reglueing.

A hook-scraper having a removable blade is perhaps the best tool for the preliminary work. Any type of scraper is possible, but the kind described works quicker and is more rapidly sharpened than most other varieties.

Small surfaces, such as places where veneer has chipped away, can be scraped clean with a chisel of the appropriate size.

If the surfaces are irregular, as in a break which has been previously glued, it is usually better to wash the old glue away. The quickest way is to wet all such surfaces with cold water and cover them with wet cloths and leave them for about an hour, after which time the glue will be softened and may easily be washed off with hot water: that is, provided the glue is soluble in water—and this is no longer always the case, due to the introduction of new types of glue many of which are waterproof. In this case the use of the scraper is the only practical alternative, although lacquer thinners will dissolve some kinds of glue and may be tried if the nature of the break seems to warrant it.

Before proceeding further it is necessary to allow the parts to dry, especially if much soaking or steaming has been necessary, as small pieces may have swollen enough to spoil their fit. The scraper should therefore be used when speed is important.

The joints should now be fitted together to see if they are quite clean; mortices may be cleaned out with a chisel, if necessary, and dowel holes with a twist drill of the appropriate size. This is not usually done, unless the joint fails to fit together perfectly.

Dowels usually remain fast in one side and should be gripped with pliers and tested for firmness. If found loose, one side should be marked, they should then be withdrawn and immediately glued back in exactly the same position. This may be thought unnecessary, but most dowels become slightly strained in one or other direction and if turned half round may throw out the joint by an appreciable amount. This will make extra work in the long run.

In the case of breaks it is usually necessary to remove some small pieces which may prevent the joint from going together perfectly, such as pointed splinters which have become burred over and chips which have become loose or displaced; in this case they should be glued back in position if they are large enough to weaken the joint materially. Usually a few minutes with a very small chisel or gouge suffices to see the joint go perfectly together.

Restoring components

The various parts being clean and easily handled, it is a simple matter to make good any damage which may have occurred to them or to replace such as are not worth repair.

Should many additional pieces be required, even though they be very small, such as pieces to build up a chipped corner, it is well worth while making a cutting-out list and preparing all necessary material ready for fitting.

An example of such a cutting-out list is given below:

This list applies, of course, to a chest of drawers and should be as comprehensive as possible, including new hardware, glass, veneer, leather and cloth, etc, as it will be useful also in making out costs.

The 'growing on' of new wood where corners have been knocked off etc, is one in which a good deal of care is well repaid.

The repair man should acquire and stock as large a variety as possible of woods of all kinds. This stock may consist of pieces of old furniture bought and dismantled for the purpose; old box desks serve very well for the purpose and can often be bought at a sufficiently low price.

The pieces chosen to be grafted on should match the parent stock as closely as possible both in colour and grain. The colour should be, if anything, lighter, as it can readily be darkened in polishing. With regard to grain, a study should be made of the effect of cutting in relation to direction of the annular rings and medullary rays. Quarter-cut oak and edge-grained softwood, for instance, are cut along the rays, while plain oak and figured fir are cut at right angles to them or tangentially. All other woods are affected more or less by the direction of cut, and a much better match can be made if this is taken into consideration; for instance Illus 9A represents a typical board. To the right is the pattern of grain which is found when the surface cut is at a tangent to the heart of the tree as revealed by the end cut: moving to the left the lines become progressively closer and more like the figure produced by a radial cut.

CUTTING OUT LIST

Description	No	Thickness in inches	Width in inches	Length in inches
Right front corner of top	1	¼	¾	1½
Left front foot	1	¾	1	2
Cock beads on top drawer	2	⅛	⅜	4
,, ,, second drawer	1	⅛	⅞	10
,, ,, third drawer	1	⅛	⅜	3
,, ,, bottom drawer	1	⅛	⅜	9
Sundry patches to frame facings	1	⅛	⅞	24
Pieces to build up lower edges of drawer sides	8	⅜	1	16½
Inlay ⅛ in square boxwood				72

In many woods, particularly mahogany, due to varying directions of spiral and convoluted growth a light and dark effect is produced having a beautiful lustrous appearance which is revealed only in this area unless the cut is truly radial. The variation in shade is due to the differences in the angle which the grain makes with the surface as revealed on the edge of the two vertical cuts in the drawing: the dark area to the left is where the viewer looks into the pores of the grain, while in the one to the right is seen the fibres of the grain looking away and reflecting the light. Because of this effect, if one marks a dark part and then turns the board end for end, it will now be seen as a light area. This is what gives it its depth and lustre and, if the job warrants it, the need for matching the grain in all its aspects.

When a large abrasion or burn in a conspicuous place on solid wood is to be repaired, a very nearly perfect match may be achieved by cutting the patch from the wood itself immediately below the damage. In order to ensure the best possible job, it is essential that it be inlaid at exactly the same angle; to achieve this proceed as follows. With different coloured pencils (Chinagraph are good) draw two lines, parallel to the edge crossing the centre of the damage as in Illus 9B. Turn it over and repeat on the underside immediately below. Now lay out an area large enough for the patch C, cut across the grain with the end of a tenon saw, nick the sides, enlarge the end cut and split out the square. Now the split side is the upper one and so it is necessary to square up the lines at each end and join up across the top; to avoid confusion erase

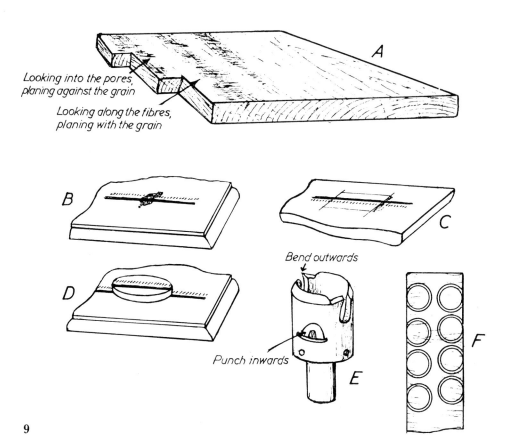

Looking into the pores, planing against the grain

Looking along the fibres, planing with the grain

A

B

C

D

Bend outwards

Punch inwards

E

F

9

them from below. You now have only to cut the patch to an ellipse with bevelled edge, D, set in place with lines overlapping, and mark round with a scriber and inlay. The hole below should of course also be filled with a plain patch.

If the fault is small, a plug cutter can be used to cut the patch from the underside and it can be fitted in a few minutes. In this case it is even more important to lay out the coloured lines so that the disc may be correctly orientated, for it is very easy to misjudge the direction of the grain on such a small area and, should it be reversed, there is the possibility of seeing a light disc on a dark stripe when viewed from one end and a dark disc on a light stripe from the other.

Plug cutters are rather expensive but home-made ones capable of cutting up to fifty plugs at a sharpening are easily made. The material is the tube from an old bicycle frame, especially the tapered ones extending to the back wheel. Simply cut pieces about one inch long with the required internal diameter at the small end. A large one has been chosen for illustration mounted on a wooden mandrel fitted tightly and pinned in place. The way it is sharpened is clear from Illus 9E; the two teeth which clear away the waste wood are bent outwards like the tooth of a saw and are filed just below the sharpened arcs which cut the plug itself. The escapement is done with a hacksaw cut below a

A

BROKEN CORNER

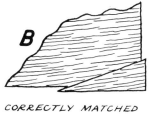

B

CORRECTLY MATCHED

C

WRONG

VICTORIAN CHAIR

D

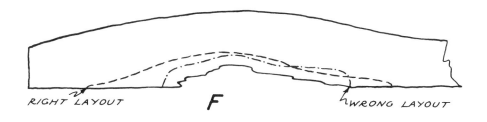

CUT

E

NEW PIECE

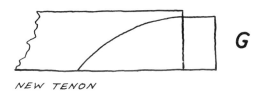

RIGHT LAYOUT   **F**   WRONG LAYOUT

G

NEW TENON

10

filed bevel with the corner punched inwards to taper the plug for easy insertion. The smaller cutters are mounted either on a piece of rod or a cap-screw with nut turned to fit and soldered in place. ⅜in, ½in and ⅝in are the handiest sizes.

Cutting plugs for ordinary purposes is best done on a drill press out of a piece of wood with grain running across; the cuts being on the edge as indicated in F. This will allow the waste material to get away without plugging up the cutter. When the cutting is finished, the wood which remains attached to the plug is cut away with a bandsaw, the saw-marks lining up with the grain. If done with grain the other way, it is easy to confuse the saw-marks with the grain.

With damage to corners or edges the type of joint will vary; the simplest being made by planing the damaged area to a straight line, fitting a patch and glueing it in place as shown in Illus 10A, B and C. If well done the result will be perfectly satisfactory and can hardly be improved upon. The conditions to be fulfilled are:

1 the wood shall match;
2 the grain of both woods shall continue in the same direction, and
3 the joint shall truly fit.

If the joint is likely to be subject to stress, it is sometimes practical to strengthen it with screws put in in such a way as to leave the heads covered. This can be achieved either by the use of plugs with the grain running across the diameter or by other parts of the piece, as, for example, in a chair where the top back rail having been splintered the new piece may be strengthened with screws as shown in Illus 10D. The holes should be bored before the joint is glued, and it is usually advantageous to start the drilling from the glued face, that is in the opposite direction to that in which the screw is driven.

It may be screwed after the glue is dry or at the time of glueing. The former permits more accurate drilling for the thread of the screw, first using the shank-size drill to form a centre.

Occasionally a large piece is missing from an old table-top due to a knot or piece of curved grain having been there. A new piece can be fitted with a joint following the grain in a fairly simple way as follows:

Having selected the best match for grain, place it under the break; and having lined up the figure as well as possible, mark the edge of the break. Now decide how much of the ragged edge must be cut away and draw a line beside the first allowing for this. Now with the thinnest brads tack the new piece on top of the old in the same position as it was under it and cut along the second line with a fine bandsaw, thus cutting both pieces to the same curve. They may now be glued and dowelled together.

The only care in laying out the cut is to remember that the thickness of the cut will spoil the joint if any two parts of the line approach parallel, Illus 10E and F.

When veneered stock is damaged in such a way as to involve the core it is usually practical to cut away both veneer and core and replace them with one fairly thick piece. Veneer patching will be considered in a later chapter.

When joints are to be made which will be subject to considerable stress, the mechanical layout of the joining surfaces should receive careful thought. Illus 11 contains some suggestions on this point.

The longer these scarfs are, of course, the stronger they will be, but three times the thickness should be considered a minimum whenever possible. The question of whether they should slope from top left to bottom right or vice versa will depend on two considerations—first, the direction of the grain, and secondly, the direction of the principal stress.

Should the grain slope as in Illus 11A and B, the scarf should be cut as in B; the reason for this is fairly obvious. But if it is straight or nearly so, as in C and D, the direction of the principal stress should influence the angle. This stress is indicated by the weight W, and the stronger joint would be D, because it must be remembered that wood is a more or less flexible substance and as it bends a very large part of the stress is concentrated on the end of the joint. This having given way as suggested in the sketch, the effect is for the new piece to peel off, whereas in D the whole glue area is taking the load. In addition to this, anyone who has a knowledge of levers will see that there is less stress at X on D than X on C.

E, F and G are scarfs in which an extra piece of wood has been added, usually to make good a place which has been broken up by former repairs. Where one face goes together well, such as the lower side of F, the scarfs may be cut on left and right, the remaining broken part glued up and then the filler fitted afterwards. This is particularly applicable to curved chair parts, which may be lined up by assembling with other parts in the first glueing. G is slightly weaker but usually quite all right if found to be preferable. H and I are double scarfs or splices and though they look complicated are more easily cut and fitted than may seem possible, especially when a bandsaw is used.

J is a multiple dowelled joint. This is usually applied to comparatively large surfaces where maximum strength is not necessary. If two or more surfaces line up, the position of the dowels can easily be marked with a gauge, but in many cases the easiest way to mark is by making depressions on one part held in the vice with a centre punch, putting small balls (ball bearings ⅛in) in them, placing the other part in position and giving it a tap with the mallet. This makes very clear marks and is a quick and good method.

While it must be admitted that the majority of cases give no choice in the kind of scarf to be used, it is well to know which is the best when a choice is available.

The cutting and fitting of these joints is simple enough when the material is of a rectangular section and not attached to a piece of furniture, but a description of the fitting of the scarf illustrated in the photograph L might be helpful (see Illus 11L).

Here the back leg had broken at the point where a screw attached the leg to the seat. This break though jagged was less than ½in long, so it was decided to pull it as far apart as possible, glue it together and, when dry, fit in the scarf as

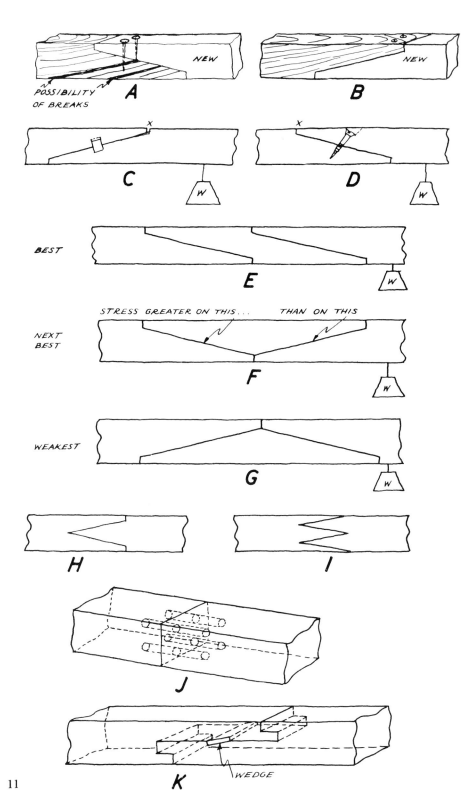

A

POSSIBILITY
OF BREAKS

NEW

B

NEW

C

D

BEST

E

NEXT
BEST

STRESS GREATER ON THIS... THAN ON THIS

F

WEAKEST

G

H

I

J

K

WEDGE

L

shown, the screw through the new wood giving added strength.

The glue being dry and the screw removed, the next thing was to mark off the length of the scarf, 3½ in each side of the break. Three cuts were then made, one at the break about ¾ in deep and at each end ³⁄₁₆ in deep. The job was now to chisel two plane surfaces connecting these cuts without breaking the glued joint by too much mallet work. To ease the cutting, two more saw-cuts were made each side of the centre, and most of the wood could then be fairly easily split away.

It now remained to produce the two flat surfaces with the chisel. Now this is not too difficult if a perfectly sharp, perfectly flat wide chisel is available; in fact, that is the secret of the job. A fairly short 1½ in bevelled chisel was used, and each surface was started by levelling an area the width of the chisel at the shallow end of the cut and lining it up with the centre depth. As long as the chisel is kept flat on a flat surface and the cut is not too heavy it will follow very closely to that plane; thus by keeping the cut very shallow the two surfaces can be continued to the centre. It is now well to check them with two strips ½ in × ½ in × 4in or so laid across them to see that they are not in winding — that is they must seem parallel when viewed so that one almost hides the other; if they are not, then one or other surface should be cut until they are correct.

The piece to be let in should now be selected and cut to size allowing ⅛ in extra width and ¼ in extra depth to allow plenty of material for fitting the joining surfaces. It must now be cut so that it fits into the recess at each end, when the position of the deepest part of the cut can be marked and the distance measured giving the line of cut for the two sloping surfaces. These are easily cut with a bandsaw and fitted with a plane.

Sometimes this fitting is so easy that there appears to be nothing to it, but at other times it will not seem to fit at all and it is often very difficult to find what it is that interferes with it. The first thing to examine is the corners, to be sure that they are clean and not stopped by rough sawing or with small splinters. Then one surface can be coated with poster paint — red is good — and the other rubbed in position, when the points of contact may be noted, and the high spots either chiselled or planed away. Poster paint is chosen because oil paint would spoil the subsequent adhesion of the glue

When ordinary scarfs such as C or D in Illus 11 are cramped up there is a tendency for the joints at the end to open up, due to the glue lubricating the inclined surfaces and causing them to slide as pressure is applied. To counter-act this a short piece of dowel may be fitted as at C with the holes bored very slightly uphill, or a screw at an angle as shown at D may be fitted.

The last joint in Illus 11K is common in Oriental work and though complicated can be very easily cut on a saw table. It is pulled up and locked by a transverse wedge and can be cleaned up almost immediately after glueing. The replacement of broken-off tenons is a simple matter, especially if a circular saw is available. The rail is merely slotted the thickness of the tenon and a new one glued in position, perhaps with a screw to secure it so that the rest of the glueing will not be held up.

In many cases it is well to have the slot end in a curve formed by the saw, as in Illus 11G, especially if the rail is light or if the upper side shows. Knowing the diameter of the saw and marking the curve with a compass, the new tenon is easily fitted to this. If done by hand this would be simply a straight slope, the slot being cut with tenon saw and chisel.

If the tenon broken off is clean at the shoulder and remains firm in the mortice, it may be repaired by fitting two or three dowels without removing the tenon.

Broken-off dowels are removed by cutting off flush, boring a hole in the dowel slightly smaller and then with a ⅛ in chisel splitting the tube thus formed into the centre. Once freed it can usually be withdrawn, but if obstinate it can always be cleaned out with a full-sized bit when enough has been cut away to give it a start.

Glueing up

Hot glues   The process of glueing consists of coating both surfaces with glue and then putting them together and holding them in position for a certain length of time. This involves the use of glue and cramps of various kinds. Let us first consider the glues.

There is a considerable and increasing variety of glues available to the cabinet-maker, and most of them will give good results if properly used.

First, the old-fashioned hot glue made of leather trimmings and other animal material is perhaps the most useful. It is almost exclusively used by the author. It is bought in the form of cakes, beads or powdered into yellow crystals something like brown sugar.

If the cake form is used it must first be broken into small pieces by putting it into a sack or heavy canvas bag, which can be made for the purpose, and pounding it with a hammer.

A glue-pot like a double boiler is necessary, preferably with two inner containers, one to be in use and the other for preparing the next batch. The inner pots are two-thirds filled with glue and then filled with water and left until the glue has absorbed the water, about twelve hours for the cake, three for the bead and half an hour for the powdered kind. The powdered sort should be stirred until it thickens.

The glue may now be heated but must never boil, this being the reason for the double boiler. The water in the outer pot is also useful for washing off the surplus glue that squeezes out of the joints. This initial heating is called cooking, and a scum usually forms on the top. This should be removed with a spoon, and then the liquid should be stirred until it is of an even consistency. When hot it should be quite fluid but not watery. When cold it should be a hard jelly into which the finger can be inserted only with some difficulty. Water must be frequently added to the glue, when it is being used, in order to counteract the evaporation which takes place and also to adjust the consistency for the particular work in hand. For instance, a chip of veneer which cannot be easily cramped would call for thick and hot glue, while in working glue under a loose veneer, which is to be put down with a hot caul, much more water would be added. Water should also be added when much time is to elapse between glueing and cramping.

It is most important that all cramping should be finished before the glue has jellied. The time available can be extended by warming the work before starting, and it is common in cabinet shops to see work stacked around the heater in winter time for this purpose, especially in veneer jobs. It has the added advantage of helping the glue to penetrate deeper into the wood.

Most artisans like the usages of their apprenticeship. The author is no exception and for that reason may be prejudiced in favour of hot glue. The following advantages may be claimed for it:

1 It has stood the test of time. The author could produce a number of rubbed glue joints over two hundred years old which were never disturbed.

2 It is as strong across the grain as most furniture woods and equal to or stronger than nearly all other glues.
3 It is the cheapest practical glue.
4 It is quicker to apply than most others.
5 It does not stain.
6 It can be washed off with hot water.
7 In using it on old joints the same type of glue is already in the pores of the wood, and it is reasonable to suppose that a better bond is formed than with two different substances.
8 In the case of veneer, if a part is found not down (unstuck), it can be put down with a hot caul.
9 The smell is delightful.

Its disadvantages may be summarised as follows:
1 It must be heated.
2 The time available between application and cramping is limited. On the other hand, this makes for speed.
3 It is neither moisture- nor bacteria-resistant, properties not particularly applicable to furniture.

Fish glues   The next kinds are the common liquid glues made of parts of fish. These are the handiest available, as they require no preparation except, possibly, warming up slightly in cold weather. Their properties are similar to those of hot glue except that they give ample time for assembly, but they are much more expensive and are somewhat harder to spread.

Synthetic glues   The third class includes the casein and the water-setting synthetic resin and similar chemical glues. They are usually waterproof and bacteria-resistant, but most stain the wood quite severely.

Directions for mixing and using come with each brand and they should be followed with the greatest accuracy, for in some kinds 10 per cent too much water seems to rob the bond of 90 per cent of its strength.

A good plan is to weigh a suitable amount of the powder into a tall glass jar and carefully mark the level. Empty it and then weigh in the required amount of water, marking its level thus — W; now add the brand of glue and keep for future use. The glass can be easily marked with paint on the outside.

The two ingredients must now be mixed. A fork is as good as anything for mixing, and the stirring should be continued until the mixture is perfectly smooth. A piece of bent wire in the chuck of the drill press at slow speed makes a very good mechanical mixer, and it can be left to do the mixing while other jobs are attended to.

Plenty of time is available for cramping up, etc, but there is little other advantage for our purpose, for the repair man wants a glue which is ready all day long, while most of these glues should be used within two hours of mixing and some in an even shorter period. Also the waterproof qualities of the glue make it very hard to clean off should the joint ever need reglueing or if any surplus glue has been missed while washing before the glue has set.

Other glues   The last type of glue to be considered is that which is dissolved in solvents similar to lacquer thinner and sold as model aeroplane cement, household glue and liquid solder. These are the quickest-setting glues known to the author and the most transparent.

They are useful for glueing down small chips in light-coloured wood and are quite good for bonding clean metal to clean wood, but they are not suitable for general use.

Cramps and handscrews   The various types of cramps are illustrated in the photographs in Illus 12.

There appears to be some confusion about the two words cramp and clamp. According to some dictionaries they are synonymous, but in this work, cramp refers to an appliance to force joints together, while clamps are pieces of wood designed to stiffen or prevent a board from warping.

A is a common bar or sash cramp and is available in various lengths. They are usually bought in pairs and have the advantage over the pipe kind in that the loose jaw is not liable to slide around and also they are possibly a little quicker to set.

B consists of a pair of attachments fitted to a piece of ¾in black pipe. It is important to use black (ungalvanised) as the adjustable jaw is subject both to getting stuck when you want to move it, and to slipping when the pressure is applied if used on galvanised pipe. However, it will serve if the black is not available, for it can always be shifted with a hammer and does not slip until some wear has taken place on both the pipe and the steel clips on the jaw.

It is quite often necessary to have a cramp with jaws long enough to reach over some obstacle such as the curved rails of some chairs or legs with applied ornaments in front. This has been achieved in C by fitting wooden extensions to the jaws by boring 1⅛in holes through oak blocks 1¾in × 3½in × 4¾in, cutting them to shape and screwing them to the jaws as shown.

The G-cramps are shown to suggest a useful range of sizes and shapes. The smallest has a 2in opening and the largest a 6in one. These are liable to mark the work unless pinch blocks (pieces of wood interposed between the cramp and the work) are used, and for this reason are not so handy as handscrews. On the other hand they can get into places out of the reach of a handscrew.

The handscrews E, F and G are probably more used by the author than all the other types put together, as there is no bother with pinch blocks and they are capable of reaching farther across a piece of work than other kinds. Moreover, by manipulating the two screws, pressure may be applied at any point from the screw to the end of the jaws. These are made in various sizes, ranging from 8in jaws to 12in jaws. They may be easily made at home if a box and tap are available.

H is simply a strip of rubber cut from a car's inner tube and is used for binding broken parts together. Very great pressure may be applied with this

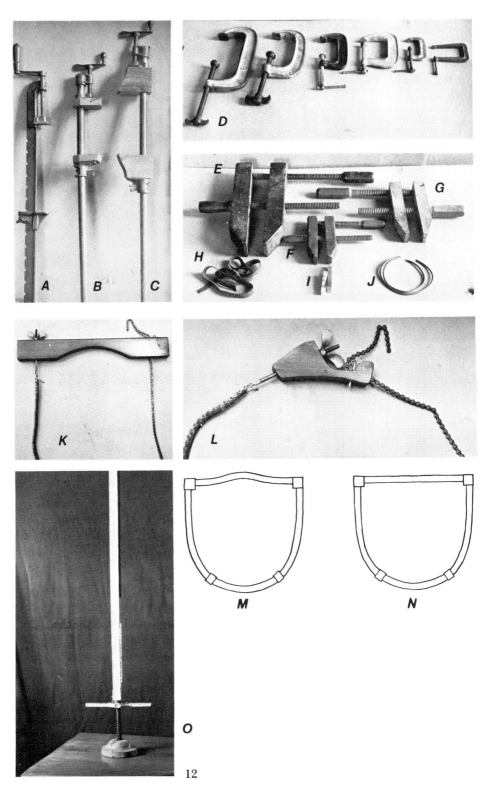

method without marring the work for a 5-10lb pull is multiplied with each turn of the binding. It is most often used on legs and turning.

I is a common clothes peg and is used to hold down pieces of veneer at the edge of a board. Longer jaws may be made to fit the springs to add to their usefulness.

J is a ring cut out of an upholstery spring and is used for the same purpose except that it may be adjusted to a very much larger range by simply bending it to the desired shape. A score or more of these should be cut by means of a hammer, a cold chisel and a block of iron. The cut is usually left sharp as it will then grip on a pinch block and can often be made to hold on an inclined surface where the mark will not show.

K is a bicycle-chain cramp, an invention of the author, consisting of a bar with eight holes (to make it adjustable for various widths of chairs), a ⅜in threaded rod attached to a bicycle chain and a large wing nut. It is used for chair seats having a plan similar to those in M and N. In use, the bar is attached to the front rail and legs (previously glued up) by means of G-cramps. The bolt is then passed through the appropriate hole and the wing nut started. The sides and back are then glued and assembled, the chain passed round and threaded through the hole on the opposite end of the bar and pulled tight. It is then held by inserting a nail through the chain as shown. All that remains is to tighten up on the wing nut until the joints have been pulled up home.

L makes use of the same equipment except that the shaped wooden coupling has been used in place of the bar to enable it to be used on circular or elliptical frames.

In order to prevent the chain marking the work as it is tightened, a leather strap should be laced to the inside at the end fitted with the screw. At the fixed end it does not seem to mark except around a projection when it should be covered.

It is occasionally necessary to put pressure on a top in a position inaccessible to a cramp (usually to put down veneer). The simplest method is to shore it down from the ceiling. A shore is a piece of wood slightly longer than the distance from the caul to the ceiling and it is simply jammed between the two, and with it great pressure may be applied by driving the upper end towards the position in which it will be perpendicular.

A more elaborate gadget may be made with a screw having the effect of a jack and an adjustable post continuing it up to the ceiling, see O.

Although the work of glueing up is probably the simplest part of the entire job, there is plenty of room for bungling. If it is at all complicated, it is well to divide it into sub-assemblies allowing these to dry before proceeding.

Most glue joints are left till the following day but six hours is usually sufficient if care is used in handling, so permitting two glueings the same day.

As hot glue must be cramped up before it has had time to cool sufficiently to jelly, the process must be carried out in a deft, unhesitating and logical manner. In order to do this a complete plan of procedure should be figured out to the last motion, the various pieces should be laid out either on the bench or on a board on trestles together with cramps and saddles. If it so happens that all the joints have not already been tested for fit, the job should be assembled dry and cramped up before setting.

When all is ready apply glue first on mortices and dowel holes; it will stay hot here longer than on exposed surfaces such as tenons. Now coat the tenons, not forgetting the shoulders, which, if properly glued, may add as much as 50 per cent to the strength of the joint. Go on assembling in the order planned without hurry but without pause or false move. Apply the cramps and tighten until the joint is home. *Do not* apply unnecessary pressure for two reasons, first it may starve the joint by forcing out too much glue, and secondly it may place the joint under stress which will cause it to spring back slightly when the cramp is removed, thus weakening the partly set glue.

Now wash and scrape off all surplus glue with hot water and a chisel. This is another reason for glueing sub-assemblies first, for once the glue is cold it takes twice as long to wash off. For instance, in glueing up a chair frame, the front legs to front rail may be one operation, the back may be better done in two, the legs to the seat rail being the first and the splat and top rail the second. Finally the side seat rails and stretchers are glued into the front and back.

Glue is usually set in about four hours, but it does not attain its maximum strength for several days and so it is well not to deliver a repair which is likely to be subject to much stress until two or three days after glueing.

The application of cramps to a great many jobs is impracticable without the use of saddles, but their preparation is usually a fairly simple problem, though one is tempted to do without them owing to the fact that they seem to be work for which there is nothing to show. This, however, should not deter the man of experience, for he will have found that the lack of them has not only spoilt the joint but often marred the work by the cramp digging in, thus involving much more work than would have been the case had the saddles been made.

The following are some examples of such appliances (Illus 13):

Illus 13A, B and C are used in glueing up the broken leaf of a drop-leaf table. This curved shape cannot be properly pulled up without a saddle if dowels are used.

On the upper side it is simply a piece of soft wood bandsawn to shape with a slat nailed on each side to prevent it slipping off, A. Either B or C will serve to protect the rule joint and centralise the pressure, for if a plain strip only is used the top will be found to cup on the upper side when the cramps are tightened. Saddle B is simply a piece of 1in × 1in with a suitable groove, C consists of a strip of plywood nailed to a piece of 1in × 1in with a piece of dowelling tacked in the appropriate place, D is similar to B but made to fit the central top of a drop-leaf table with rule joint.

This principle applies to any moulded edge where the pressure applied by the cramp would otherwise be received close to one surface, such as E, while with F and G a simple strip is sufficient.

H and I are for cramping shaped legs which are dowelled in position, and

44

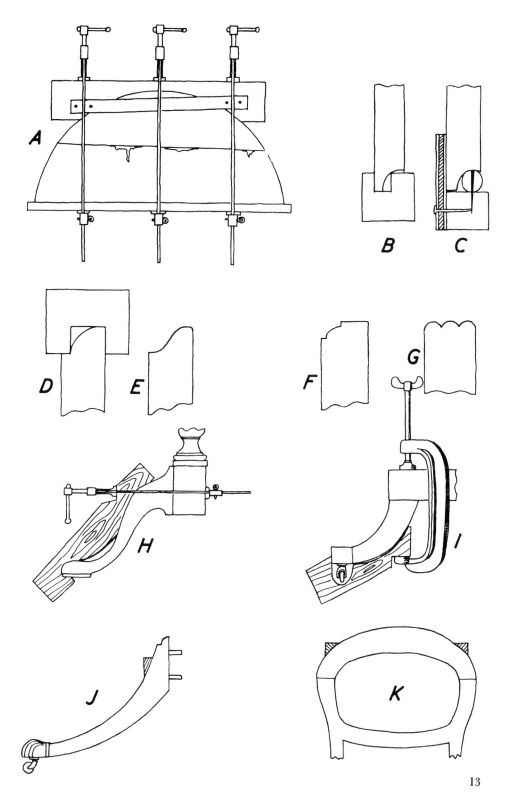

A

B C

D E F G

H I

J K

they are best cut out of seven-ply so as not to split. In some cases, such as H, it is a help to fasten the saddle to the leg with a small G-cramp before starting to glue up.

When making a new part to replace a broken one it is occasionally a good idea to leave suitable projections to take the cramp, these to be removed after glueing. The shaded portions of the Duncan Phyfe style leg, J, and the Victorian chair back, K, are examples of this practice. Saddles could of course be made for both these jobs, but a little time is saved in this way.

It might be well to mention that both H and J are more often dovetailed and are removed by driving straight down. The end of the dovetail can be seen on the bottom of the column unless it is covered by a turned ornament.

While the glue is hot it is a good time to fill any holes that may be found with sawdust and glue. All that is necessary is to put a dab of glue into the hole and then rub in the sawdust with the finger leaving the patch slightly raised if possible. This is the quickest method of filling nail-holes, screw-heads, etc.

Sometimes it is necessary for a number of reasons to introduce glue into a joint without taking it apart. This is not to be recommended if it is possible to dismantle the joint, for only so can the entire surfaces of contact be coated. However, the little device about to be described has proved very useful and successful.

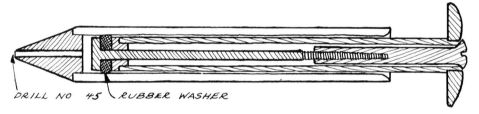

DRILL NO 45 — RUBBER WASHER

14

A hole is bored into the bottom of the mortice or other place from an inconspicuous place and the glue pumped in with the syringe pictured in Illus 14.

This is the third and most successful syringe made by the author. The cylinder consists of a piece of brass tube with a solid brass nozzle soldered in and drilled with a No 45 drill. The plunger is another tube fitting the cylinder at the end of which is a rubber washer which when compressed by tightening the hollow screw in the handle, presses against the cylinder walls, thus making a seal. The sketch should make this clear.

Levelling and sandpapering

If a repair is to be made as perfect as possible, it must be cleaned up with as much care and skill as the original piece received from the artisan who made it.

46

An old cabinet-maker on examining a certain piece of furniture once remarked, 'It is a sound piece of work, but it has "Carpenter" written all over it.' When asked to explain he stressed the difference in the way it had been cleaned up.

A carpenter is a fine craftsman, used to handling tools and wood and much of his knowledge and skill is a closed book to a cabinet-maker, but the latter is called upon to produce a much finer finish.

This is mentioned in case anyone should dismiss this part of the work as a simple matter. To take a piece of rough wood with a figured grain and produce a perfectly smooth flat surface on it by hand in a reasonable time is the work of one who has gone a long way towards being a skilled craftsman.

To achieve this result on flat surfaces the following tools are used: planes, scrapers and abrasive papers, garnet preferred. On shaped work draw-knife, spokeshaves, compass plane, rasps, files and carving tools may be added.

While planing a flat area, the surface should be frequently felt with the left hand, passing it across the work palm down. Waves and high spots quite invisible to the eye can be felt in this way. A straight-edge should also be used across the grain, or if the plane is straight it can be used tilting it so that its edge permits light to be seen in the low spots. This is continued until it is as perfect as the plane can make it. When necessary, turn the wood round and thus plane certain areas in the opposite direction due to the convolutions of the grain, and in rare cases plane across the grain.

After planing, the cabinet scraper is used to remove both the imperceptible ridges between each plane cut and also roughnesses due to the impossibility of getting the plane to operate in the right direction required by all parts of the figure. This tool is a piece of steel about $\frac{1}{32}$in × $2\frac{1}{2}$in × 5in, and most old cabinet-makers claim that there are very few able to sharpen it but themselves. There is indeed quite a knack in it, but it is one which should be acquired. The following suggestions may be found useful.

The narrow edges must first be filed and oilstoned until they are perfectly square and sharp, burrs being removed by rubbing the flat surface on the oilstone. A magnification of the end view should now be as Illus 15A. It is now held on end on the bench and each cutting edge receives three strokes with a burnisher or back of a chisel from the bench upwards. The burnisher is held square with the first stroke and canted towards the cutting edge with the second and slightly more with the third. The end view should now be as B, presenting two very sharp short cutting edges. It is now ready for use. When dull, it is laid flat on the edge of the bench and the cutting edges flattened down with the burnisher, producing the effect shown at C. It may now be sharpened again with the burnisher, but with the final stroke canted at a greater angle from the square. This may be repeated three or four times until the end view will be somewhat as D, when, of course, the filing and oilstoning must be repeated.

In use the scraper is held with both thumbs close to the centre and the fingers around the two ends. It is inclined away from the user at an angle

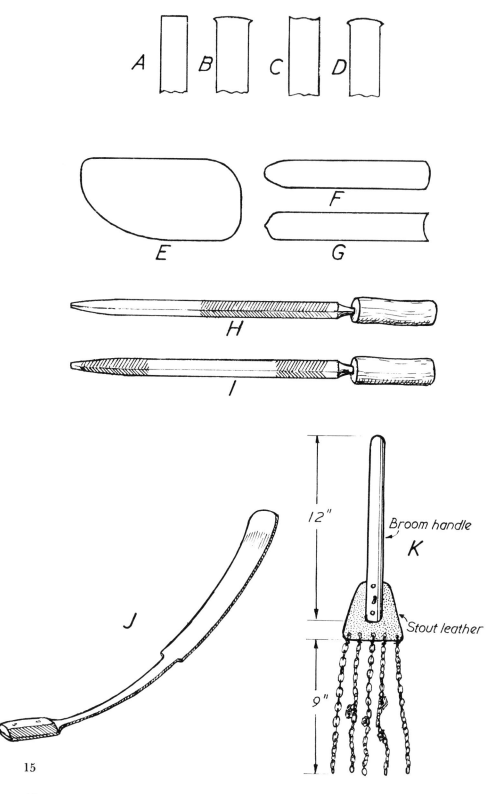

A

B

C

D

E

F

G

H

I

J

12"

Broom handle

K

Stout leather

9"

15

sufficient for it to bite and thrust away to make a cut, or in special cases it may be held in any way that suits. The direction of scraping, relative to the grain of the wood, should be constantly varied to prevent forming ridges. Again the hand must be used to feel the surface while it is frequently examined for imperfections preferably with an oblique light.

Sandpaper   The final operation is with sandpaper wrapped round a cork-composition block, starting with middle 2, continuing with fine 2 or 1½ and finishing with 1 or 0. After using each grade the surface should be inspected so that the imperfections may be progressively eliminated.

Sandpapering, sanding and papering are all common terms for smoothing wood with abrasive paper. Sandpaper was formerly true to its name, employing sand as the abrasive grit; now glass, flint, garnet and aloxite are commonly used for wood and emery for metal. Backings have a wide range of weights and include both cloth and paper: two are commonly used in this work, 'cabinet' and 'finishing', terms which refer to the thickness of the paper rather than the fineness of the abrasive. Below will be found a table of comparative British, Continental and American gradings; the last referring to the number of openings per inch of the mesh through which the grit was sieved. It will be noted that grade 1 is recommended for use with both 'cabinet' and 'finishing' backings.

Abrasive paper gradings

British	Continental	American	
M2 coarse	4	80 ⎫	'Cabinet', for preparing
F2 medium	3	120 ⎬	the wood
1 extra fine	1	150 ⎭	'Finishing', for use
1 extra fine	1	150 ⎱	during the polishing
Flour	00	240 ⎰	process

Measurements of volume
Useful for keeping a record of stains, fillers etc.
Approximations sufficient for practical purposes

Metric	British and Canadian	US
4.55 litres	= 1 gallon = 4 quarts	
3.75 litres	=	1 gallon = 4 quarts
1.14 litres	= 1 quart = 5 cups	
946cc	=	1 quart = 4 cups
236cc	=	1 cup = 8oz
30cc	=	1oz = 2 tablespoons
224cc	= 1 cup = 8oz	
28cc	= 1oz = 2 tablespoons	
15cc	= 1 tablespoon = 4 teaspoons	
4cc	= 1 teaspoon	

49

Sandpapering is a dusty, tiring and tedious job, but it may be reduced to a minimum if the planing and scraping are thoroughly done.

Small insets on both curved and straight work can often be more easily handled with files than with chisels and planes, for though the method is slower there is no danger of splitting chips out by misjudging the direction of the grain.

If the old surface adjoining the patch has faded, and repolishing is not intended, the very greatest care will have to be taken to avoid removing any of the old wood. Should any of it be cut away in levelling, particularly in the case of rosewood, it will appear as a dark purple-looking stain which cannot be bleached out. Mahogany is not quite so bad, but its natural redness will contrast with the golden colour of the faded wood.

It is important, of course, that the surface of the patch be above that of the old wood.

Before planing it is well to cover the surrounding wood with paper; the author uses strips of gummed brown paper. With this protection the major part of the work can be carried out, after which the paper is removed and the final levelling completed with a fine file.

In handling shaped work such as the back leg or other parts of chairs, it is well to remember that these were cut out with a saw in the first place and the corners so formed used as a guide in rounding and moulding. For this reason it is usually best to work a new piece to a square section before rounding up. The flattest surface should be first shaped to its neighbours, then the convex surface at right angles to it. These two shapings can be done with a plane. Now set a calliper to the thickness and work the remaining two surfaces until the appropriate width and thickness are correct.

If the member is moulded, the various members can be pencilled in and the quirks (ie small angular grooves) cut in with a V- or parting tool. Next the concave members should be cut with a gouge and finally the convex members should be rounded in to these cuts and any other shaping which seems necessary should be done with spokeshave, scraper, files and sandpaper.

In sandpapering such work it will probably be found easiest to use the fingers as a pad instead of wrapping the paper round a cork block.

The removal of the old finish   The factors on which a decision must be based regarding the retention or removal of the existing surface have been covered in Chapter 1, page 7. Quite often the treatment will vary; ends may be quite satisfactory; front may only need cleaning and a few patches touching up while the top may have had so much work done on it that it must be taken down to a new surface. Maybe also the customer will have given specific instructions.

If the restorer is also the owner and he feels some doubt as to how far he should go, he will likely proceed as follows. First, hot water and pot cleaners; wire wool (steel wool in America) impregnated with detergents. This will quickly reveal the nature of the finish and whether a surface colour-coat has

50

been applied; also it will remove old wax and dirt which would retard the action of a solvent. Perhaps he is now satisfied; if not and a colour-coat appears to cover the original polish he will probably try to remove a corner of it with methylated spirits applied with fine wire wool and the softened coat wiped off with paper towelling. Does the surface beneath look promising? If not, waste no more time, for removal down to the wood is indicated. If it does look satisfactory, continue the process all over leaving the colour as even as possible and transferring some of the softened polish to any patches or bare places. Set aside to dry before levelling with garnet finishing paper.

If it is a typical North American varnish finish with a checked surface, and a minimal job is wanted, it may be fused together by the application of a heavy coat of commercial amalgamator or a mixture of one part toluol to three parts alcohol. The success of the method depends on a number of factors including the thickness of the varnish, the amount of deterioration and subsequent treatment in the home and by other finishers, but it sometimes works wonders though some sanding and more polishing are nearly always required. The result however, at best, is a varnish finish and should not be used on good work. Incidentally, the mixture may be used to liquefy varnish which has become jellied in the tin.

It is more likely that the reason for the colour-coat is still a dead, lack-lustre appearance so further work is indicated. This time use a cabinet scraper on a small area: maybe there is richness below the coating, the dead appearance being due to deterioration of the coating only; if not, further scraping and the application of a little raw linseed oil will be the final test; it well may be that the quality hoped for is just not there and it is foolish to throw good money after bad (time being money), so even up the colour and finish off as quickly as possible.

If the decision is to remove the finish, it may be better to use a commercial varnish remover commonly called a stripper especially if it is a varnish- or spray-coated job. As usually indicated on the label, a heavy coat is applied with a brush; one allows about twenty minutes for it to do its work and then, with a wide putty knife, the softened guck is lifted off and transferred to old newspapers. On carving and mouldings, old sacking is used. Unlike the instructions on the label, however, the process may have to be repeated four or five times. The final cleaning is done with fine wire wool and spirits as described above.

In some places, firms engaged in repolishing have large tanks of solvent into which furniture such as a chair may be immersed thus greatly facilitating removal of finish. When this is the case, it is usually economical to have the firms do the work.

In many jobs it is largely a matter of individual preference whether to use scraper or solvents and a combination of the two is often the best way, using the scraper mainly on the flat surfaces.

In addition to the rectangular cabinet scraper already described, a number of special shapes are found in the toolchest. The first is likely to be one with the corners rounded as in E, Illus 15, each one having been ground or filed for some special job. F and G are about five inches long and were made out of old framesaw blades; the left-hand end of F was shaped to fit the flutes of a pair of columns, while G cleaned the groove between the reeds of a bedpost. When a special shape is needed, one makes it from the one nearest.

H and I are made by grinding off the serrations from two triangular saw-files in the places indicated producing three cutting edges. Both are good for cabriole legs and spindles: H is handy for getting into corners and frets; I can be used with both hands without cutting one's fingers on the sharpened point. For rough work such as cleaning off old glue, the Scarston hook scraper is a useful tool but is rather coarse for fine work, in fact it may cut right through thin, knife-cut veneer especially if there is any weakness in the glue joint.

After scraping there usually remains finish in various places which can now be better handled with solvents.

The wood now being bare, there are three conditions which indicate further work before staining and polishing:
1 the promise of figure and lustre beneath a faded surface,
2 the appearance of white filler in the grain, and
3 when solid wood is so battered that time may be saved by planing.
Procedure with 1 and 3 has already been indicated, but 2 requires some explanation.

A collector had a name for a certain type of cheap though attractive reproduction made perhaps from 100 years ago until the time of World War I; he called it Tottenham Court Road furniture. His daughter, a dealer, still uses the term and has passed it on to others so that it has become well recognized. No doubt it was made in many places but if one can believe old cabinet-makers, much of it was produced in small workshops in the East End of London; mostly by hand with incredible speed. When finished it was put on a hand-barrow (like a costermonger's) and hawked to the smaller retailers in the more fashionable road. The material was, of course, of the cheapest, and was veneered with the thinnest knife-cut laid very skilfully with the hammer: often it would feature a fair amount of inlay where it would have the greatest effect. In order to sell it had to be small, well proportioned; the drawers hand-dovetailed and well finished. By now, much of it is old enough to deceive the novice and so it finds its way to the workshop of the restorer where, if he is not wise to it, he may find himself undertaking to make a silk purse out of a sow's ear.

The main reason why it is mentioned here is that it is often a prime example of the effect of plaster of Paris used as a grain filler; it shows up particularly in areas which have become bleached by exposure to sunlight as a yellow patch flaked by lighter streaks in the grain. When the surface finish has been removed, the contrast between filler and wood is greatly increased and it is almost impossible to remove it without removing wood to the depth of the filler, which could well be the thickness of the veneer.

Of course, these light-coloured fillers were originally made translucent by the application of raw linseed oil, but being oxidized it will not work a second time, nor is the problem confined to the furniture described. With solid wood it may be more economical to plane the tops and fronts at the start, and reasonably thick veneer can be scraped or taken down with a sander.

If the surface has had a normal amount of wear and abuse, it is helpful to give it a good sponging with hot water before the final sandpapering in order to swell up the dents: if this is not done they may well become bumps after staining and further sanding will remove the stain from them.

When a new part, such as a new leg on a Windsor chair, has been fitted to an old and battered piece there is no reason why it should not be faked to match its neighbour. The most obvious step is to simulate the wear with sandpaper and even a spokeshave or rasp. Stretchers worn by the feet can have very deep depressions and the smaller details of turning on the outer side are often quite worn off. These should be carefully copied and corners rounded.

Even when these details have been matched the part may still look out of place through being too smooth. To rectify this give it a good beating with a piece of chain; the kind used to tether a goat made into three or four loops may be used. The cat-o-five-tails shown in Illus 15K was made for this purpose. The operation is best done between the water staining and the filler because the dents will not be raised by the water and the filler will colour them naturally. The leg will then look happier with its dog-bitten neighbours.

Colouring and polishing

The more modern methods of polishing furniture have already been described and, in view of the fact that pieces of the period are now being regarded as antiques, it is reasonable to suggest that the same process should be used in their restoration. To cover their use, however, is not only beyond the scope of this work, but their application cannot be successfully undertaken without well-equipped separate workshops and so the finishes to be considered will be restricted to waxes and French polish.

In order to match the repair to the old surface one should first consider the four factors which come into play; they are as follows:

The nature and colour of the wood itself—by age, chemical action or stain

The colour of the substance which fills the pores

The colour of the surface film

The kind and degree of polish from the open grain of some oak finishes, the wax, the dulled or egg-shell surface to the high polish

To achieve a match, one or more of the following processes are necessary:

Raising dents by means of steam

Filling holes with composition

Staining

Bleaching

Filling the grain

French polish $\left\{\begin{array}{l}\text{Fadding-up} \\ \text{Bodying-in and surface colouring} \\ \text{Further bodying-up} \\ \text{Spiriting-out}\end{array}\right.$ $\left.\begin{array}{l} \\ \\ \end{array}\right\}$ Or wax-polishing

Dull or egg-shell finish

Genuine wax-polishing

Short cuts

Occasionally all these steps need to be taken but more often the problem is more simple. The most common repair job is handled with a filler stain, bodying-up so that the colour can be seen, blending the shade with coloured polishes, and a final body, finished as clean as possible without spiriting-out.

The tools and materials used are both numerous and varied; there is a range of kits on the market containing both equipment and instructions. A list of materials and a description of the author's portable kit will be found in Illus 17. The processes mentioned above will now be considered separately.

Raising dents with steam   If, as an experiment, the surface of a piece of wood is dented with a ball-pein hammer but not fractured, and then boiled in water for a few minutes, the depression will be found to have swelled up again level with the surrounding surface. This fact enables many of the dents in old furniture to be raised and made good without having to be filled.

The first consideration is to get the water into the wood through the polish (assuming that it has not been removed). This is achieved by cutting a number of slits with a razor blade in the direction of the grain and then making a little puddle of water over the dent. In about ten to fifteen minutes it should have soaked in.

Heat is now applied in the form of an electric iron if it is a large area, a soldering iron or a burning-in tool according to the amount of work to be done. A small piece of rag is soaked with water, placed on the dent and the heat applied to it until the water boils. This is repeated until the dent is as level as possible.

If the job is to be refinished using a water stain, it is well to treat all dents in this way or at least sponge the surface with hot water between scraping and sanding because, if the surface is levelled to the bottom of such dents it will be found later that, after staining, the water in the stain will have caused them to swell thus forming raised bumps which will be a continuous nuisance both because sandpapering will rub through the stain on them and also because they will show in the finished job. Should these raised patches occur it is best to wash the stain off as much as possible with hot water, level down with three grades of sandpaper and start over again.

Filling holes with composition   Small holes may be filled with composition at any time during the polishing process and normally the earlier the better. Sometimes, however, it is better to wait till after fadding-up because the colour to be matched will then be more apparent, especially if stain is to be used. Also, unless the patch is very well levelled, the wood surrounding it may be sealed thereby preventing the stain from penetrating.

The material to be used is called stick shellac or stopping and is available in a variety of colours both opaque and translucent. In its opaque form it is almost identical to good sealing wax which, if the colour is right, may be used as a substitute. A piece of button shellac will also do when an orange translucent colour is needed.

The author's burning-in tool is made from half of the spring from an old harmonium, Illus 15J. A piece of brass is riveted to the lower end to hold the heat, and above, it is waisted to discourage the passage of heat to the handle. Any piece of steel such as the blade of a table knife will do, and electric burning-in tools are now available.

If the hole is only a scratch in the surface film, the translucent should be used; but if wood is missing, the lightest tone in the finished job should be matched, erring if at all on the lighter side.

The method of application is to heat the blade of the tool in the flame of a spirit lamp and, with it, melt off the corner of the stick and press it into the hole to be filled; then smooth it over. If the hole is old and dirty, it should be cleaned and roughened with the point of a small knife in order to give better adhesion.

When cool, the surface must be levelled with a file or chisel. The chisel should be perfectly sharp but the angle of the cutting edge comparatively obtuse, about 40°.

It may now be finished with sandpaper; if on a polished surface it will help to lubricate it with raw linseed oil.

Staining The colour of nearly all wood is a combination of three basic colours, red, yellow and black. Less obvious but occasionally useful is green, which can be the answer when the match seems almost impossible. Almost any colour can be matched with a mixture of these colours plus the addition of pigment. In short, wood colours are usually a combination of a dye and a paint.

The dye part may be either a chemical acting on the wood and changing its colour such as potassium bichromate, potassium permanganate or ammonia; a dye dissolved in water such as solutions of the proprietary water-stain crystals; a dye dissolved in benzine or similar solvent sold as penetrating stains, or in alcohol such as Bismarck brown. The table overleaf gives the stains and pigments used by the author.

The chemical stains do not usually mix with the aniline, but pigments may be mixed with most stains to modify, strengthen or cloud up the colour. Pigments are also added to the filler and may be used in shading colour-coats, so that it is well to be wary in using them until the confidence of experience has been achieved.

The good points of water stains are as follows. They are cheap, quickly

	Black	Brown	Red	Yellow	Green	Bleach
Chemical	Iron dissolved in vinegar	Ammonia Washing soda Potassium permanganate Potassium bichromate				Patent bleaches Oxalic acid solution
Water	Chinese ink Indian ink	Aztec brown ink and other coloured inks Water-stain crystals available in all colours Cloth dyes as sold for domestic use				
Penetrating	Available in various colours each brand having its own nomenclature Some brands of shoe dyes also good					
Spirit	Spirit black Nigrosine	Spirit walnut aniline	Bismarck brown Dragons blood	Picric acid Tumeric Aniline yellow	Aniline green	
Pigments	Lamp black	Vandyke brown Raw umber Burnt umber	Rose pink Burnt sienna Red lead Red oxide	Raw sienna Yellow ochre Chrome yellow	Chrome green	

applied with brush and sponge, less fugitive, more penetrating and thus less easily sandpapered through during subsequent operations. But they raise the grain and old bruises and, in the case of chemical stains, cannot be readily washed off.

The penetrating stains are more easily handled and can be considerably lightened by washing with benzine, petrol or turpentine.

The spirit stains are made up with very thin shellac and are seldom used as a basic stain as they are so hard to handle, but they are invaluable for colouring-up and blending.

Bleaching Today there are proprietary brands of bleaches which are very much more powerful than the old ones, but their composition is secret.

SECOND APPLICATION	FIRST APPLICATION				
	Natural	Soda	Biohro	Potassium Permanganate	Iron-vinegar
Soda					
Biohro					
P.P					
I-V					

Sample board for stains on oak

16

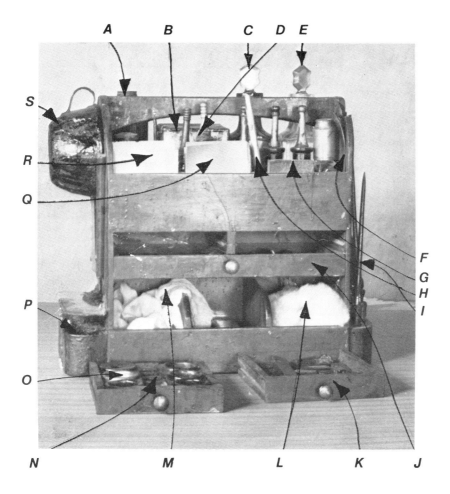

STRING WRAPPED AND GLUED

METAL TUBE WITH
DISC SOLDERED ON BOTTOM

A. Walnut penetrating stain.
B. Tin containing rubbers.
C. Spirit.
D. Shellac.
E. Left to right in bottles:
   1. Stopping, e.g. Brummer (Sealer, e.g. Rez American). Also used as vehicle for bronze powders. 2. India ink. 3 to 7. Bottles, with wooden stoppers identified by their turning, containing coloured shellac. 3. Yellow. 4. Green. 5. Red. 6. Brown. 7. Black. 8. Spirit lamp.
F. Burning-in tool.
G. Cork block.
H. Knife.
I. On end:
   ¾'' chisel blade. Brushes kept in alcohol and turpentine.
J. Artist's oil colours and bronze powders.
K. Stick shellac.
L. Cotton batting.
M. Clothes, steel wool.
N. Dry colours:
   Lamp black. Burnt umber. Raw umber. Raw sienna. Yellow ochre. Red lead.
O. Gramophone needle cups in which to mix colours.
P. In cups: rottenstone, pumice powder, raw linseed oil.
Q. No 1 Garnet finishing paper (U.S. 150).
R. Flour finishing paper (U.S. 240).
S. Shellac cup.

17

A saturated solution of oxalic acid was always recommended in old books and it is very effective in taking out some ink stains, iron stains in oak etc; in short it may be tried and will sometimes work. Before polishing the acid should be killed by the application of an alkali such as a weak solution of washing soda. Calcium chloride is also occasionally successful.

To keep a finish light a preliminary coat of glue-size is recommended. If necessary, pigment may be added to match the colour in the pores. It might surprise many people to realise that if one takes a board and oils one end, adds glue-size to the other and leaves the middle untouched, three contrasting shades will be revealed on polishing.

Many woods, for example walnut, rosewood and satinwood, are seldom stained except to colour sapwood and even up the tone. Others, such as beech and birch are porous enough to respond perfectly well with a single coat of aniline water or penetrating stain.

In the case of mahogany or oak and those woods which are often used with it such as elm, ash and chestnut the author prefers to achieve the colour in several stages starting with a chemical stain. Mahogany is relatively simple; a preliminary stain of 'bichro', rubbed down and then perhaps modified with an aniline wash will suffice. 'Bichro', a saturated solution of bichromate of potash thinned with water, produces quite a good average colour on most mahoganies. It is helpful to make up a sample board divided into squares as follows: first square, full strength; second, $\frac{2}{3}$ bichro, $\frac{1}{3}$ water; third, half and half; fourth, 1 bichro, 2 water; fifth, 1 bichro, 4 water. Mahoganies respond differently, some of the near-mahoganies not at all, but this will provide at least some sort of a guide.

Oak colours naturally very slowly; pieces 100 years old show very little change and so really dark oak is a treasure to be used sparingly. For this reason new wood has to be used for the larger replacements and it is desirable that the colour should not only match but that the wood itself be changed as deeply as possible so that it may stand up to the sanding, rubbing, polishing and at least some abuse. To achieve this the author normally uses one or two coats of chemical stain; a coat of aniline water stain, a fairly heavily coloured filler and often some colour in the fadding-up operation with sanding between all coats.

The chemicals used are as follows: washing soda solution, a medium brown; keep a saturated solution in a quart bottle and thin with an equal quantity of water. Bichro, a reddish brown, half and half as for mahogany. Potassium permanganate, a dark walnut shade somewhat difficult to apply evenly, a teaspoon to a cup of water made up fresh and stirred with a nylon brush (it will eat up animal bristles, natural sponges and play havoc with the skin). Iron-and-vinegar, a very cold black; put a handful of old nails in a quart bottle and fill with vinegar; after about a week it will be ready for use.

Again it is useful to make sample boards; one for white and one for red oak as they respond differently. Lay them out as indicated on page 56 then coat the vertical bands with the stain indicated above: allow to dry and repeat with

58

the horizontal ones. This will produce four single stains and sixteen colours resulting from two coats. The effect of all water stains is greatly strengthened if applied hot; in fact, as with ivory, the greatest penetration is achieved if the piece can be boiled in it, which is occasionally useful in ebonizing small turnings.

Old-timers will remember the 'fumed oak' which was fashionable early in this century. It was achieved by subjecting the furniture to the fumes of ammonia derived from a solution listed as 880-ammonia. Though of limited use in patching, it is perhaps the best foundation stain for oak and may be worth trying when there is enough new wood to warrant it. It is a rather greenish brown but very penetrating and gets everywhere, drawer sides, backs and bottoms etc. Small pieces can be fumed in an old tin trunk or similar container; larger pieces can be covered with a sort of tent made of transparent plastic sheeting so arranged that it touches the surface as little as possible and is sealed to the floor by weighting the edges with pieces of board.

Ammonia is a very powerful gas and, if inhaled at full strength, can have dangerous and painful effects: before uncorking the bottle proceed as follows. Place a shallow bowl in a convenient place with the bottle beside it. Rehearse the action of filling the bowl with liquid, sliding it beneath the plastic or placing it within the box, closing or sealing the opening and recorking. Assure yourself that this can be done in fifteen seconds then take a deep breath, uncork the bottle and carry out the manoeuvre as planned, turn and walk away half-a-dozen paces before inhaling. Instructions usually include a sample piece of wood which can be removed so that the action can be stopped when it has become dark enough but the author usually leaves it overnight. 880-ammonia can also be used with a brush; outside with a breeze.

Let us now, as an example, consider staining a chair. A piece of ¾ in plywood, 30in by 48in, on a pair of saw-horses provides a platform for the more convenient handling of smaller pieces. Rubber gloves are suggested.

Place the chair on the board. A bowl of stain, a 2in brush and a piece of absorbent cloth or a sponge should be at hand. First plan the operation — this usually means starting at a predetermined place, working round and finishing with the most important parts. Tilt the chair to the left; coat the seat rail from the back to the front; down the back of the front leg, the side, the front, the side facing the other front leg; across the front rail, the other front leg, side rail, back leg from the seat down, back rail and other leg. Now the back in similar fashion and finally the seat. Now take the cloth and moisten it with stain either from the bowl or by mopping up the wettest places, then follow the course of the brush going lightly at first and more heavily as it becomes wetter, straightening and evening as you go. Lighter areas which have not absorbed sufficient stain can be coated again with the brush and left. Keep at it until the best possible effect has been achieved.

Filling the grain   Fillers consist of three main ingredients, the first being a liquid known as a vehicle which will harden and tie the solid matter to the wood. It may be water to which glue has been added, linseed oil or a thin form of varnish. In the author's case it is usually one part of marine-spar varnish thinned with two or three parts turpentine: it is kept in a quart gin bottle and labelled 'MIX'.

Second, a powder to form the bulk of the filler, the most satisfactory substance being powdered silica, a crystalline mineral; finely powdered pumice is also good.

Third, pigments for colouring. Vandyke brown and rose pink are the favourite ones for new work being those causing the least amount of cloudiness. With antiques, however, a substitute for the grime and soot is sometimes needed so one or more of the pigments on page 56 may be used.

This type of filler is available ready mixed in various colours and is known as a 'paste wood filler'. A substitute for the thinned varnish vehicle is sold as a 'sealer', and it sometimes incorporates a powerful insecticide, pentachloro-phenol, which is useful if active woodworm is suspected.

When enhancing the beauty of the wood rather than matching the finish is the aim the filler should be kept as translucent as possible and coloured to a shade only slightly darker than the tone of the wood. If a slight darkening is tolerable a modicum of raw linseed oil added to the vehicle will be an advantage.

The filler, which should be of the consistency of custard, is scrubbed in across the grain with an old, short-bristled brush. After a certain length of time it is rubbed in with a piece of sacking (burlap in North America) and the surplus wiped off as cleanly as possible. The length of time between application and wipe-off will vary with the nature of the vehicle and the room temperature. If too short not only will there be a tendency to wipe the material out of the grain but also subsequent shrinkage will further reduce its effectiveness. It is better however to err in this direction than to leave it too long when it will be very difficult to get it clean. As a general rule one should watch the part first coated, and as soon as it dulls start wiping. With good management the wiping will take the same time as the brushing and so the work can proceed in two or three stages. If left too long the sacking can be moistened with turpentine to facilitate the cleaning.

In matching patches and replacements such as a new leg or stretcher, the approach is somewhat different, for the filler may be made to take the place of an accumulation of polishes and dirt. Most early oak and walnut has been subject to coal fires which each winter have deposited an infinitely thin film of tar and soot. In 200 years this can represent a fairly thick and opaque coat, especially in the hollows of carvings, turnings and mouldings. For this therefore, instead of striving for clarity, the opaque pigments such as lamp black, raw and burnt umber and raw sienna are required. The application is also different, the brushing-in may be the same but it is perhaps simply straightened out with the brush and allowed to dry. More likely some wiping will be needed on the areas which would be worn and dusted; in fact it may include the whole range from painting to the treatment for maximum clarity.

The common procedure for a few patches on a number of jobs might be as follows. Put a teaspoon of silica or fine pumice or both in an old tin; now choose the lightest patch, perhaps in mahogany. Maybe the surrounding wood has faded to a shade calling for yellow, so add a pinch of yellow ochre or raw sienna. Now add some of the chosen vehicle from the bottle and mix it up with the brush; try a dab on the patch, rub in and wipe off with a paper towel; perhaps it is too yellow and needs a touch of Vandyke brown; now it is too dark, so more silica and vehicle; this continues until satisfactory. The next job is walnut and possibly the same colour will do; it is more likely that raw umber will be needed. In similar manner continue till the darkest patch has been coated. It is most likely that all the wiping can be done with paper towels.

The inside fronts of veneered drawers, the backs of bookcases and the insides of cupboards were usually finished, when of softwood, with a kind of paint made of glue-size and pigment. When these have been patched, a similar paint can be made by adding pigment and vehicle to the remainder of the filler; burnt sienna is often suitable.

It is not worth while mixing a filler for a very small job; a dab of linseed oil rubbed in with 150- or 180-paper will fill the pores with powdered wood. A little pigment on the finger or artist's oil colour may be rubbed in if necessary and the French polishing process started.

French polish   Jenkins (see Sources of Supply) lists twenty-five kinds of French polish. Spon's *Workshop Receipts* has ten which, in addition to shellac and spirits-of-wine (ethyl alcohol) include the following: gums — copal, arabic, benzoin, sandarach, mastic, elemi and dragon; and virgin wax. Both old polishers and books concur that alcohol and shellac are the only really essential ingredients. Mainly because French polish has not been readily available on Vancouver Island the author cuts (dissolves) his own; about 2½lb to the gallon of denatured ethyl alcohol. Each gallon bottle is dated when mixed and, having enough to last about eighteen months the one in use is normally over a year old. In addition he keeps gum-benzoin solution (also called glaze) which he occasionally adds to the rubber when a particularly bright polish seems required; and gum-sandarach solution which, when added to the shellac in the proportion of one to three, makes it both harder and clearer. White or bleached shellac has been robbed of some of its durability and is not recommended: also it has a very limited bottle-life after which it may dry but not harden.

Polish as it comes is about right for most of the process. When fadding starts, particularly when mouldings, turnings and carvings are involved, it should be thinned with alcohol so as to penetrate more readily to the inner corners. Again, towards the end of the process when lighter and more sweeping strokes are being used, it should be progressively thinned so as to counteract the evaporation and hardening of the rubber as well.

Fadding-up   Take a piece of cotton wool (cotton batten in America) which, when folded and squeezed, makes into an object about the size of an egg, large or small according to the job. Dip it into a cup of French polish, squeeze out the surplus and start covering the surface by a wiping and rubbing motion following a predetermined plan as described for staining. There should be enough work to take at least ten minutes before repeating the process.

If carried out with gay abandon this can easily result in a horrible treacle-tart effect and so is often omitted from books of instruction; but there is no other practical way of getting into the inner corners of mouldings, turnings and carvings or, for instance, the pierced openings of a riband-back chair.

The fad should be squeezed hard after dipping and worked until it ceases to yield its polish even when considerable pressure is used. From time to time, raw linseed oil is transferred to the face of the fad, no more than a drop at a time. Apart from the spray gun there is no quicker way of building up a finish and it used to be the common way of finishing coffins.

For finishing turnings in the lathe there is nothing better than an old, well worn fad. If it is at all moist do not dip it. With the lathe in motion cover the work from end to end squeezing it into every corner and hollow. Follow it with the left hand, whose friction will warm and smooth the surface; continue to repeat the action for perhaps a minute when there will be quite a good polish. After half-an-hour, sand and go over it again; for many jobs this will suffice though a third time may be better.

The fad is a short-lived thing because it is continually being manipulated; pulled out to pass through frets, pointed to get into corners then flattened to be applied perhaps round a cabriole leg. Raw linseed oil should be used, but sparingly; an egg-cup half full should last all day.

When worn out a new fad must of course be made, but retain at least one old one in a tin in case it is needed in an awkward place, for a turning or for shading.

For the author its main function is to reach those places which are beyond his skill with a covered rubber. As soon as they have a reasonable body, the work is set aside to harden for at least half a day.

Two further applications might be mentioned. After a very dirty piece of furniture has been thoroughly scrubbed with detergents, hot water and abrasives and has been allowed to dry, it will have a weathered appearance even though the foundation polish may still be sound. Very often the life may be brought back with a fad in a few minutes especially after an application of raw linseed oil with a pad or rag—for this the polish is thinned. It is likely that the more conspicuous places will need further sanding and polishing but it may well suffice for frames, legs and ends.

The other application is needed for the finishing of the interiors of such things as boxes and drawers. This is an awkward job: after washing if necessary, the surfaces should be first oiled with a brush to get into the corners, wiped out with tissue paper then gone over with the fad with the action and effect of drying it out. No fine polish is needed here; just enough to give it a clean finished look.

Bodying-in and surface colouring   This is the beginning of French polishing proper and may be used on the bare wood if it is sufficiently good and well matched and if the operator has sufficient skill. Normally however it follows the processes already described.

First the fadded-up surface must be smoothed and levelled with fine garnet finishing paper. This is the most important sanding in the finishing process, for after this it is to be kept to a minimum for fear of disturbing any colouring. First tear the paper into pieces 2¾ in × 4½ in (one-eighth sheet) and hold it between thumb and first finger and between third and little fingers, the three fingers forming the pad. These fingers are the most sensitive part of the human body and so can feel any roughness through the paper and also any edge, which must be avoided for fear of cutting through to the bare wood beneath the stain. Apprentices who used to work for days at this unpleasant job would bandage their little finger to prevent it becoming raw through abrasion.

During this process more faults are likely to be revealed and they should now be filled with stick shellac or stopping as already described.

The bodying-in process can now be started; the rubber being normally the same sort of cotton wool as was used for the fad. The author however prefers to use wool; perhaps the filling from an old wool comforter or raw wool obtained from a farmer. It will retain its absorbency much longer and is more resilient than cotton and for this reason should be first sewn into a little bag made of knitted cotton underwear material.

The cover must be either fine linen or cotton; modern synthetic materials including 50 per cent cotton mixtures are not satisfactory because they seem to form an impervious film before the rubber is half worked out, causing it to slide over the work without effect. Since without a label they are hard to tell from pure cotton, they may be suspected if the work is not proceeding in a normal way. The cotton wool or wool is charged with thin polish either by dipping or by pouring on the polish from a bottle with a grooved cork. It is placed on the cover which may be about the size of a man's handkerchief and the surplus cloth twisted up behind it and held in the palm of the hand, the thumb and fingers holding and shaping the face from which the polish is to pass on to the wood. It should be wrinkle free and pointed beneath the fingers. A few drops of raw linseed oil must be applied to the surface of the rubber to prevent sticking.

The rubber must never be allowed to rest on the work, or it will stick to the surface and bring away the polish that has already been deposited. On large surfaces the rubbing must be done with a progressive circular motion, beginning in one corner, proceeding horizontally backwards and forwards (always overlapping the lines of rubbing) and finishing in the opposite corner. Proceed in the manner described for fadding, the rubber being removed from its cover for dipping up as required and moved to an unworn part of the cover as long as it will last. Work out each rubber; the pressure should be perfectly even and sufficient to cause the polish to pass on to the work, but leave no sign of wetness; it must increase as the rubber dries out until the combined pressure of both hands, one above the other, is used. Particular attention should be paid to the corners by passing the rubber right off the work — this counteracts the tendency of the novice to miss them.

At this time apply only enough polish to 'see your colour' (this can be better experienced than described) and then start the colouring-up.

Most colouring is done with an artist's small camel-hair brush, or pencil as it may be called. A couple of brushfuls of polish, one of a mixture of black and red shellac and a little pigment picked up with the brush may be the start. The brush is now dabbed onto the place to be coloured and the shade compared. Does it require more red, black or yellow? Is it too clear or too cloudy, too light or too dark? If adjustments are necessary, a rubber should be used to wipe it off. By the time the shade is right it is likely that enough will have been added to provide sufficient for the whole job.

The colour should be on the light side, so the light patch will need two or three coats while other parts can be brought to colour with one. If the colour is too dark when applied, it may be at once spread with the hand — this will also pick up some of the colour. Going over a wet patch a second time before it is dry must, of course, be avoided. Three or four minutes are sufficient for it to dry. Puddles of colour must be avoided for they dry with a dark rim.

Dark patches can be lightened by giving them coats of yellow ochre, red lead or chrome yellow, though it is better at times to make them part of the figure by bringing the grain around them as suggested in Illus 18A. If this piece of faking looks too isolated in a plain piece of wood the figure may be accentuated in another area not too far away, to give a better balance to the piece.

Illus 18B is designed to show how a poorly matched patch can be blended in with colour so that it is less noticeable. The grain of the main wood and also the patch should be carried across the joint by colouring-in. A mixture containing more pigment is generally used for this purpose.

Any missing inlay will have been repaired before the polishing began; Illus 18C suggests how a banding of ebony and boxwood may be simulated with pen and Indian ink on a plain insert. If a banding of some fancy wood such as tulipwood or kingwood needs repair and the actual wood is unobtainable, another wood with similar basic colouring such as yew may be substituted, and the grain faked in with coloured polish applied with a brush.

Larger areas can also be shaded by adding colour to the rubber, or perhaps a worn fad can be used. Even a touch of pigment is sometimes effective: after applying it to the fad or rubber it should first be worked on the back of a piece of sandpaper to even it and to judge its probable effect. Although the intent is to finish the colouring as soon as possible it often happens that it continues for some time when one realises that perhaps a faded end is still on the light side.

Further bodying-up Now follows more bodying-in; the circular motion which covers a band from four to six inches wide can be changed to a figure-of-eight motion covering twice as much. This is alternated by straight sweeps

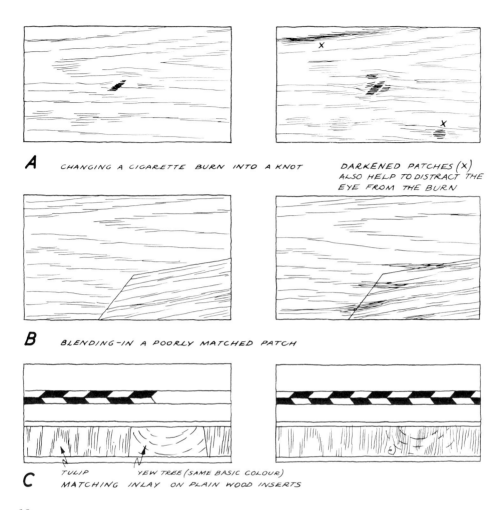

A CHANGING A CIGARETTE BURN INTO A KNOT

DARKENED PATCHES (X)
ALSO HELP TO DISTRACT THE
EYE FROM THE BURN

B BLENDING-IN A POORLY MATCHED PATCH

TULIP   YEW TREE (SAME BASIC COLOUR)
C MATCHING INLAY ON PLAIN WOOD INSERTS

18

the length of the top passing off the edge at the end of each stroke and gliding onto the work on the return. Now increase the figure-of-eights to the entire width or length of the board.

This requires hard physical effort and there will be a strong temptation to substitute a wetter rubber for the pressure required to work it right out before recharging. This may result in the type of French polishing deplored by R. W. Symonds.

Fine pumice powder tied in a piece of cloth called a pounce can be very sparingly dusted on the surface when the rubber is about half worked out continuing also with the occasional drop of linseed oil.

Although an expert may handle his rubber with such skill that the surface never becomes wet, the amateur and occasional polisher will likely find that he has misjudged the relationship between amount of liquid and pressure applied, with the result that particles of dust will stick and whips will be left after the passage of the rubber. When these are noticed, pause for a five-minute rest then remove the roughness with the finest paper moistened with oil and with light pressure and continue.

When the straight strokes cannot be seen in the curved ones or vice-versa the finish will probably be good enough for most jobs, but highly finished pieces, particularly in satinwood or rosewood, may need spiriting-out.

Spiriting-out   As in any other type of work the final stage is dependent for its success on the preliminary work. The surface must be perfect in every respect, except for the smear of oil tracing the last motion of the rubber. Any other defect will remain and be more apparent after the spiriting-out.

The operation is simple. Methylated spirit (ethyl alcohol) is poured into a saucer so that it may be easily absorbed by a new piece of cotton wool. A piece of cotton cloth is placed over it and a rubber formed; this is squeezed in the hand to distribute the liquid. If too wet it is dried on a piece of paper. It is tried on the cheek, but what the correct degree of wetness is, is impossible to describe. When ready it is quickly passed over the work in long sweeping strokes with feather-weight pressure at first, increasing the pressure as the rubber is worked out. The cloth must be frequently changed as it absorbs the oil. In five to ten minutes the work should be bright.

Dull or egg-shell finish   If the polish is too bright or glassy it can be dulled by means of a moderately soft brush (such as is used for boot polishing) and very fine pumice powder, finishing with a soft cloth. Carvings, turnings and mouldings get the same treatment and great care should be exercised to get the residue of the powder out of the corners.

Genuine wax polishing   It is often said that a patinated surface cannot be successfully matched, and the author felt this to be true for it was not until after twenty years' experience that he found a way to produce a satisfactory copy.

As is so often the case, the solution was very simple. It happened that a Chippendale chair had come in with the back broken. This had been repaired with old wood of a very good match for both colour and texture so that very little colouring was necessary, except where there was a little dirt in the crevices of the carving.

An electric sad-iron was placed in the vice, sole up and heated, a block of beeswax was rubbed over it so that it became covered with a thin layer of molten wax, this was sprinkled with raw umber, a very good dirt colour. A shoe brush was rubbed into this mixture and held in it until the bristles had time to warm up thoroughly. It was then removed, and the repaired part of the chair was given a vigorous brushing. The brush quickly cooled off, but it was soon warmed up again and the brushing repeated until the whole of the repaired area had been covered.

The result of this was so successful, both in appearance and feel, that the owner was delighted, for in spite of the fine patina which he thought could not be matched he could not pick out the damaged chair from the set.

Since that time this process has been used on a great many pieces of furniture including walnut and oak.

It has been found that the surface is less hard than a genuine patina, but it is thought that time will have the effect of hardening it, especially if it gets continued care and is occasionally waxed in the ordinary way.

In handling flat surfaces it was found that the wax was inclined to build up into little lumps; this was overcome by playing the flame of a bunsen burner on them and then brushing them out. The burner was, of course, attached to the gas main by a rubber tube.

This is a match only for a true patina, but most wax finishes are in combination with other kinds of polish, leaving the grain more or less open finished with a coat of wax.

Such a finish requires similar treatment and may be carried out by following the processes described in this chapter as far as the colouring-up, after which it should receive a fairly heavy coat of shellac with a brush and then be rubbed down with fine steel wool.

The final finish is one or more coats of paste wax polished with a piece of silk or, if available, a power-operated brush polisher.

The amount of filler and shellac in the first bodying-up will depend on the amount to which the grain has to be filled.

Short cuts   In doing work where the price has to be kept as low as possible, it is worth remembering that it is quicker to match with pigment than with transparent colour, and so the start may be made with a heavily coloured filler. This may be followed with a rather wet rubber, for it is quicker to use than a brush if any sort of levelling is wanted.

The only way to save time in colouring-up is to use more pigment in the mixture, for the nearer it approaches the nature of a paint the less will be its variation in colour. Transparent colours vary from the lightest tint to the darkest according to the thickness of the coat or coats and so they must be built up to the required darkness of each colour area with care and skill.

After colouring all that is needed is a coat of flat varnish. This minimises the faults instead of exaggerating them as would a glossy polish. If time does not admit of the varnish drying, a similar effect may be had with a coat of shellac rubbed dull with steel wool.

This chapter has dealt with the six steps which form the basis essential to furniture repairing in general. These steps were as follows:

Dismantling
Cleaning joints
Restoring components
Glueing up
Levelling and sandpapering
Colouring and polishing

In Chapters 4, 5 and 6 the principles enunciated will be applied in detail to different kinds of construction, for example:

Chairs, of various types

Carcase work

Drawers, repairing and refitting

Chapter 7 describes veneering, marquetry and mosaic bandings; Chapter 8 deals with miscellaneous problems such as turnery, mouldings, worm-eaten wood, lacquer work etc, and Chapter 9 with the making and colouring of metal fittings.

Chapters 10 and 11 give examples, with illustrations, of a number of specific jobs which have passed through the author's hands, and describes the numerous problems which he encountered and how he dealt with them.

4 Chair Repair

Owing to the fact that chairs are limited in weight for reasons of easy handling and good proportion they are more heavily loaded for their strength than any other kind of furniture, with the result that they form the major part of the work of the repairer.

In view of this fact a man who values his reputation will realise that his best work will be put to the hardest test, and so he will strengthen the chair in any way possible consistent with good practice and satisfactory appearance.

In assessing the various methods used for this purpose it is necessary first to consider the stresses applied to a chair in both use and abuse.

The worst treatment it may be expected to take is when a heavy man or woman throws himself or herself back in it to such an extent that the front legs leave the ground. This is by no means an uncommon thing, and every chair which has been reglued should be tested in this way.

Now the greatest stress is concentrated where the seat rail joins the back leg, and the joint here is the most common one to fail. It should be noted that it is the top part of the tenon which takes the weight and will therefore be the first to give way. Then again there is the tendency of the back leg to break in half. Here again the point of greatest stress is in the same place. At this point the leg is also weakened by mortices.

The weight on the top back rail will place a stress on the joint at each side, and the joint will start opening in the front and not at the back.

Other stresses will be applied to a chair when it is knocked over backwards; when it comes into contact with obstacles in being carried; when it is dragged about while someone is sitting in it and so on; but these are unpredictable and cannot be particularly guarded against.

To return to the seat rail and back leg joint, a common form of brace is an angular piece of metal screwed to the underside of the rail and back leg as indicated in Illus 19A. This is practically useless as it will spring enough to allow the top part of the tenon to pull out far enough to break the glue. When that has happened it will not be stiff enough to prevent the joint from being loose. If it were placed above the rail as in B, it would do more good for its screws would have to be drawn or else it would have to be bent out of shape before the joint could open and it would be out of sight in an upholstered

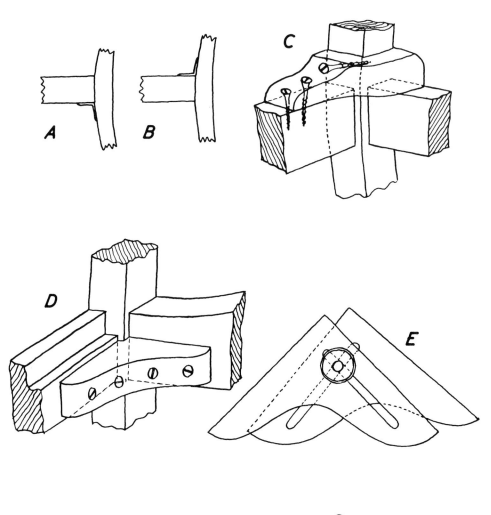

19

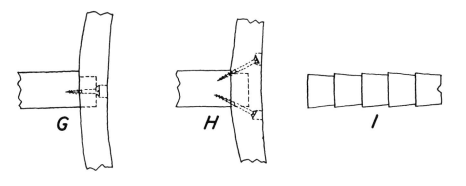

chair. Even here it would have the disadvantages of all such ironwork, that is, that it does not offer much resistance to a very slight movement, and a slight movement is all that is necessary to start weakening the tenon or dowelled joint. If the reader doubts this, he should try screwing an iron bracket on a board, also a piece of wood with glue and screws; mark their positions carefully and try moving them $\frac{1}{16}$ in with a hammer, striking each alternately a similar blow. Each blow will slightly move the metal, but the wood will remain in position until it receives a blow sufficiently hard to break the glue.

The most effective form of brace is that shown at C, which should be cut out of a piece of maple or beech about 1in thick and fitted very carefully to the top of the rail and the front edge of the leg. The joints on the back rail and inside of the leg should also be good but are not quite so important. The leg here should, of course, be scraped so as to give a clean surface for the glue and the screw-holes should be bored to the full depth of the screws.

This brace gives added strength where the load is greatest; it gives support above the mortice, thus relieving this weakened part of some of its stress; also it enables the upholsterer to make a neater job of his gimp around the back legs.

In chairs having a slip seat, that is a seat upholstered on a frame and fitting into a recess in the chair, this type of brace cannot be used for it would show. The best that can be done in this case is to fit a block to the inside of the side and back rails around the leg as shown at D. This is the most common kind and if carefully fitted, which is rarely done, adds a good deal to the strength of the joints.

A little tool which can easily be made is shown at E and F. It consists of two thin plates cut out of hard sheet-brass and fastened together with a short bolt and knurled nut. The head of the bolt, which should be as large as possible, is filed so that it leaves a slight projection fitting into the slot in the lower plate to prevent it turning when the wing nut is tightened.

This device is fitted around the leg where the brace is to go, each plate against a rail, and the nut tightened. It may now be removed, laid flat on a suitable piece of wood and the corner block marked out. After cutting, a few strokes with a smoothing plane usually suffice to make the fit perfect. The small braces notched into the rails inside the top edges across each corner of old upholstered chairs are designed to relieve the tenons of the strain of the upholsterer's webbing, a stress of several hundred pounds with tight webs and a heavy weight sitting on them. These braces should always be put back, and if found slack, new ones should be fitted, that is unless the larger corner braces occupy their places.

A fairly common practice is to put screws through the back leg into the rail; this is to make a repair without dismantling, and quite often they fail completely in their object by being countersunk so deeply that the heads are in the mortice with the screw in the tenon as shown at G.

Should it be felt that screws are the only recourse available they should be put in as indicated at H where they will not only go through solid wood but will

A

B

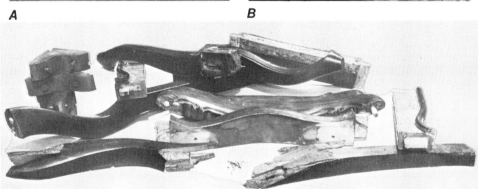

C

20

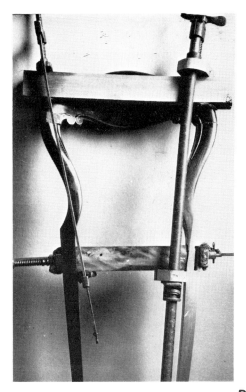

D

E

F

also hold where the stress is greatest. If plugs are glued into the holes bored to accommodate the heads they will not be unsightly. These plugs can be turned on the lathe with the grain across and are usually made as shown in Illus 19I.

Repairs to a Victorian chair

The work to be carried out on this chair is typical of such work, and a description of each step of the repair will be attempted.

The first consideration is to examine the chair in the presence of the customer and to point out each fault so that he or she will appreciate the work to be done.

An examination of the photograph in Illus 20A, will reveal some of the faults, others can only be found by testing for firmness etc. Here is a list of the faults.

1 Back leg broken off.
2 All joints in the seat are loose.
3 The top rail of the back is loose and has been badly patched on the left hand (compare A and F, Illus 20).
4 The top end of the broken leg has been patched and the patch is loose, B.

The first thing to do is to remove the upholstery. This is best done with an old ½ in chisel and a mallet. The blade of the chisel is tucked under the head of the tack and the handle is given a light blow with a mallet, at the same time depressing the chisel. With practice this flips the tack out. This takes more time than customers realise, for there are upwards of three hundred tacks in an ordinary dining-chair, and all those which do not break off should be removed.

The corner blocks are next marked and unscrewed, the screws are put back in their holes in the blocks as they may vary in length and thickness, and it saves time to have them where they will fit. Old glue may also be scraped off them and then they can be put away until the chair has been put together again.

The top back rail is next removed without difficulty, but the seat frame is a different matter for it has been nailed in all directions. However, it responds to the various methods described in Chapter 3 and is dismantled without damage except for the broken back leg, which is so full of nails embedded in glue etc, that by the time it is apart it is so splintered that it is necessary to replace the lower half. Part of the tenon on the left-hand side rail in front is also found to have been broken away.

The various parts are now cleaned, first with a scraper on the flat surfaces, not omitting the inside surfaces of the seat rails where the corner braces would have to be glued; the other parts are washed with hot water.

There are five places requiring new wood: part of the tenon, the lower half of the back leg, the upper end of the same leg at the back, a chip off the top rail on the left hand where the curve of the back forms a point and the lower

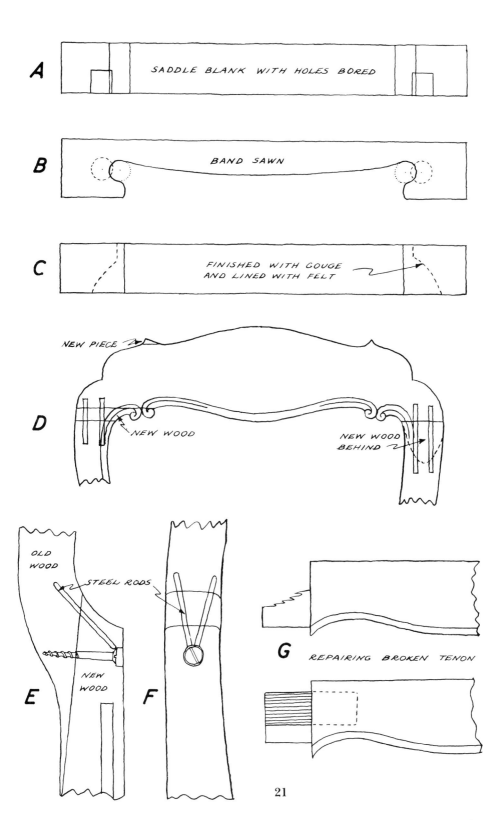

A   SADDLE BLANK WITH HOLES BORED

B   BAND SAWN

C   FINISHED WITH GOUGE AND LINED WITH FELT

D   NEW PIECE   NEW WOOD   NEW WOOD BEHIND

E   OLD WOOD   STEEL RODS   NEW WOOD

F

G   REPAIRING BROKEN TENON

21

edge on the same side where a poor job of fitting and carving has been done.

No old wood is available for the back leg, so new mahogany has to be used. The joint used is shown in the sketch, Illus 21, E and F. First the new part is cut out and the joint made, it is then screwed with a 1¾in No 12 steel screw and carefully tested against the other leg for alignment etc. When satisfactory, it is taken apart, glued, screwed and cramped together. The next day two ³⁄₁₆in holes are bored diverging from the ½in countersink for the screw-head and occupying the positions shown in the sketch. Two steel pins are then driven into them, the screw replaced and the countersink plugged.

The mortices are then cut and the leg is cleaned up. The mortice for the back rail is square with the face, but that for the side rail is at an angle (Illus 22A). In some cases the tenon is cut on an angle and the mortice square, as in 22B.

The upper part of the same leg at the back is simply planed off level, and a suitable piece of old wood glued and rubbed into position.

The badly carved up repair on the left of the top back rail is knocked off and

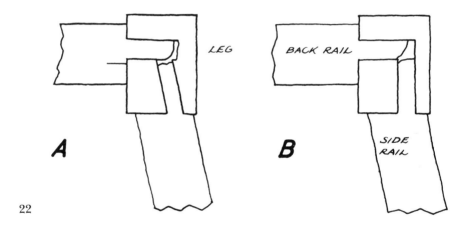

22

replaced with mahogany of similar colour as is also the chip at the top. The former in the rough may be seen in D.

The broken tenon is repaired by boring out a mortice in the rail and glueing a piece of oak into it (Illus 21G).

The front rail and legs are in good condition and so are glued and assembled on the first day and set aside.

The top back rail and back legs having been made good are prepared for assembly. The seat rail is first fitted and the legs secured to it, dry, with a cramp. The top rail is then tried in position and the joining surfaces planed or chiselled until the joint on both sides is satisfactory. When dismantled, only one dowel is found in each side, but originally there were two and as new wood formed one side of each pair of joining surfaces it is decided to fit two to each side and make them long enough to strengthen the joint between the new and old wood. Thus the dowels on the left are made extra long in the top rail and those on the right passed through the patch behind and well down into the leg, Illus 21D.

Opposite the new wood on each side is an old surface containing two dowels; one has been cut off smooth and one is broken off just below the surface. Their positions have to be marked on their opposite surfaces. The flush one is marked with a centre punch, and a small ball bearing is placed in the cavity thus formed. The top rail is then placed in position and given a light blow; the balls make a very clean and clear imprint. The dowel broken below the surface is too ragged for this method and so a finishing nail is driven into it as near the centre as possible, cut off just above the surface and then bent to the exact centre. This serves the same purpose as the balls, although it takes a little longer to fix. The old dowels are then bored out as well as the new dowel holes and new dowels are fitted.

In order to cramp down the top back rail a saddle has to be made. A piece of oak 2½in × 2½in × 20in is used and four 1¼in holes are bored as shown in A and B (Illus 21). It is then cut out with a bandsaw, and the two ends hollowed out with a gouge, C. Finally these points of contact are lined with felt. In use it may be seen in D (Illus 20).

The back, when dry, is carved up and sandpapered and then the seat frame is assembled. The corner brackets are reglued and screwed, and added strength is given by means of braces described earlier in this chapter; they may be seen in E (Illus 20), which shows the chair ready for the polisher, while F is the finished job.

When the side rails have become weakened by tack-holes these parts should receive a liberal coating of hot thin glue well brushed in. This will help to restore some of the lost strength and the ability to hold tacks.

In cramping up the side rails of this type of chair the cramps are liable to slip off the back legs owing to the fact that they are often at an angle to the back rail. In this case a saddle should be used, such as that shown in Illus 24A.

Repairs to back leg of a Duncan Phyfe chair

Another way of repairing a chair leg is illustrated in Illus 23.

A is the leg which has been broken and patched up a number of times in various ways and is now so split that the bad part must be cut away.

B is a cardboard made from the good leg on the opposite side.

C shows the leg with the damaged part cut away in such a manner as to give the largest glue area possible and with the two cut surfaces when placed in position forming a wedge. The pattern is then laid on a board about ¾in × 6in × 3ft and the two pieces cramped into their respective positions on it. A tapered piece is then fitted into the gap with its grain exactly following that in the leg itself. It is always easier to fit a tapered piece than a parallel one, for it can be cut with excess length on the thick end and this will allow plenty of material for planing away to make a perfect joint. When satisfactory

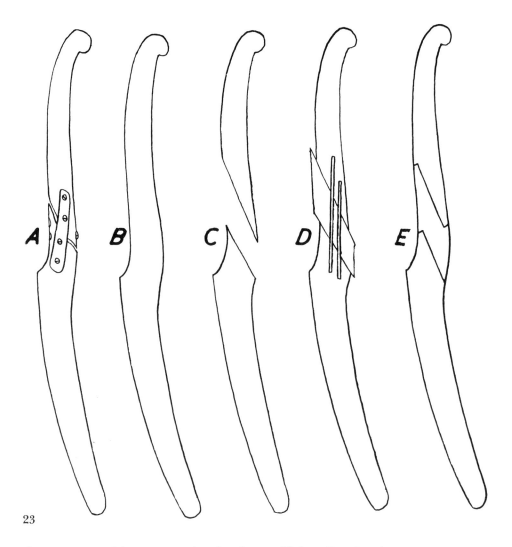

23

the excess wood is cut away leaving just sufficient for cleaning up.

It is next glued to the upper piece with two dabs of glue about the size of a normal, square postage stamp. When it is dry, two parallel $\frac{5}{16}$ in holes are drilled through the new piece upwards into the old. It is then permanently glued to the lower part, checking the alignment against the pattern. The next morning the upper joint is broken and the two holes continued downwards into the lower part.

Two cold-rolled steel rods are then cut to fit the holes, and the leg is assembled, glued and cramped up; a sectional view is shown at D.

Some would advocate the cutting of the joints as at E in order to avoid the feather edge which is liable to catch in things and so give trouble.

This objection is valid only when the glue starts to fail or when poorly fitted; for when well done the straight joint is not perceptible to the hand when passed over it nor to the eye, except for variations of colour and grain.

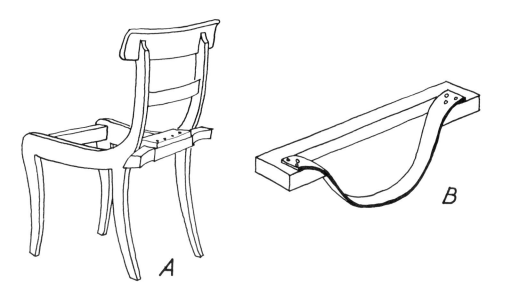

A

B

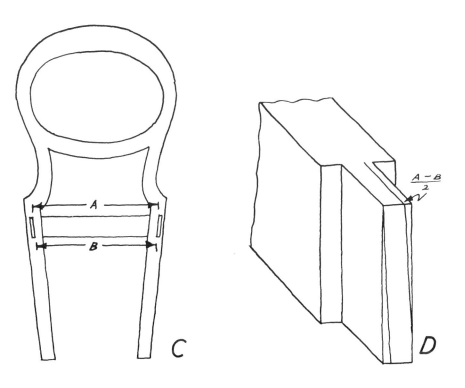

C

D

$$\frac{A-B}{2}$$

The stopped scarf, as at E, requires much more skill and time to make a perfect fit, the glue area is slightly less and therefore the finished job is weaker.

The type of saddle used for glueing up the side rails of these chairs is shown in Illus 24A. It is cramped onto the back seat rail with a G-cramp and prevents the cramp sliding down the inclined surface and spoiling the back leg. If the surface touching the back leg is rounded and covered with ½in felt, it will accommodate a variety of chairs.

In renewing the side rails of old chairs, the fact that the back tenons are not quite vertical can be easily overlooked.

In marking out, the following method may be used: add to the thickness of the back tenons half A minus B (Illus 24 (C)), then complete the laying out as shown in (D).

If they are to be cut by machine, make them the extra thickness and then plane to angle with a rebate plane.

Ladder-back chairs

The repair of this type of chair may require the solution of two problems: (1) to make good the seat joints without removing the rush, and (2) to bend the horizontal curved 'rungs' of the back.

With regard to the first problem it will usually be found that in an old chair the rush seat will be capable of considerable stretch. If the legs are forced apart by the use of a light car jack there will be room to get glue around the pins and, by means of a glue syringe (see description on page 46), into the holes in the leg. The pins are then forced into the gluey holes and the other ends attended to. The first side attended to may be cramped up and the jack moved to the other side until all are done.

New rungs may be steamed and bent between two forms; these should be made out of a piece of soft wood about 3in × 6in × 20in. The wood should be cut to a radius of about two-thirds that of the finished rungs in order to allow for the straightening which takes place when they are taken out. Three or four may be bent at one time, placing them all together between the forms, and forcing the forms together in the vice. After this they may be held together

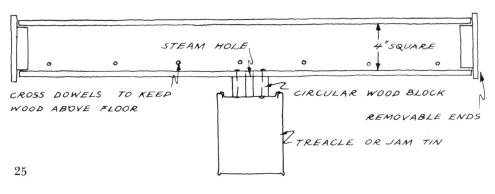

STEAM HOLE   4"SQUARE

CROSS DOWELS TO KEEP WOOD ABOVE FLOOR

CIRCULAR WOOD BLOCK

REMOVABLE ENDS

TREACLE OR JAM TIN

25

with a couple of cramps and set aside for a day or two to set.

A steam box can be made very simply by nailing together a box about 3in × 4in × 4ft long (see Illus 25). Each end should be fitted with a removable plug so that strips can be steamed in the middle by passing them right through and stopping the openings with cloth.

A hole is bored in the centre of the 3in side, and a corresponding hole in the lid of a treacle tin. This is nailed to the box, with a block of wood (also having a hole through it) between the box and the lid, to fill the depression in the lid.

The tin is half filled with water and the box fitted to it, and the whole thing put on a hot-plate.

When the water has been boiling long enough to have the interior of the box thoroughly heated up, the rungs may be put in. About twenty minutes inside the box is usually sufficient for thin wood.

It might be worth while warning against kiln-dried lumber which is very hard to bend. Old ladder-back chairs had the rungs cleft from a billet in the woods, where they were steamed, bent and left to season in that form.

Hepplewhite—shield and oval-back chairs

An examination of Illus 4 should explain the result of shrinkage in this type of chair, and the oval back shown in Illus 26A is of similar construction.

When these chairs are to be repaired they should be cleaned and put together dry. If there are gaps at the side joints of the top rail, it should be adjusted so that these two gaps are the same on both sides. They can now be carefully measured and the same amount removed from the shoulder at the bottom of the centre splat; this will enable the chair to go together without strain.

When the splat is so wide that there is a considerable difference in length between its sides and centre the upper shoulder may need fitting to the top rail. Shrinkage will have caused the rail to be straighter, and also by shortening the splat its curve will be greater.

The saddle suitable for oval backs is shown in Illus 26A and consists of a strap (a piece of leather belting in this case) nailed to a piece of wood. Illus 24 (B) shows a view of this upside down.

Shield backs can be cramped with only a felt pad on each side.

Inherently weak parts

Repairs are occasionally asked for on parts which are so pierced and carved that they could not be expected to stand up to wear even if they had not been damaged. In these cases there is little prospect of making a repair which will enhance the repairer's reputation.

There are three courses available in such a case:

26

B C

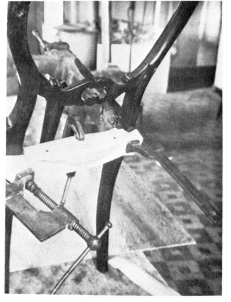

A

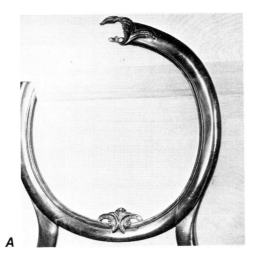

A

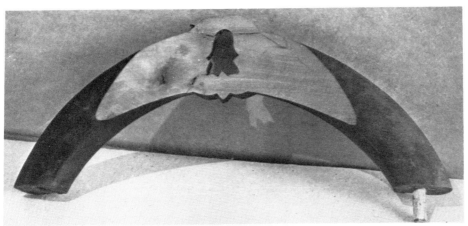

B
C

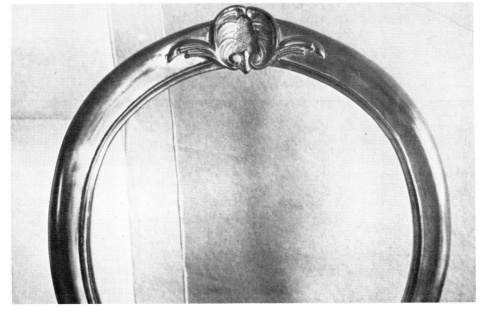

1 To make the repair as well as possible, but to take no responsibility for it.
2 To use metal braces, a method which will be considered later.
3 To change the design and reconstruct in such a way as to make a strong serviceable part, first obtaining the customer's sanction.

An example of the last is shown in Illus 27. Here was a piece which had been broken and repaired many times, and so it was decided to convert it from a pierced into a relief carving.

The first thing was to glue up the break as well as possible and to replace the chips missing in front, then to remove sufficient wood from behind to form a flat surface leaving the carved face about ½ in thick (Illus 27B). This may be done on a jointer, taking care that the fingers do not get hurt even if the glued joint should break. A suitable piece of wood was next fitted and holes bored for two short, ¼ in positioning dowels to prevent slipping when cramping up. The opening in the centre was then marked, and after taking apart this area was gouged over and frosted with carver's punches so that it would not look too flat. It might also have been coloured and polished if a particularly clean job had been required.

The rest of the work was straightforward and, as may be seen from the last photograph, does not appear incongruous.

Another part occasionally giving the same trouble is the middle back rail of similar chairs, such as the one pictured in B, Illus 26. These may be strengthened by fitting a piece of mahogany about $\frac{3}{16}$ in thick bent to the curve and glued to the back of the rail. Here again the part seen through the piercing may be gouged up and frosted.

In other cases, parts of the carving itself may be replaced with similar pieces of heavier section. This can sometimes be done with little apparent change by adding the material where it is not often seen.

The use of metal braces

The use of unsightly exposed metal braces on chairs is usually the recourse of the poor artisan and should have no place in first-class work.

In spite of this it often provides the only alternative to discarding an article which is not considered worthy of the expense of a good job. If well done, it should make the piece serviceable for many years without being too ugly.

The metal to be used should be sufficiently stiff to bear the whole weight that might have been expected to be borne by the wood. Thin plates of soft metal are worthless except where their function is solely to withstand tensile stress. The stiffest ordinary metal is steel, though duralumin is not much less stiff and has the advantage of being lighter, rustless and capable of being easily cut with a skip-tooth bandsaw. This also applies to brass which should be obtained in its hard form; it is available in soft, half-hard and hard forms.

Most braces are analogous to A and B (Illus 28). When the pressure is downward at the ends, the metal on A will be in tension and the joint will be

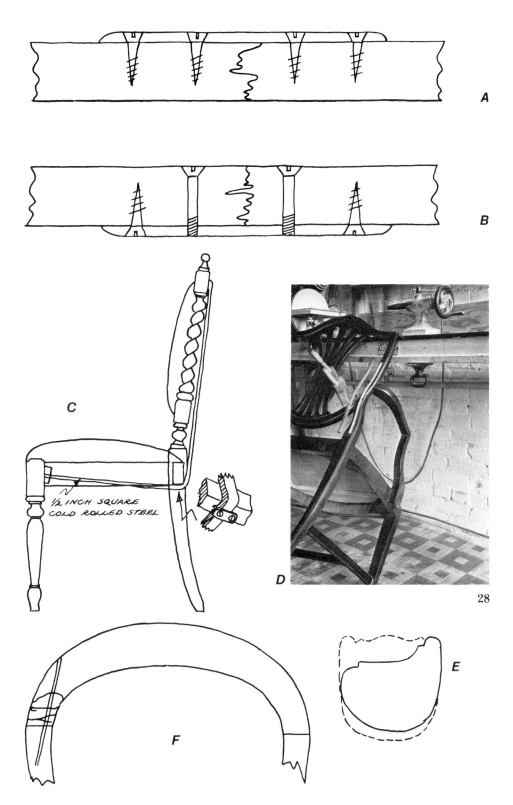

A

B

C

½ INCH SQUARE
COLD ROLLED STEEL

D

28

E

F

quite strong especially if the screw-holes be bored slightly away from the centre in the wood, thus tending to put a slight pull on the metal. This is often impractical owing to the fact that it would be on the face side of the wood and so would spoil its appearance. In this case B must be resorted to, and it is here that it is so essential that it be stiff enough to support the whole weight without assistance from the wood. If it is capable of bending, say, $\frac{1}{16}$ in with the pressure likely to be put on it, this will be enough to break the joint in the wood after which it will have to take all the weight. The method of fastening shown, using machine screws threaded into the metal, is much to be preferred to using wood screws as shown in A, because thinner screws may be used thus weakening less both the wood and the metal. The weight is also taken from the full thickness of the wood. It has the disadvantage of marring the face, but the screw-heads may be counter-bored $\frac{1}{8}$ in deep and plugged, or if the wood is too thin they should be countersunk slightly below the surface and covered with composition.

Illus 28D shows a more elaborate repair made by inlaying a piece of $\frac{3}{8}$ in square cold-rolled steel. This was a case of an attempt to make a mass-produced chair in the Hepplewhite style. A section of the frame of the shield back is shown in Illus 28E, with the correct section in dotted lines; this form was used to enable it to be cut on a shaper. This section plus the housing and screw hole for the arm added to the soft mahogany used was beyond a normal repair and so the metal had to be used. After it had been bent to the desired shape it was let in almost flush, screwed with a long screw into the arm, its principal tie, and with three other small screws. It was then filed slightly, rounding at the back, and painted to match the wood.

Cold-rolled steel in both round and square section can be readily obtained from a hardware concern and is quite inexpensive. It is a very useful article to have in stock.

Illus 28C shows a method of supporting a chair back by means of a steel rod. This chair was broken at the turned part of the back legs just above the seat, and it was all so badly worm-eaten that it seemed hardly worth attempting a repair. However, it had sentimental value, and so it was decided to try the use of a metal brace.

The woodwork was first dowelled together with large dowels, soaking plenty of glue into the worm holes, after which the back was to be held by a $\frac{1}{2}$ in square cold-rolled steel rod capable of supporting it without the wood. The metal was first taken to a blacksmith, who bent it at right angles cold, as heating might have left it softer. The lower arm was made long enough nearly to touch the inside of the front rail, the upper was bent slightly to conform with the curve of the back and let into the lower edge of the top back rail and screwed there. The front end was let into a block screwed to the inside of the front rail and pinned to it. Support under the back seat rail was effected by means of a $\frac{1}{8}$ in $\times$ $\frac{3}{4}$ in $\times$ $1\frac{1}{4}$ in brass plate with stout screws on each side of the bar; this was to prevent weakening it by boring holes at this its point of greatest stress.

86

In fitting, the two back fastenings were secured first, the front block having been previously placed in position but not screwed. It was then slightly depressed so that the back should be sprung slightly forward to counteract the weight of a person leaning back, and then the block was screwed down. Lastly a hole was drilled through both block and bar, and a nail driven through it to prevent it slipping back.

This was not unsightly for a little padding was added to the upholstery of the back and the metal covered up with cloth, except for a small piece between the seat and back which was painted to match.

Steel dowels are often a great help, especially where a cheap job is required. Holes may be bored through parts which have been shattered and glued up and rods inserted in them which are capable of carrying the weight independently of the wood. Such an example is shown in Illus 28F, which represents the back rail of a Victorian chair. The wood at the left would be cut away and replaced if a good job was required, but if it is glued up as well as possible and strengthened with the $\frac{5}{16}$ in rod as shown it should probably give a good service.

If the joint is apart, it is always best to bore the upper part of the hole from the broken part upwards, glue up and then finish it downwards. This ensures that the hole is in the best position at the most important part, namely, the break.

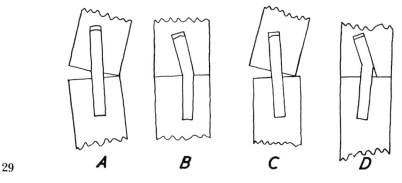

29   A   B   C   D

The use of glue on the metal is not advised. Its adhesion is slight and it makes insertion of the metal difficult owing to the pressure of the trapped air. A slight space should be left between the top of the rod and the wooden plug to allow for shrinkage.

Steel may also be used in place of wood in the conventional dowelling practice. If the two holes are not quite in line, the dowel may be taken out and put in the vice and bent slightly to bring the two surfaces together. In this case if the surfaces are not flush they may at the same time be improved by making the bend above or below the joint as the case may be. A, B, C and D (Illus 29) may help to make this plain though it is to be hoped that the holes will not be so far out.

The use of a rod in repair of turnings will be considered in the chapter devoted to that work.

87

5 Carcase Work

A carcase is essentially a box. Placed upon a plinth or feet, capped with a cornice and fitted with doors, it becomes a bookcase, wardrobe or cupboard. Fitted with drawers it is a chest of drawers, and in combination it may be a desk, cabinet or sideboard.

Up to the latter part of the seventeenth century many carcases had framed and panelled ends, but after the introduction of walnut in England the more common practice was to make them of boards, jointed when necessary and either solid or veneered.

Most of the work on them is straightforward and requires no comment. They are easily dismantled, ends rejointed and so on, but when they have been poorly made and then veneered they are something of a problem.

The proper methods of construction may be found in any good book on cabinet-making, but Illus 30 shows practices which, though not good, are quite common in cheap old chests of drawers. The ends, top and bottom are usually dovetailed together with large, lonely dovetails, the material being deal, more or less knotty. The rails between the drawers are mostly dovetailed in from the front, the back part being supported in the groove which takes the runner. Often this groove is omitted, the runner simply being glued and nailed to the sides. Dust boards were usually fitted, for it was a common belief that they were only found in good chests, and also to prevent access to a lower locked drawer by removing an unlocked upper one. D, E, F and G are other methods of fitting these rails. D was the earliest, the dust boards fitting into grooves in the carcase sides and also forming the runners. E was the best, the dovetail being entered from the runner groove and driven forward.

Having cleaned up the framework, the ends were next veneered with a veneer hammer, and also the front edges either with the grain or cross banded, thus covering the joints. Around the edge of the top was nailed and glued a strip of deal to form the overhang. This was also veneered, sometimes with thick veneer which could be rounded slightly. Finally the top itself was veneered and the base moulding mitred, glued and nailed round the lower edge of the carcase instead of under it as it should be. The feet, if any, were glued to the lower edge of the base mould, which thus supported the whole weight of the chest.

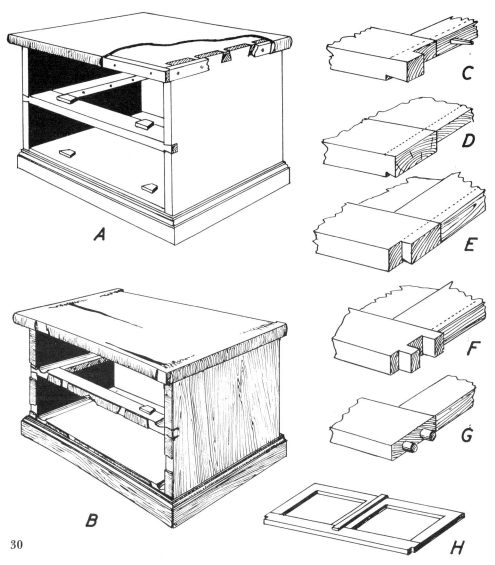

A

B

C

D

E

F

G

H

30

The result of this is depicted in Illus 30B. The top and ends have shrunk somewhat, and the cross pieces which formed the overhang of the top have forced the top strip away and shattered the veneer for some distance from each edge on the near side, or caused a split in the top and end, usually at a joint in one of them. The base mould is similarly pushed away in the front corners and may have become so loosened that it has given way under the weight of the chest and contents. The rails between the drawers will probably also be loosened, breaking the veneer covering the joints. The runners may also be loose and may be forcing the back away if they were cut long enough. It is likely they will also be deeply worn by the motion of the drawers, and some of the stops will be missing. The cross veneering is seldom perfect on the front edges especially where the rails are worn by the joints and also where the lock bolts have done damage by being either forced or having the drawer shut when in the locked position. The dust boards may have dropped because the sides have become barrel shaped thus letting them drop out of their grooves.

Such are the main faults to be looked for which are not covered by other chapters in this work. Now for their repair.

The treatment of the front corners of the top and veneer damage might consist of cutting back the front edge of the end cross pieces enough to enable the front piece to go back into position and then reglueing both joints. In other cases this piece may be loosened from the top veneer with a thin blade and removed entirely. The front strip can now be glued and cramped back into place and then the end strip replaced, re-laying the top veneer on it with a caul and a number of small G-cramps. The damage to the veneer can be filled with sawdust and glue and made fairly presentable by a good polisher.

If, however, the veneer is badly damaged and a good job is required, the method shown in Illus 31A may be tried. First the end strip is removed, and the front glued in place. The top is then rebated ¼in deep and sufficiently far back to remove all damaged veneer, leaving a mitre in front as shown. Strips are now cut across the end of a wide board to form new ends to the top, the back half is shown in place in Illus 31A, the grain following that of the top.

This, when levelled off, will not only look reasonable, but can swell and shrink with the carcase. If a better appearance is required, a strip of veneer of equal width can be removed from the front edge and replaced with cross banding, the joint between centre and border being emphasised with an inlay of ebony or boxwood, as in Illus 31B.

If the ends are split, they can usually be glued by inserting glue with a palette knife and cramping up, but it is well to see first if they will go together for they are sometimes held apart by the drawer runners and the base mould as well as by the top strip, and these may have to be removed. Then again, they may have been filled with anything from strips of wood to putty and these should, of course, be cleaned out.

The base mould will simply need removing and reglueing in its proper place, the surplus being cut off at the back.

If, however, the customer should be sufficiently interested in the piece to pay for it, the bottoms of the carcase ends may be cut off flush with the bottom drawer-rail and a frame made the size of the bottom of the chest, the moulding and feet being glued to it in such a way that a lip is formed for the carcase to sit in. This in turn is screwed in place firmly along its front edge and with slots elsewhere to allow movement across each end (Illus 31C).

The rails between the drawers and the runners are the next to receive attention; if they are loose they should be reglued, first examining the carcase end to see if they have been nailed. If this is the case the nails can usually be punched right into the rail so as to get them out of the way. The veneer covering the dovetails is usually so damaged that it will need replacing, but if not, it should first be removed with a palette knife or with something similar.

When they are badly worn by the drawer sides, pieces should be let in as

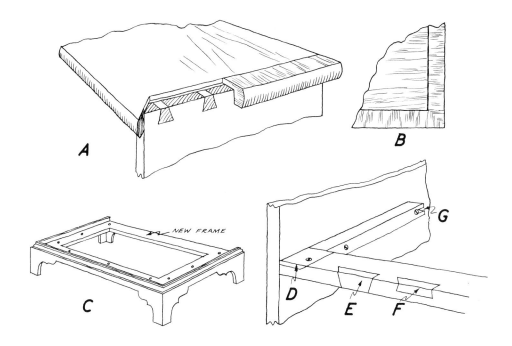

A   B

NEW FRAME

C   D   E   F   G

31

shown in Illus 31D. This will effect a great improvement in the running of the drawers. In some cases they may be extended so that they project into a slot cut in the carcase side, thus strengthening the joint at this point. When of solid wood, they may be patched when necessary by letting pieces in. The tapered dovetailed patches shown at E and F enable the job to be cleaned up immediately.

The worn runners are usually best replaced, both from the point of view of making a satisfactory job and to save time. If they need holding at the back end they should be slotted and screwed as shown at G. The front end should be butted against the rail and firmly glued and screwed as this will help to take the shock of the drawer as it is banged in against its stops.

The new runners also form the cure for loose dust boards for they may be made wider than the originals and with deeper grooves. If they are of the type marked D (Illus 30), and are coming out of their grooves at the back, a method will have to be found to straighten the carcase sides and keep them from spreading. This may be accomplished by fitting a new back which may be either a single piece of plywood or, if the job warrants it, a framed and panelled back using the old boards for the panels. In either case the carcase should be measured and the back fitted so that it will be about $\frac{1}{8}$in wider inside at the back than at the front so as to be sure that the drawers will have clearance.

6 Drawer Work

A short history of the construction and ornamentation of drawers may be of interest, and this will embody a description of the various types to be met with.

Up to the Jacobean period, mid-seventeenth century, they were nailed together with hand-wrought nails, the boards of the bottom running front to back and nailed into a rebate in the lower side of the front (Illus 32A).

Runners attached to the carcase sides supported the drawers by means of grooves ploughed in their sides. This was a very satisfactory method which has been in use ever since in cases where the rails between the drawers are undesirable, as in collectors' cabinets, etc. The reason for its abandonment was probably because the sides had to be very much heavier than when the later methods were used and this was objectionable both from the point of view of cost and also of good proportion, in the lighter types of furniture then being introduced.

Ornamentation might be in the form of carving, crude inlay or an arrangement of applied panels outlined with mouldings (Illus 32A).

Towards the end of the seventeenth century the introduction of walnut-veneered furniture created a great change in the craft, as at B. Dovetailing had become the more common corner joint, the grooved side was giving place to the thinner one running on its lower edge, but the bottoms still had the grain running from front to back.

Rails between the drawers were cross banded, the earlier ones being worked into one or two beads and later the drawers were lipped to cover the joint. In *The Present State of Old English Furniture*, Mr R. W. Symonds dates these three types approximately as follows: single bead 1690-1705, double bead 1700-15 and lipped drawers 1715-35, as shown in Illus 32C.

Now lipped drawers of this early date give trouble because the lip acts as a stop when the drawer is closed and so in time is liable to break away. Its construction is pictured in Illus 32D. The front, usually of oak, was first fitted to the opening and then rebated about $\frac{1}{2}$ in $\times$ $\frac{3}{16}$ in all round. It was then through-dovetailed, and the drawer was put together. The lip, of walnut, was then fitted and glued in position, the grain running across. Finally the front was veneered. The drawing shows a common pattern with burr centre, herringbone surround and cross-banded edge. Sometimes the dovetailing was

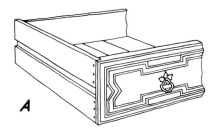

A

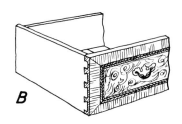

B

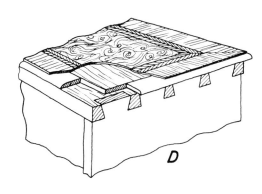

D

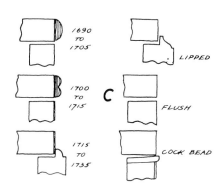

1690
TO
1705

1700
TO
1715

1715
TO
1735

LIPPED

FLUSH

COCK BEAD

C

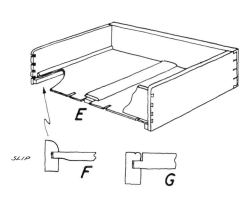

E

SLIP

F

G

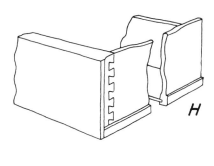

H

I

K

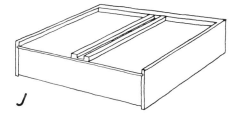

J

lapped, making a better job, for the lip was not then glued to end grain.

The wear on the lower edges of drawer sides and the shrinkage of bottom boards evoked the introduction of a change of construction. This consisted of the fitting of grooved slips glued to the inside lower edges of the sides both to accommodate the bottoms and double the wearing surface. The grain of the bottoms now ran in the same direction as that of the front and in wide drawers was in two panels divided by a centre muntin E, Illus 32. This came in about the time of the introduction of mahogany (1710) and continued up to the present time. Properly fitted, these should be glued into the groove in the front and be free to swell and shrink under the back, beyond which they should project ¼ in and to which they should be attached by screws in slots. The dovetails also became narrower and more numerous, especially in nineteenth-century England, when this fineness was carried to the point of weakness. In Scotland and Europe they were commonly much coarser while those of Colonial North America are usually of the golden mean of proportion.

Illus 32G shows an uncommon, though excellent form of drawer bottom occasionally found in nineteenth-century furniture of the best quality, almost always in solid mahogany.

The lipped front drawer continued to be in vogue for a long time after the introduction of mahogany, though no longer was it separate from the front which was usually of solid wood. Around the middle of the century, however, veneered fronts became more common and cock beads were introduced and have remained popular up to the present time. They both covered the edge of the veneer and broke the joint so that a slight variation of flushness was not apparent, a most desirable feature, for the veneer was very likely to twist the front a little.

The most common practice now is to machine-dovetail the drawers, groove the sides to avoid the expense of fitting slips and use plywood for the bottom.

Some time ago, particularly in America, it became fashionable to stain and varnish the sides and insides of drawers. Unless special precautions are taken, not only will the surface become scored in pulling the drawer in and out but its rosiny nature will make smooth running almost impossible. To avoid these disadvantages, the construction pictured in H was adopted.

The sides were set in about ⅛ in, and strips glued at their lower edges to take the rubbing and guide the drawer. These strips were not polished. The top edges were rounded along the major part of their length, leaving a raised part at the back to take the weight of the drawer when fully extended. The fitter had only these small pieces and the strips to plane if any easing was necessary.

Another innovation, achieving much the same result, was to glue a grooved centre strip from front to back on the bottom J, or use a grooved centre muntin K and attach a strip, made to be a sliding fit, to the frame beneath it. This works very well indeed and is to be recommended especially in cases where the drawer is long but shallow from front to back. Here again the sides need not come in contact with the carcase except on their lower edges and the top edge at the back.

Drawer repair—oak drawers

Starting with the oldest type as in Illus 32A, the grooves in the sides and their corresponding runners become much worn and rounded so that they may drop and jam. The best way to make this good is first to square out the groove, being careful to see that it still remains parallel to the edges. This will make it wider, of course, and new runners will have to be fitted somewhat wider than the originals. In many cases the old ones may be prised out of their dovetails or notches and entirely replaced, while in other cases it is easier to cut away the worn part and glue and screw a new and wider face onto the old.

Often the mouldings on the fronts will be found to have been reglued or nailed and their mitres will be a very poor fit. This is usually due to the shrinkage of the front, and there are two remedies. One is to widen the front to its original width, when it is probable that the mouldings, when cleaned, will need very little fitting. This widening may be done by ripping a ¼ in strip from the top edge and glueing a strip of new wood under it. The mouldings will cover it leaving the old top edge.

In narrower drawers where shrinkage is less, it will probably be better to take a few shavings off the ends of the vertical mouldings and facings to bring them to a fit.

The gaps in the bottom boards which run from front to back should be left, it is the way the makers intended them to be. If they were all glued together and new wood added to make up the loss of width by shrinkage, it would be detrimental to the piece for a collector and trouble from swelling during a damp spell might also occur.

Drawer repair—walnut and mahogany

Illus 32B requires no special comment, but the lipped drawer D often gives trouble because warping or twisting of the front causes only a small part of the lip to take the impact when a person slams the drawer in. It is comparatively simple to glue down the lip and replace any missing veneer, but the trouble is likely to recur unless other means of stopping it are provided. This may be accomplished by fitting ordinary stops on the rail below. If there is not sufficient clearance below the bottom, they may be placed in such a way as to catch the top edge of the front. Alternatively, by removing the back of the carcase, they may be placed behind the back edge of the drawer sides.

The parts most commonly needing attention are the lower edges of the sides. These often become so much worn that the bottoms scrape on the stops beneath and become deeply grooved thereby.

If the wear is not down to the groove in the drawer side or slip, it is a simple matter to reduce the surface to a flat and straight edge and glue on a strip to make up the deficiency. Hard maple is a very satisfactory material and a few brads will expedite the job, but, if this is done, care should be taken that they do not touch the drawer bottom. The heads should also be punched in, for if left flush they will, after a little wear, project and groove the runners. It is not uncommon to find them projecting $\frac{1}{4}$ in with corresponding groove in runner and rail.

In the case of a grooved side it is sometimes necessary to cut it away to the upper side of the groove and fit a rebated piece, preferably of $\frac{3}{4}$ in material, thus forming a new groove and a wider wearing surface (Illus 32I).

With the earlier type, with the grain of the bottom going from front to back, a strip glued on each side, $1\frac{1}{2}$ in wide and thick enough to take up the slack, will be found satisfactory.

The author repaired a drawer of the kind having its sides grooved to receive the bottom, in which the side was so thin (and therefore the groove for the bottom so shallow) that the bottom, which was also thin, when sprung by moderate weight simply slipped out of its groove. To repair this condition, nails had been driven through the sides into the bottom and glue blocks fitted all round.

The time spent in doing this was probably more than that required for a proper job, which consisted of removing the bottom, fitting slips and glueing them in position, fitting a centre muntin to add stiffness and then cutting the bottom into two panels and re-assembling.

After a drawer job, it is well to coat all sliding surfaces inside the carcase and outside of the drawer with floor wax. This will make a vast improvement in running qualities.

Fitting drawers

All that is necessary to make a drawer run easily is to plane sufficient wood from those places which are causing it to bind, a simple enough task; yet it is surprising how much wood is often taken from places which are not causing the trouble.

The common procedure is to work the drawer in and out about a dozen times and then examine the rubbing surfaces for shiny places. A few shavings from these will usually ease the drawer. If it does not make a considerable improvement, the following suggestions might be followed. Hold the drawer at arm's length in such a way as to get the upper edges of the sides in line so as to be sure that they are parallel. Quite often they are not, due either to a twisted front or improper glueing of the sides. If they are not, it will be found that the top back edge of one side and the bottom back edge of the other will be shiny. Before correcting this it is well to see how the front lines up in order that it may be adjusted so that it is as flush as possible, or, if twisted, so that it is out evenly on both sides. If planing from the lower edge is chosen, that is all that will be necessary provided that it does not cause the stop to foul the bottom, for the drawer will rest evenly on its runners when in, and the one side will hold it when out. If, however, the top edge is to be reduced, that side should be refaced-up on the lower edge so as to make it again parallel, for weight in the drawer will place it under constant stress and cause the top front edge of the opposite side to press upwards.

In some cases it is practical to adjust the runners to the drawer, and occasionally it will be found that the runners are out of parallel causing the same effect.

If the drawer seems to be in order, the carcase should be examined. Glue in corners is a common impediment; nails which have caused splits should also be looked for.

Occasionally it is found that the carcase sides have warped inwards making it narrow half-way back, and sometimes the back is narrower than the front. These faults may be ascertained by cutting a stick the length of the drawer front and testing the inside of the carcase with it. They can generally be corrected by fitting a piece between the runners sufficiently long to force the sides out enough to give clearance.

Dragging of the bottoms on the stops has already been mentioned, but occasionally the top edge of the back will also drag. If this is the case, about $\frac{1}{4}$ in should be removed from it, for this is considered the correct clearance for an ordinary-sized drawer.

7 Veneer, Marquetry and Inlay

The art of veneering is a very ancient one and may have two objects, either to decorate a surface or to disguise inferior workmanship and material.

In addition to applying a rare and beautiful veneer on a specially prepared ground, the first object may be achieved by making use of the fact that all the pieces of a stack of veneers from one piece of wood, known in the trade as a flitch or parcel, are very similar to one another and may therefore be pieced together in a variety of ways producing matching patterns quite impossible to obtain with solid wood.

Then again, wood of a twisty nature which would be too unstable for use in the solid can be successfully used as veneer.

Veneers were originally cut with a handsaw and were about $\frac{1}{8}$ in thick, but were often thinned to about $\frac{1}{16}$ in in cleaning up. Later, circular saws were used, and an old friend describes a veneer cutter in Yorkshire in about 1880 who used an 8ft diameter wooden saw for the purpose. This wooden saw had a steel cutting edge screwed to it in segments about 4in wide. It was flat on the face side and bevelled on the back, the veneer being flexible enough to bend away from the thicker part as it came off.

In the nineteenth century a machine was introduced to cut veneers with a knife, slicing it in layers of any thickness required.

This is the common modern practice and is carried out in two ways. The first is to slice the log in the same way as a saw cuts boards. This produces a figure having variety in its width and similar to the old saw-cut veneers. This is known as sliced veneer. The second is to mount the log in a form of lathe known as a peeler. As the log revolves, a knife is advanced against it peeling off a band as long as the log with the grain and of continuous width across until the whole of the log, except the centre, has been cut. The figure of this rotary-cut veneer is very unvaried as it mostly shows the annular rings on the flat, and so it should not be used for repairs to antiques.

Next to chair repair, loose and missing veneer provides the largest amount of work for the repairer and in many cases gives the greatest improvement for the time spent.

First let us consider glueing down loose veneer. The presence of loose veneer may be detected in a number of ways; each loose area should be clearly

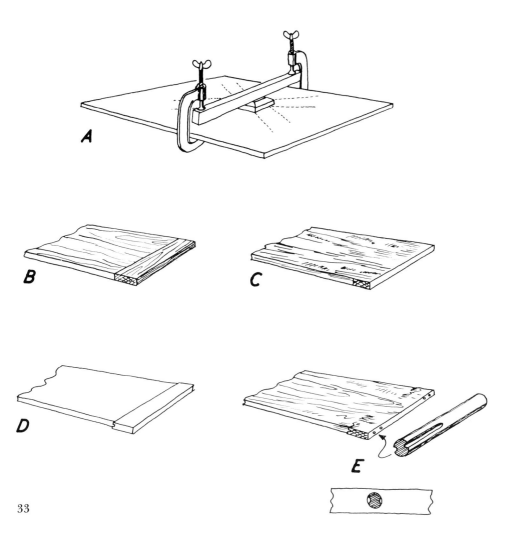

33

marked with chalk as soon as it is found, its boundaries carefully outlined and later marked with parallel lines so that its position may be located while it is covered with a caul (Illus 33A).

The first way to detect loose veneer is to look for raised or blistered areas, and these should be tested by tapping with the fingernail. The difference in sound between loose and solid veneer is quite obvious. The hand should then be passed quickly and lightly backwards and forwards over the area to be tested with the palm down. A hissing sound is heard as it passes a loose area. This is then more carefully located by finger tapping.

All loose places being now marked, cauls consisting of pieces of wood slightly larger than the loose areas should be prepared and arrangements made to apply pressure to them so that they may force the veneer down after the glue has been applied.

This is simple enough when the place is near the edge. G-cramps, hand-screws and other devices already described solve the problem, but when the blister is near the centre, more elaborate measures must be taken.

The simplest method is to put weights on the caul, but owing to the fact that cramps apply a pressure of 200lb or more it is usually hard to find suitable weights to equal them.

And so probably the most common way is to use two cramps and cross-bars as shown in Illus 33A. The caul should be bevelled in such a way that the bar rests only in the centre, otherwise an unequal tightening of the cramps may cause pressure only on one side.

Another way is to shore it down from the ceiling, that is to say, a piece of wood is cut a trifle longer than the distance from the caul to the ceiling and jammed between the two. Tremendous pressure may be applied in this way as all boat builders know, but there is a danger of spoiling the ceiling, and so, if necessary, a board to spread the pressure may be nailed to the top end of the shore. For those who like making tools, a kind of inverted jack may be made with screw to apply the pressure (Illus 12, O).

The use of either of these methods involves the danger of splitting the top or panel. If this is thought to be possible, the under side should be supported either by a cross-bar or by shoring from beneath.

Cauls and cramping arrangements being now ready, the cauls should be placed by the fire or other heat to warm and the job of introducing the glue commenced. The most common method is to use a palette or table knife, dip it in the glue and work it about beneath the veneer (which has been previously slit), repeating the process until sufficient glue has been inserted and then rub the surface with the fingers moistened with warm water in such a way as to work it into the most remote corners of the loose area.

A piece of wax paper is then placed over the patch to prevent sticking, followed by the hot caul cramped down according to plan.

Another method is to introduce the glue by means of the syringe described on page 46. This is particularly useful when the place is away from the edge of a polished top in otherwise good condition as it saves the trouble of slitting the veneer and so having to repolish. Two holes are bored through the core from beneath, one at each end of the patch, and thin hot glue is forced into one of them, the air escaping from the other. As before, the surface of the veneer should be rubbed to spread and even out the glue before cauling down.

When the cramping up is going to be a lengthy process, a piece of sheet lead a little larger than the caul should be prepared and heated. This is best done by laying it on top of an iron stove or a piece of ¼in boiler plate on an electric or gas ring. It should be hot enough to sizzle when splashed, but not to scorch the wrong end of a match when pressed against it. It is inserted between the caul and the wax paper.

This is also used to put down veneer which has been cauled but has failed to adhere properly. It will usually put it down even after it has had several days to dry without further wetting, but if it is desired to flatten old areas which have had glue worked under the veneer and which, due to poor cauling, is lumpy, it is necessary to sand the finish off and cover with a wet cloth for an hour or two, or even overnight for a bad case with thick veneer. The lead, if hot enough, will soften the glue enough to enable the surplus to be squeezed out.

Laying veneer on curved surfaces

There are a number of ways to caul veneer on curved surfaces, the simplest being to use a pad of felt, sponge rubber, cotton wool or several layers of cloth between the wooden pinch block and the wax paper or lead. This serves very well for small areas of slight curvature. Should the area be long but slightly bowed, such as the front of a bow-front drawer, a thin caul may be bent to do the job. It is cramped first in the centre of the loose veneer and then cramps are added each side until it is all pulled down. A piece of 3-ply with the outer grain across is good for this purpose. In many cases, however, the cauls must be bandsawn to fit the curve.

The problem of making a caul accurately fit the veneered surface is not always an easy one, especially when the ground has warped or has been damaged; and so a certain amount of padding is usually used, though, when the best possible work is required, the caul should be accurately fitted and smoothly finished, since the surface of the veneer will be a fairly accurate reverse of it. The cauls used for veneering mouldings during the nineteenth century were fitted by covering a piece of the moulding with sandpaper of the same thickness as the veneer to be used and with this the final finishing of the caul was accomplished. Of course when the sandpaper was replaced with the veneer the fit was perfect. This principle may be used in repair work, the sandpaper being placed over the veneer on the moulding; but as in this case the veneer is already in position, the sandpaper must be used as part of the caul, the simplest way being to glue its grit side to the caul. This I have recently used in replacing veneer on a waterfall bed-end.

Cauling veneer on curved work with sand-bag

Another method particularly useful on shaped work is the sand-bag. Any bag full of sand is useful, but a strong sack of 8oz cotton duck, about 10in × 20in, is recommended. This is about two-thirds filled with sand and the mouth is sewn up. If filled too full, it will not so easily adapt itself to the shapes required.

The sand takes a considerable time to warm and so it should be put in a warm place, preferably an oven, some time before it is to be used.

Let us assume that part of a drawer front has loose veneer. A piece of 2in × 12in board is placed on trestles and the hot sand-bag on it. The drawer front is pressed on to it leaving an indentation corresponding to its contours. One or more cramps are used to add to the pressure and hold it in position. Everything being in order the cramps are removed, the glue introduced, the patch covered with paper and the front replaced on the sand-bag and cramped up.

Repair of ground work before laying veneer

Although most loose veneer is a result of failure of the glue, it is quite often the outward and visible sign of more serious faults in the ground on which it is laid. This may take the form of anything from a simple crack to a ground completely eaten away by insects or rot, but it is most often caused by shrinkage. Whatever it may be, it is inadvisable to lay the veneer until the wood beneath has been made good, otherwise it will be but a temporary repair.

The most common case of this kind is that of a board clamped across the ends with a piece of ¾ in × 2in material grooved on and then veneered; Sheraton sideboard doors and desk falls being very common examples of this construction. Illus 33B depicts such a piece before veneering, C is the finished job, D the core after shrinkage has taken place and E the resultant damage to the veneer. It is shattered and broken away near the outer edge, farther in it has become split into narrow strips which have bent to conform to the movement while the centre is in good condition. The first step is to reglue the clamp by dowelling each end.

This can be made to force glue along the tongued joint at the same time. Dowel holes are bored through the clamp into the panel for about an inch and the dowels are also grooved back a similar amount. The holes are about half filled with thin glue and the dowels driven home, the grooves being towards the sides of the board. This forces the glue out of the hole and along the joint each way for some distance. It is well to apply cramps, for the glue may have forced the clamp away to some extent.

For a cheap job, glue and sawdust may be now used to fill the cracks and openings and, when dry, levelled and polished. In other cases a certain amount of new veneer may have to be let in to fill missing parts, while the best result may be obtained by cross banding the border, as already explained for carcase tops on page 90. This has the additional advantage of providing plenty of veneer for other repairs on the same piece, and covering any building up of the main board that may have been necessary to restore it to its original width.

Other examples of similar nature are very numerous and range from tea caddy tops to piano fronts, but the most important thing is to recognise the fact that the ground must first be made sound before the veneer can be fixed. It should be explained to the customer and then carried out to the satisfaction of all.

Marquetry

Marquetry is a wood mosaic in the form of a pattern built up of different veneers pieced together and laid on a wooden core or ground. It differs from inlay in that the background and pattern are both of veneer and are first assembled and then glued down. With inlay the pattern is cut out and let into recesses cut in the ground.

If an area of marquetry is so damaged as to need a complete replacement, make a careful drawing of the original design (by tracing or otherwise) as accurately as possible and on thin paper: on this drawing mark each section with an initial showing its wood. Take as many pieces of thin paper as there are different woods, interleave these with new carbon sheets, place the drawing on top and pin down on a drawing-board. Trace all the lines of the drawing (including the initials) firmly with a sharp, hard pencil: the lower tracings may need strengthening with a thin pencil line. The result should be a series of identical tracings, all with clear thin lines. Mark each sheet with the name of one of the woods.

Now, from—say—the mahogany sheet, cut out all the mahogany sections, leaving ⅛in margin round each: paste these, edge to edge, on to a piece of cheap thick veneer. Cut a piece of plywood to the same size, and sandwich, between these two, one or more pieces of mahogany veneer. Pin through this sandwich with fine veneer pins (between the sections as well as round the outside, but not too near the lines): nip off the points of the pins and clench with a light hammer. Fine holes should be drilled for the pins, so as not to split the veneers. Make similar sandwiches of all the other woods.

Pin the original drawing onto a board.

Cut each sandwich in turn with a fretsaw, or a fine jigsaw. Follow the outlines carefully and do not encroach over them. When all are cut out, fix each section of this 'jigsaw puzzle' onto the original drawing with a dab of paste. They should all be found to fit accurately, with no visible saw-lines between, but a touch with a fine file may be needed here and there. When the puzzle is complete, glue a piece of paper over the whole surface: when dry, lift from the drawing, clean off the back, and lay as a simple veneer.

If each of your sandwiches has contained more than one piece of the appropriate veneer, the additional pieces will be available to make so many replicas of the original.

if no more than an odd piece, here and there, is missing, it is only necessary to make rubbings of the vacant spaces with cobbler's heelball on thin paper: then, using these like the tracings, proceed as above. This applies also to missing pieces of inlay in solid wood.

Making mosaic bandings, etc

Although inlay centres, stringing and banding can be bought in a great variety of patterns, it is a rare thing to be able to match any but the simplest kinds from stock.

The making of mosaic bandings is not too difficult, but in the ordinary way the methods to be described are only worth while when a fairly large quantity is required. However, they can be modified to make up smaller quantities.

In order to explain these methods three patterns have been selected and are pictured in Illus 34. No 1 is a common cross banding usually of tulip or

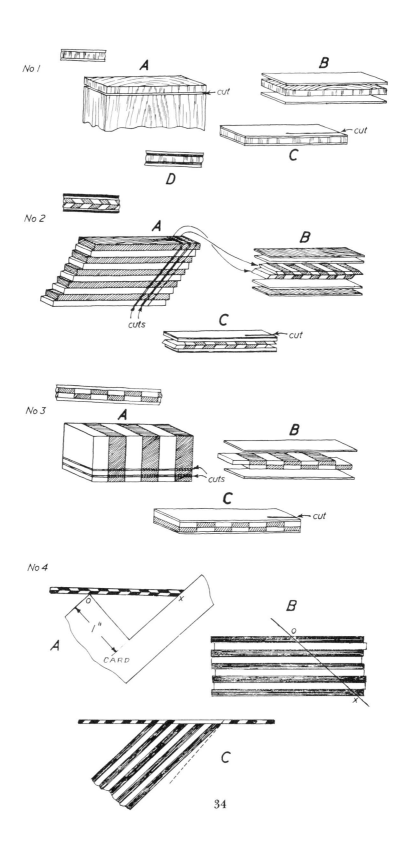

No 1

A

B

C

D

cut

cut

No 2

A

B

C

cuts

cut

cut

No 3

A

B

C

cuts

cut

cut

No 4

A

B

C

O

x

1"

CARD

O

x

34

satinwood with boxwood or holly lines each side. First a board of the centre wood is taken, for tulip or kingwood yew tree makes a fair substitute while birch or maple can be coloured fairly well to match satinwood. The end grain of this is planed square and true and a piece or pieces are cut off the width of the cross banding A. Next a piece of boxwood veneer is glued on each side as in B or in the case of satinwood more than likely a veneer of ebony will be interposed between the satinwood and the boxwood on each side, producing the pattern marked D. When dry all that remains is to cut off the banding in strips, C.

No 2 is a black-and-white herringbone effect. First a little stack of black and white veneers are glued together, A. These must be got to the thickness of the herringbone of the pattern. Next the end of the stack must be planed to the correct angle, which can be checked by matching up with pattern. It is then cut off in layers, which are then laid together in pairs so that the alternate patterns may match each other perfectly, B. Other pairs following to the left of those are sketched as necessary. The white and black outer veneers can also be laid and the whole thing cramped up, but if any doubt is felt about the thickness of the herringbone part, it is better to omit the side veneers until this has been checked and possibly corrected by planing down, after which the outer veneers can be laid either together or in pairs. All that remains is to cut off the strips, C.

The method in No 3 should be fairly obvious from the above, as indeed with any of the bandings.

If only a very small piece of mosaic banding is needed, it can be made up directly with veneers: eg by glueing strips of alternate black and white veneer onto paper, shooting the ends (either square or diagonally as the case may be), cutting off a strip with a cutting gauge, or with a sharp knife against a metal straightedge, and building up with side lines as necessary.

For instance, if a piece of inlay were needed to match A, No 4 Illus 34, the procedure might be as follows. First determine the number of strips per inch by cutting a piece of card, lining it up as shown and counting the number of segments between O and X: nine in this case. Now obtain or prepare black and white strips which, laid side by side, make nine to the inch. A convenient number (not necessarily nine) should now be strongly glued to a piece of brown paper between two strips tacked to a board, B.

When thoroughly dry, clean up the face and mark a line at such an angle that OX is equal to OX in A. Cut with a dovetail saw, check against the existing inlay and if necessary make spacing match by adjusting the angle with a plane. All that now remains is to gauge and cut a sufficient number of strips and glue side by side in pairs.

It is always desirable to make more of the original striped band than required and to save the unused part, for each one can be made to cover a fair range of spacings by altering the angle as shown in C. The slight difference in angle as indicated by the dotted line would not be noticeable.

It should not be assumed that the light-coloured part of inlay is necessarily boxwood. If it is used in patching, particularly in eighteenth-century furniture when various other woods were used, its hardness and yellow colour may produce a poor match not easily toned down to the more mellow shades of the original: this is especially true if, as sometimes happens, it has become worm-eaten.

For the purposes of matching colour, it is useful and interesting to make what might be called garden timber: holly, hawthorn, apple, pear, cherry and laburnum; these being listed in order from light to dark. The author's collection includes yew tree, arbutus (both plain and burl) and berberis which is a bright orange yellow. Of all these hawthorn is the most useful being both hard, fine grained and also likely to be the shade required.

Quite small logs can be used. When received from the gardener they should be barked and sawn down the centre to minimise checking. When dry it is the author's practice to true and square them roughly; cut a few pieces of fairly thick saw-cut veneer and leave the remainder for future cutting as required. The veneers are put into a drawer marked 'Odd saw-cut veneers' which is kept for matching purposes.

Metal inlay

Loose brass inlay is one of the more difficult jobs. The metal is usually buckled or even broken when the job comes in and the wood into which it is inlaid has often shrunk until it no longer fits.

The first step is to lift the metal out of its recess. This should be done with a thin wedge such as a palette knife (Illus 35B), otherwise the upward pull will bend the strip, A. Great care should be taken for most of the metal is very soft. The loose part being now removed, it is necessary to clean the dirt out of the groove. This is best done with a narrow chisel. Now straighten out the bends and kinks which may have occurred. If it is bad it is advisable to remove the bent part entirely, if necessary cutting it away from the good part with a jeweller's saw, ie a metal-cutting fretsaw. After this it should be made as flat as possible and then tried in position. More than likely something will have to be done to allow it to fit across the grain: either metal or wood will have to be removed in places, especially if it is a fretted inlay such as that shown in C, which shows the effect of shrinkage of wood and the steps necessary to refit the metal. Of course, in the case of plain metal strips, only the ends would have to be filed.

All that should be necessary now is to glue the inlay back, but much grief and failure has induced the writer to take the added precaution of pinning down all loose ends and doubtful places such as those which tend to spring up.

The procedure of pinning is as follows. Three thicknesses of hard brass wire are procured, the smallest being about the thickness of a common pin; indeed, brass pins will do for this size. From these a number of brads are made by tapering the wire to about the shape shown in D and about ¾ in long. This

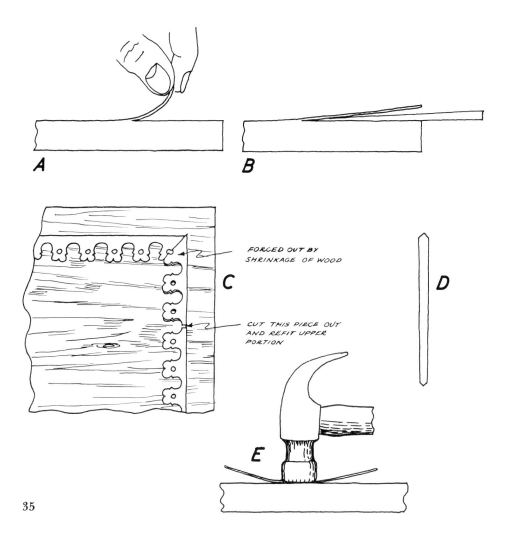

A

B

FORCED OUT BY
SHRINKAGE OF WOOD

C

D

CUT THIS PIECE OUT
AND REFIT UPPER
PORTION

E

35

may be done by filing them as they revolve in a chuck or holding them in a drill against an emery wheel. Three drills slightly smaller than the wires are used and holes are drilled where necessary, the size being appropriate to the width and thickness of the inlay. A caul is then prepared so that the metal may be forced in without bending, for if it is hammered in it becomes bent during the process, as suggested in E. The strongest adhesive for the purpose is Bostik cement; next liquid glues. Hot glue is not recommended.

Once the glueing and cramping have been finished the caul should be removed and the appropriate pins driven into the holes, watching carefully and tapping gently until the inlay is pressed down nearly flush with the wood, and not driving so hard that the pin forms a depression in the metal. The latter would necessitate a great deal of filing and papering to get it out. Now examine carefully and, if necessary, drill and put in additional pins to bring down any other high spots. Set aside to dry for two days: the cement takes longer to dry, shrink and harden beneath the metal. Any faults in the wood can now be filled with stick shellac, the pins nipped off and the whole thing filed and sanded to a smooth, flush surface. If the wood is rosewood, as is common, and the whole top is not to be refinished, great care should be taken to leave the surface intact. Any removal of the wood will expose the darker colour beneath.

If carefully carried out, the pinning is completely invisible after polishing.

Short cuts

For a cheap job, missing brass may be filled with composition and gilded with leaf or bronze. The leaf makes quite a good job, but the bronze, though it may look well from certain angles, will strongly contrast with the brass from others. Loose corners of brass inlay may be put down by slipping a flake of shellac underneath and pressing the corners down with a burning-in tool sufficiently hot to warm the brass to melt the shellac beneath it. The tool should be held patiently until it has quite cooled off.

8 Miscellaneous

Turnery

The peculiar characteristics of turned work provide both facilities by which repairs may be made and problems in cramping. The use of strips cut from automobile inner tubes has proved a solution to most of these problems. Great pressure may be applied and in a way which does not mar the wood. These strips should be from ⅜in to ½in wide and around 2ft long. In use they stretch to three times their length and are also much reduced in width.

If the break be clean and long and the part of sufficient dimensions for strength, a simple glue joint will be sufficient. In binding it up the following suggestions are made; if the rubber were taken straight round the break as shown in Illus 36A, the pressure would cause the break to slide along its inclined surface as pictured. This may be counteracted either by placing a sash cramp on the two ends of the part, and by this means compressing it to its correct length, or else by applying the binding at an angle as shown at B. The use of the two nails shown is rarely necessary for the rubber itself has quite a good grip on the wood and the angle of the break is rarely as great as that shown. Illus 36C shows a more common application in which the various bindings counteract one another and the joint is brought to alignment by increasing the turns and pressure as required. For instance, those at 1 and 2 have a tendency to pull the joint so that the leg will be shorter, while those at 3 and 4 will have the opposite effect. The binding should be done in groups piled on top of one another as shown, with gaps between, both to enable the joint to be examined for alignment and also to permit the glue to dry.

After two or three hours it should be removed, for it has a tendency to stick to the polish, and it also excludes the air, thus delaying the drying of the glue.

When the break is such that when glued up it is not considered sufficiently strong, it is best strengthened with a dowel. The difficulty here is to get the holes perfectly lined up. If the break is near one end, as in example D, the hole may be bored right through the short part, starting it at the break and boring from O to P. The break is now glued together, binding or cramping if necessary, or as is often the case just pressing the broken parts together. When thoroughly dry, and taking care not to break the joint, the hole is continued

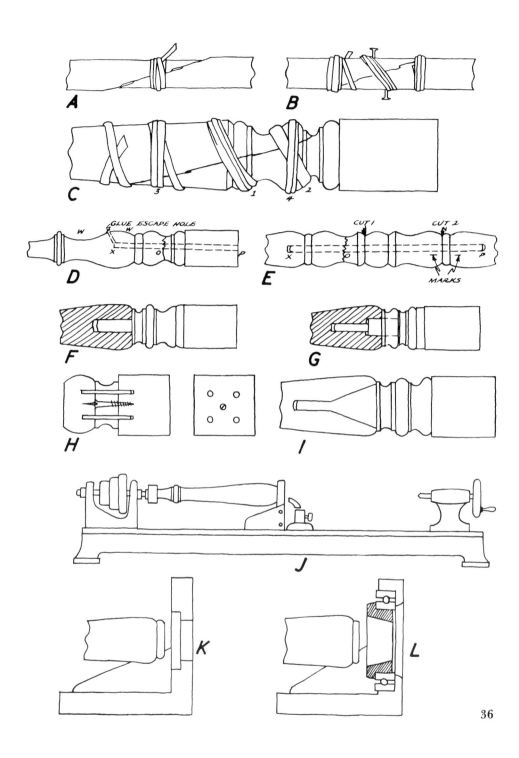

from *O* to *X*, passing the bit through the hole already bored, which forms a guide and continuing to a place at which the turning is as large as possible, and not at such places, for instance, as those marked W, for the weakness caused by the bottom of the hole would add to the inherent weaknesses of these places. A dowel should now be fitted so that it will go to the bottom of the hole without forcing; a groove the full length cut with a V-tool or the corner of a rebate plane will allow the air and surplus glue to escape. Glue should be put in the hole as well as on the dowel, and it should be forced steadily home with a sash cramp. In many cases, especially with long dowels during cold weather and always with steel dowels, a small hole should be bored from behind into the bottom of the dowel hole, for it is very easy to split a leg with the pressure of glue should the groove be inadequate or stopped up.

The dowel itself may be either a common piece of hardwood dowelling, a piece cleft from hickory or hard oak and carefully turned in the lathe (the cleaving is, of course, to ensure that the grain is perfectly straight) or a piece of cold-rolled steel rod, according to the requirements of the job and the customer.

When the break is too far from an end for the above method, the following procedure is generally effective; pictured in example E.

The general idea is to bore a long hole into the break, cut a piece off at some suitable place such as either cut 1 or cut 2 in the bored part, glue up the break and then through the hole and continuing in the opposite direction complete the dowel hole.

In other words, referring to E, the hole is bored from the break O to P where the turning is thick, two marks are made each side of the selected cut, cut 2 in this case. The turn is cut off here with a fine dovetail saw, the break O is glued up and then the hole OX is bored and finally a dowel is fitted and the whole thing is glued up, turning the cut part so as to line up the two marks. In choosing the position of the cut, it is advantageous to have it between 2in and 3in from the break so as to give sufficient length to guide the bit and keep it in line. If it is less than 2in, great care should be taken to see that the hole follows the axis of the turning, and for this reason it is best bored in a lathe or drill press.

F and G both suggest cases in which the piece on the right has been so badly broken that it has had to be replaced. That on the left has a plain pin, while the one on the right has a pin turned in two diameters giving added strength. In both cases, the damaged wood is cut away until there remains a sound part, and this is bored either with a single hole or a large one followed by a smaller. If the boring is accurately centred and found to be reasonably in line when tested with a piece of dowel, the new part may be completely made and glued up. If, however, this is not the case, a new piece of larger dimensions than required for the finished job should be taken and the pin merely turned and fitted to the hole. If necessary the shoulder should be chiselled to fit. This should be glued in, and when dry the whole thing should be placed in the lathe with the old part in the chuck, a piece of wood on the screw centre with a slightly tapered hole (which may be bored in it to fit the end of the turning), and the tailstock fitted with light pressure to the new. The old part adjoining the new is then centred by allowing it to revolve, marking, and then moving the new part on the tailstock by taps of a hammer as required. When it is running true, the tailstock may be tightened and the turning finished and finally the square part lined up and brought to size.

When large, short turnings are involved, it is usually better to use a number of smaller dowels; a turned pin in the centre is handy for locating the two parts, around this may be placed three or more dowels which may be easily marked by making depressions with a centre punch, placing $\frac{1}{8}$ in ball bearings in them, assembling, tapping together and thus marking the opposite side. A chalk mark is a help in putting the parts together in the same relative position.

Illus 36H is an example of a bun foot which has had the narrow part replaced. Four dowel holes were bored through the new narrow part, and a screw-hole was made in the centre. It was first screwed onto the foot and the four holes bored into the foot. Then the new part was unscrewed from the foot and screwed onto the square part above, and the holes bored through into it, after which the dowels were fitted and the whole thing glued up.

The construction of a hollow centre for a lathe makes possible the accurate boring of any turned part within its capacity. It consists in its simplest form of a wooden bracket bolted to the lathe bed, J, with a hole in it bored to fit the end of the turning which is to be drilled (Illus 36K). This hole must, of course, be well greased.

A more elaborate fitting may be made by mounting a large ball bearing in the bracket, collars are then made to adapt the bearing to the work in hand, L. This has the advantage of not marring the work, and it may also be used to form an excellent steady rest to support the centre of long turnings.

In practice, the left-hand end of the piece to be bored is held in a wooden chuck while the other end revolves in the hollow centre. The tool rest is, of course, to the right of this. The hole is started with turning tools and carried to a depth of two inches or more after which it is continued with a bit or drill. The late Charles Whitfield of Victoria, BC used to bore 6ft bed-posts in this manner to convert them into standard lamps. He preferred a spoon bit for the purpose.

The method of boring the conical hole in the joint marked I is now easily understood. The boring of the hole is, of course, the first operation, after which the new part is turned up and fitted by simply taking it out of the lathe and trying it in its hole. By thrusting it in and twisting it a few times, the places where it touches become shiny. These spots are eased off with the turning tool, the part removed from the lathe again and the process repeated until a good fit is achieved. This is the strongest joint for this purpose.

Twist

When it is necessary to copy a twisted leg, first turn the twisted part to the correct outside diameter and smooth and parallel it.

Now observe whether it is a single or double twist, or, in mechanics' parlance, a one- or two-start thread. Place a piece of lath along and mark each place where the twist touches it; even these points out with dividers and then divide them again by four. Mark these points on the turned part as it revolves in the lathe. There should now be four pencilled rings for each turn of the twist. Now divide the circumference into four and mark four parallel lines crossing the rings. Starting at one end, make a spiral line cutting each ring and line where they intersect, being sure that it is in the correct direction. Some legs are twisted the opposite way each side. If the twist is double, start at opposite sides and draw the spirals through each alternate intersection, cutting the intermediate rings half-way between them. Now measure the depth of the spiral groove, and cramp two pieces of lath along a saw-blade, set back from the teeth the depth of the groove. Now make a saw-cut to this depth along the spiral line or lines. Then with chisel or draw-knife cut this into a broad V-shaped spiral groove. The bottom may now be curved with a gouge or rasp and filed, and the upper part similarly rounded over. Sandpaper will finish the job.

In laying out a twist, not a copy, a fairly good proportion is as follows: pitch 1 to 1¼ times diameter; depth of groove ¼ to ⅕ diameter.

A top rail for a Regency chair

Making a new top rail for the back of a so-called Trafalgar chair (Illus 37D) might be a bit of a challenge.

The first step is of course to make a pattern allowing extra cardboard at the back for projections to take the lathe centres. When a number of these were to be made, the blanks were provided with only a small projection at X which was intended to take the thrust of a jig which was clamped on to take the live centre. With only one required, however, the layout indicated will be found satisfactory. After getting the outline from the original, mark the axes of the two turned ends and from them lay out the projections for the centre, allowing plenty of material for turning as shown in A.

Illus 37B shows the set-up in the lathe; with a speed of about 750rpm and with light cutting it is surprising how normally the work proceeds.

The next step is to remove the projections with the bandsaw and work up the curved part. Mark each side with two lines to which the corners are to be chamfered to make an octagon before the final rounding with spokeshave and file.

Next comes the roping; in the case of the one illustrated, one strand of the one being copied was marked with a red pencil; it made one complete turn in 4½in and there were seven strands. On the new piece bands were marked every 1⅛in (quarter turn), also lines on top, bottom and each side parallel to the axis. A spiral line drawn through the intersections of these rings and lines

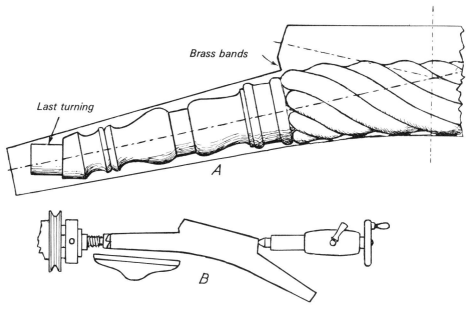

Brass bands

Last turning

A

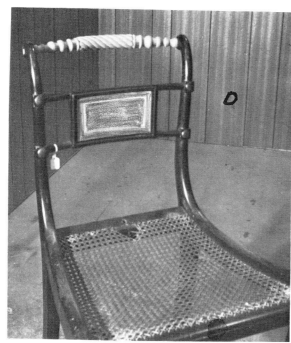

B

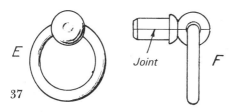

D

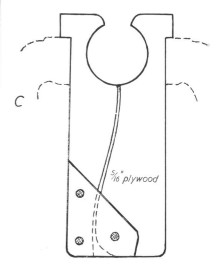

C

5/16" plywood

E

Joint

F

37

114

will indicate the centre of one strand. Each ring was then divided into seven and the layout completed.

The first step in the carving is to make a V-groove with a parting tool between each line; this is better than following the line itself because it remains as a guide. The rounding is done with a suitable gouge, convex side up, and with the same tool one lifts the handle and turns in the end of each strand as seen in A removing the small triangle with a chisel.

The pins at each end require the greatest care both in centering and turning. Make crossed saw-cuts for the spur centre, as the pressure on the tailstock must be kept as light as possible, also run the lathe at its slowest speed. Because of the obvious difficulties, it is likely that the added care will result in a satisfactory job.

The brass bands which add to the nautical appearance are cut from thin sheet; they are sometimes overlapped and secured with one nail underneath or butted and held with two. In order to hold them in place while being pinned, the clamp illustrated in C was devised; it took perhaps ten minutes to make but greatly facilitated the work and also ensured a snug fit.

A knob and ring handle for a Regency tea caddy

Another job which looks rather difficult but is really quite simple is the wooden knob and ring handle often seen on Regency tea caddies (Illus 37, E and F). Two rings can usually be made from a ¾in disc mounted on the screw-centre. First turn the outside to diameter then with a pair of dividers, mark the thickness of the ring and make a cut of an equal depth; now round the outer surface. Next move the rest to the face and work it in a similar manner: sand and cut off. You will now have a ring with the inner back corner square. To finish this make a wooden chuck, a ¾in disc of plywood will do; turn a recess in the face into which the ring will tightly fit. In this both the rounding and most of the polishing can be done. This is faceplate turning and the accepted practice is to advance the tool in a horizontal position level with the centre using a scraping action.

There are two methods of getting the ring into the knob, both of which may be found on old pieces. If the knob is in place, nick the ring from the inside with a chisel and break it; insert it and immediately glue it together again.

If the knob is also to be renewed the author prefers to make it out of a square previously glued up in two thicknesses. The hole across the joint should be drilled before turning and plugged with a piece of white wood as it is difficult to avoid splitting or shattering the edges if it is attempted afterwards. The pin should be carefully fitted to its hole as it may not be of a standard size. Old Charlie would ask for a sample hole because, in his youth, a bit would often have quite a variation from its nominal size. The knob, now being ready, may be heated, the two halves separated with a knife and the ring tried in place. Quite likely the hole will have to be flared a little with a rat-tail file to allow for the curve of the ring. By glueing it together as well as into its close-fitting hole there is very little danger of failure.

Although mainly for appearance they should be strong enough to lift the box; however, they will not stand much abuse.

Straightening warped wood

Any piece of wood at a given moisture content will, by its nature, take up a certain form. Thus a warped board is as it is because its moisture content is different from that when it was planed flat. It may be forced into a different form by mechanical pressure or by artificially changing its humidity, but it will return to its former shape when similar conditions return. For this reason steaming or wetting will only produce a temporary cure. There are, however, several real cures, each of which has a different range of application.

The first consists of forcibly pulling the wood flat and fastening it in that position. This may be used if the wood is neither too hard nor too thick and where there is either something to fasten it to, or where additional strips screwed to it will not spoil its usefulness or appearance.

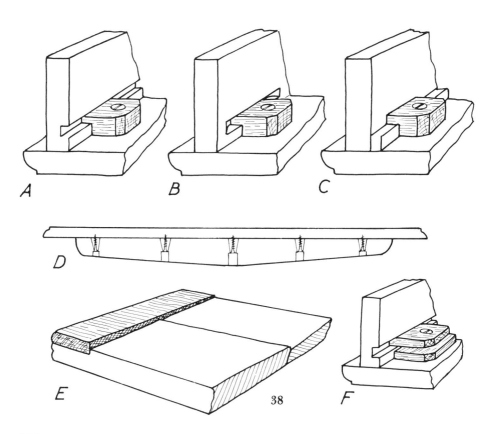

A   B   C

D

E   38   F

The most common application of this is when a table-top has warped and pulled away from the frame. Now it may be argued that the top, having once pulled the screws, will probably do it again and this is true if they are put in in the same way. In most cases where screws have pulled out, it will be found that they have been put in diagonally through the rail instead of through buttons. This has caused them to be bent sideways with each change of season until they finally pulled out or broke off. To remedy this, buttons should be fitted either in a groove (Illus 38A) in mortices, B, or on strips glued to the upper edge of the rails, C. If the top is ½in thick or less, it is better that the button be made in two thicknesses as shown at F. The lower part should be glued and rubbed into place before screwing down the upper.

In the case of drop-leaves, tripod table-tops etc, cross members can often be screwed beneath to straighten them out. When this is done they are best secured also with buttons on alternate sides, but it usually happens that this is not suitable for reasons of appearance, and they are screwed and plugged as pictured at D. Here it is well to make the end holes in the form of slots or at least larger than would be otherwise necessary, to allow for shrinkage.

Another method which is fairly often applicable is to rip the warped board into strips and then joint and glue them up again, preferably dowelling the joints. Often an additional strip has to be added to make up for the loss of width. It is then planed up true and refinished. The final result is, of course, a thinner board which is not often a detriment.

In repairing a Sheraton sofa table having a finely figured top, it was necessary to reduce the thickness to ⅜in in places to get an approximately flat surface. This was an exceptionally bad case, but a very satisfactory job was made by building up the lower surface of the edge by rebating it 1¼in wide and glueing a strip in it with the grain corresponding to that of the top. After remoulding the edge the result was all that could be wished. Illus 38E shows a view of the underside.

By Grooving, etc

Another method which is useful in veneered panels is to groove the back about two-thirds of the thickness. Either a handsaw, circular saw or plough may be used, and the grooves may be about 1in apart, more or less, according to the amount of straightening required. They are made closer where the greatest curvature exists, it usually varies considerably across one board. The board is next cramped between four cross pieces to flatten it, and strips are fitted and glued into the grooves. Another way is to fit the strips in such a way as to effect the straightening. If the grooved side is the convex side, the strips must be fitted slack and gradually reduced in thickness until the panel is flat when cramped up.

By Veneering

The fact that veneer in glueing absorbs relatively more water than the ground on which it is laid, and therefore swells more and consequently shrinks more in drying across the grain, thus pulling the veneered side into a hollow, has been a problem to cabinet-makers since veneer was introduced. Old craftsmen used to swell their wood by leaving it overnight covered with wet sawdust to counteract this pull of the veneer, and, if they were skilful and lucky, their panels dried flat, but quite often old tops are found warped with the veneer on the hollow side.

This characteristic may be used to counteract this fault and also to straighten solid wood. The procedure is, of course, to veneer the convex side. The result of this is sure, but the amount of effect is very hard to foretell; however, there are many occasions when it is the most practical method to use. For instance it is often desirable to both straighten and veneer the inside of the top of a folding card table. Before laying the veneer the surface should first be cleaned and toothed with a toothing plane or scratched with the teeth of a tenon saw used as a scraper.

If the warp is considerable, the veneer, after being coated with glue, should be well sponged with hot water on the outside; the effect will be greater if it is laid with a hammer, less effect being obtained if a press is used. If the warp is only slight the moisture in the glue will be sufficient.

If the underside does not show, laying the veneer across in strips may be tried, say 3in wide with 3in spaces between. With this method more control is possible as further strips may be laid between the first, possibly only at one end if so required. Similarly a twist may be got out by laying a veneer or strips diagonally across from corner to corner.

Making mouldings

The replacement of missing mouldings is a very common job and one which may be tackled in a variety of ways, depending on the length of moulding required and the equipment available.

When one piece only is necessary, as is the most common case, it is best to mitre the new blank to the existing moulding before starting to work the new. The outline can then be marked on the mitre, a much better method than making the mould first and mitring it afterwards.

Although the shaper or spindle moulder has become the most common tool for manufacturing mouldings, it is rarely practical for any but the simplest sections, for it would take longer to make the knife than to work it by hand.

The most common method is the use of a rebate plane, circular-saw table and hollow and round planes. As a matter of fact the hollow planes can be dispensed with, for the rounded sections can be worked with a rebate plane,

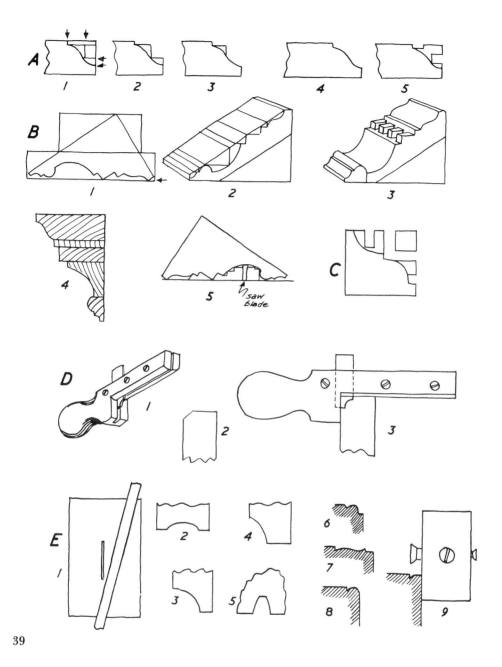

39

but it is hard to get along without a few round bottom planes. The simple mould (Illus 39A) would be worked as follows.

The first step, as in making any moulding not already mitred and marked, is to make a cardboard pattern, and from it to mark each end of the wood selected and run the four gauge lines shown by arrows the full length of the wood. Next is made the upper rebate which may be worked to size by means of a fence and depth gauge if the rebate plane is fitted with them or just worked to the gauge lines. Next the lower rebate is cut down to the middle of the hollow part as shown, followed by the round-bottomed plane down to the lower gauge line, A 3. The remaining small piece is easily worked down with either a rebate plane or a hollow-bottom plane. In using a rebate plane for this last purpose, it is a good practice to move the blade away from the corner of the mouth to avoid scratching the vertical side when doing the upper part of the rounding and the hollow when meeting it. Alternatively a plough could be used as in A 5.

The following method of moulding a cornice is that described in Thomas Sheraton's book and is often the best way for short lengths today. The extra labour involved in making it of mahogany backed by another wood instead of in one piece adds to the cost, but it often happens that old wood of sufficient thickness is not available.

Again the first step is to make the cardboard pattern and mark on it the line showing the joint of the two components. These may now be got out and glued together, B 1. The highest point of the cornice in front is then gauged, shown by arrow, a bevel is set to the angle between the face and the top, and the top is planed down to the gauge line so that the bevel fits along its full length. From this it is simple to square up the other sides. Each end is now marked from the pattern and the horizontal and vertical lines drawn in as shown. Gauge marks are scribed the length of the wood where these lines intersect the face, B 2. It is then set up on the bench in the position shown and the rebating started. Old craftsmen could start cutting a rebate on a gauge line and work it down clean and true, but few have now sufficient practice to do this. It is therefore a help to cut a rough groove about $\frac{1}{8}$ in from the upper gauge line with a V-tool or small gouge, and from this to start the rebate with the cutting edge of the plane vertical until it is carried over to the upper gauge line. After this it may be worked down to the lower one in the ordinary way. The job is finished with hollows and rounds.

B 4 shows how this same cornice can be built up with strips, a very good way in many cases, while B 3 is a combination of the two methods, for the lowest member is run separately to avoid the difficulty of working the cove against the lower projecting bead.

All the bevelling and rebating can be done with a circular saw. This may also be used to rough out the hollows as shown in B 5. Indeed, hollows of any fairly large radius can be cut by running the stock diagonally across the saw, a fence being fixed as shown in E 1, the saw being allowed to project the depth of the cut and the angle of the fence being so arranged that the difference in distance from fence to front and back of saw is the width of the arc. With this method the wood is removed in a series of cuts of less than $\frac{1}{8}$ in and E 2, 3 and 4 can be easily worked. When narrow arcs are attempted, they will be found to have flat tops as shown in E 5 and the saw will tend to bind.

The scratch stock made out of a piece of $\frac{3}{4}$ in × 2 in stock, pictured in D 1, is also a very useful tool especially for small mouldings. The blade is usually made out of a piece of old saw filed to shape. It is not bevelled but will be found to cut quite well in either direction if the corners are square and sharp. A compass-saw blade will do if an old piece of saw is not available. Whenever possible the cut should be eased by bevelling with a jack plane, D 2. Quite heavy cuts can also be made with this tool, in fact most of the mouldings of Jacobean furniture were worked in this way, but it is not only hard work but also takes a good deal of time as the blade must be frequently cleared and also sharpened. E 6, 7 and 8 are suitable sections for this tool.

E 9 depicts a handy little tool for making small beads especially on curved parts such as the backs of chairs, a detail quite common around 1800 and often found around drawer fronts in lieu of cock beading.

It simply consists of a block of hardwood with one or more screws in it. One adjusts the most suitable-sized screw in or out to fit the pattern and then cuts a V-shaped groove, using the slot in the screw as a cutting-edge, after which the bead is completed with a piece of sandpaper. Its effect is quite satisfactory.

Fretwork

If the fret is newly broken and can be laid out flat on a board, it is a fairly simple matter to glue it up. The board should be larger than the fret and should be covered with paper, preferably wax paper, to prevent them sticking together. A strip along the bottom and up one side will form a frame on which the broken parts may be assembled. As the various parts are fitted together they are held in position by driving 1in finishing nails into the board against their edges.

When it is completely assembled and any adjustments made that may have been found necessary, it is taken apart and refitted with glue in the joints giving further pressure as required by bending the nails.

If the back of the fret is not exposed, it may be strengthened by covering the paper with cloth and glueing the various pieces to it as well as to one another. Afterwards the surplus cloth is, of course, cut away.

When the work must be done in situ it is usually possible to support the pieces with wedges cut to fit the various openings as required. Other parts can be pulled together with bindings of string or with clips cut from upholstery springs.

40

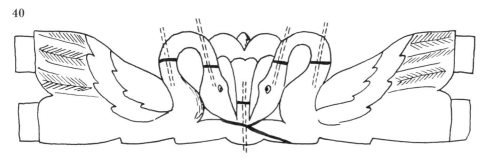

In some cases dowels can be used both to strengthen the joints and to hold the pieces in position while the work is being cramped up. Such a case is shown in the sketch (Illus 40) of the cross rail from the back of a chair. This was a poor design from the structural point of view, too much being cut away in fretting. The dark lines indicate where the breaks occurred, and the dotted lines the dowels which were $\frac{3}{16}$ in diameter. The holes were bored first from the break to the outside, then the drill was inserted part way into the hole the opposite way, the broken parts being held together, and the hole continued into the other half. With the dowels all inserted it was easy to cramp up, and the part was probably stronger than it had been when new.

Fixing cracks

Occasionally a table-top is found to have a crack, maybe a foot long, from one edge. This may be due to an accident, but more likely it will be the result of unequal shrinkage, especially in figured wood.

This can be filled with composition and polished so that it will look perfect, but after a few days a fine line will appear and this will gradually get worse until within a few months the crack will be as bad as it was in the first place. The reason for this is that the composition is not strong enough to prevent a certain amount of motion between the two joining surfaces; they must first be held rigidly and glued before filling and polishing.

Old craftsmen usually let in dovetail keys under the top (Illus 41A). This is quite a help, and, if the crack is not filled with wax and oil and can be glued and pulled together without too much force, will make a good job.

Another way is to saw down the crack, thus cleaning it out and making it of equal width. It is then filled with a piece of veneer glued in, B.

The best way in most cases, however, is to drill down the length of the crack and glue a dowel into the hole, C. By this means enough wood is removed to get past the wax that may have soaked into the sides of the crack preventing adhesion, and by its piston action the rest of the crack can be filled with glue.

The procedure is as follows: take a block about 1in × 2in the thickness of the top and bore a hole through it the size of the dowel, take two strips about a foot long and cramp the block between them at one end, start the hole in the crack and then make a chalk line straight along the crack and extending across the top. Set up a long drill, through the block, into the crack and lined up with the chalk line as shown at D, cramping the strips solidly into position. This enables the hole to be drilled accurately and at the same time holds both sides of the crack level. In glueing, the two strips are moved so that they cover the crack on both sides; the hole is filled with thin glue and the dowel forced home. By this means the glue does not run out of the crack at one place but is forced all along it. The strips may now be removed and if the crack is long, a cramp should be applied with moderate pressure.

When thoroughly dry it may be filled and polished.

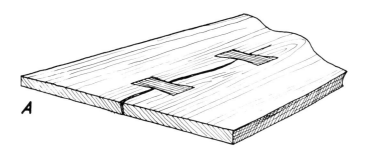

A

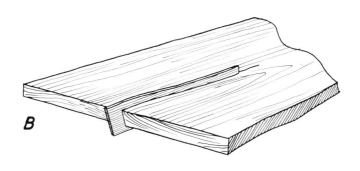

B

C

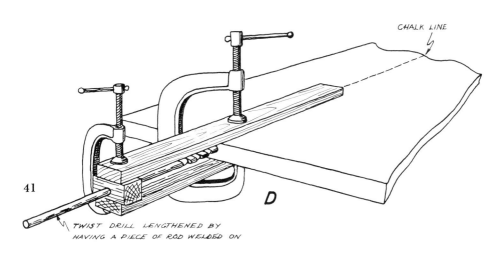

CHALK LINE

41

TWIST DRILL LENGTHENED BY
HAVING A PIECE OF ROD WELDED ON

D

123

Worm-eaten wood

A great many old pieces are worm-eaten, a condition which, contrary to popular opinion, detracts much from their value, for the connoisseur looks for old pieces in as nearly perfect a state as possible. However, if not too badly damaged, they may still give useful service especially where they are subject to no great stress.

A worm-eaten part may be replaced either entirely, or the most weakened portion may be cut away and renewed, or if sufficient strength remains it may be left but should be treated to kill the insects which do the damage.

In replacing part of a worm-eaten piece there is, of course, one main object in so doing and that is to make the article serviceable, at the same time retaining the old surface and patina.

Each job presents a different problem. Sometimes everything is replaced except a thin overlay of the old wood. This is common in the rails of chairs, only the polished surface, about ⅛ in thick, being retained. Another common case is to find a piece of sapwood falling away but the heartwood next to it quite sound. Again, the lower ends of the legs which have been standing on damp floors, possibly stored in sheds or cellars, are often crumbling away although the wood higher up may be good.

The amount to be replaced will depend on the conspicuousness of the part, the nature of the work on it, whether carved, twisted, turned etc, and the cost of replacing it, the weight it is to bear and the wishes of the customer.

To replace the whole of the perforated part is the most satisfactory course; the infection is thus completely removed and the strength almost completely restored. All that is necessary is to measure or make a cardboard pattern or patterns of the part affected, cut away until clear wood is found, make a scarf or other suitable joint, and mark it on the pattern, which may now be cut to fit the old wood and used in marking out the new.

It is, however, more common only to cut away that part which is too weakened, for there are usually a few holes in otherwise sound wood. The same practice is followed, but especial care must be used to ensure that all levelling of the joints is done on the new wood only, because it is the nature of the furniture worms and beetles to tunnel just beneath the surface and moderately heavy sandpapering will uncover these holes leaving unsightly grooves.

In passing, it might be worth mentioning that the presence of these grooves is often an indication of a spurious antique faked out of old worm-eaten beams, etc. Their presence in places which have not been repaired or refinished is an almost sure clue to a fake.

When all the glueing has been finished, *and not before,* the job of killing the insects and making the wood poisonous to them may be undertaken.

The old treatment was an application of coal oil, also known as paraffin in England and kerosine in the USA. This was considered to be effective for ten years, and some firms contracted to look after valuable carvings such as those of Grinling Gibbons by treating them every ten years.

Application may be made in a number of different ways. The carvings above mentioned were taken down from the walls and doorways they adorned and were dipped; this is probably the most effective method. However, paraffin has a most penetrating nature and will soak into most woods if applied with a brush. Another method is to force it into the holes with a syringe.

DDT may be added to the oil and probably adds to its effectiveness and increases the period of protection, but there is a firm (Rentokil Ltd) in England which manufactures a special solution guaranteed to kill all wood-boring insects and which also supplies a special syringe with which to apply it.

Laying leather and cloth

The replacement of leather desk-tops and cloth card-table coverings is a simple enough job, but one or two suggestions may be of value.

The adhesive to be used is either flour or rice paste, and for directions for preparing, see page 146. The use of glue is not recommended because it does not give time enough to do the necessary cutting and working nor will it permit the leather to slide, as will paste, while working out wrinkles etc. It may, however, be used for cloth if desired.

The first consideration is to remove the old cover and clean the wood beneath. The cover can be torn off, and this leaves a coating of paste and lint which is readily scraped off after softening with hot water. Splits and other defects must now be repaired, for a smooth and level surface must be obtained before applying the leather or cloth. Holes can be filled with sawdust or whitening and glue, while cracks should be rejointed or filled with strips of wood glued in.

Although most instructions direct that the leather should be laid first and trimmed after, the author, particularly with hide which has been previously tooled with a border, prefers to reverse the procedure. When received, a desk lining will usually have the blind outer border slightly smaller than the specified dimensions, and there will be upwards of half-an-inch of excess leather to be trimmed off.

With an old piece of furniture there may be variations due to shrinkage and sides may be curved and slightly out of square. In some cases this may be corrected by planing the edge of the recess but if not enough to spoil the appearance of the border, the leather may be cut to fit. After measuring the recess and the tooled portion of the lining, calculate the clearances necessary to centre it, lay it out with a sharp pencil, check and then cut a side and an end: lay in the recess and, if necessary, trim to fit and then mark leather and wood. From these two fitted sides, check the remaining layout, cut with knife and straight-edge and it is ready to be laid with paste, directions for which are on page 146.

For skiver, the more orthodox method may be better because, being so much thinner, there is no trouble in seeing the outline of the recess while it is being centred. So, first cover the recess with a normal coat of paste, cover it with the lining, run your finger lightly along the edge of the recess and slide it into position, now work out all the bubbles from the centre continually checking the borders for alignment. When satisfactory, the trimming is started with the point of a very sharp knife, first making a slit about an inch long against the edge of the recess: now lift the waste piece and cut across to the outside with a pair of scissors: continue with the knife against the edge of the recess while pulling the cut leather away. Thus the blade follows the edge and the leather is guided into place while any deviation is at once apparent. This method is particularly useful for curved work; both may be used for plain linings or for those which are later to be tooled by a bookbinder.

Little need be added in respect to felt or green baize except that an electric iron is useful in removing any creases or wrinkles, but it must not be too hot and must be kept moving or it will so soften the glue or paste that it may show through the cloth.

Gilt work

A gilder used to get a penny an hour more than a carver. From this it is evident that it involves much more skill than one might suppose; consequently it is clear that when a first-class job is required, the obvious course is to send the piece to an expert, if one is available. The following suggestions are therefore only meant for one who has to do the best he can without the skill, knowledge and tools required for the most successful work.

The most common gilt piece requiring attention is a mirror frame. These are usually made of wood, the carving being built up from a basic frame by glueing pieces on and carving them in a number of layers. When this was finished they were taken to the gilder who coated them with a thick layer of whiting and glue, finished with a perfectly smooth, rounded surface. This was covered with gold-leaf, the hollows matted and the raised parts burnished with agate.

In repairing, this process must be repeated, the missing parts replaced by glueing on suitable pieces of white pine or other wood, and then carving them up to match. This is followed by a coat of thin glue and then a heavy layer of whiting and glue, which is also used to fill all other small faults.

If the frame is made of plaster, this substance may be used to replace any missing parts. First the areas to be built up must be cleaned and roughened and then coated with glue. Any places which are to have considerable projections should have a ground work fitted, on which the plaster can be built up. This may either be of nails or screws or wooden pegs, which can be built up with strips of cloth moistened with glue and wound round. The plaster is mixed fairly thick, plaster of Paris, and applied with a spoon. It hardens in a few minutes and while still plastic may be modelled with the fingers or a spatula and built up with more plaster as required. Finally, after a couple of hours, it may be very easily carved with carving tools. Those long delicate scrolls and leaves which are built up on wires are best built up with the gluey strips of cloth before adding the plaster.

After a couple of days the surface may be finished off with fine sandpaper after any further carving, filing or scraping which may have been thought necessary, has been carried out.

The condition of most old gilt frames is such that the touching up may be done more effectively with bronze powders than with gold-leaf. These may be obtained in a variety of colours from brass through yellow, orange, green and red-gold to copper and also shades verging on brown. It is always better to mix with bronzing liquid immediately before application, the result will be both smoother and brighter. When dry, further colouring may be done with the shellac colours used in polishing, the most common being bismarck and the yellows antiqued with raw umber.

No matter how excellent bronze powders may be, they cannot be made to match gold-leaf in good condition and so there is no alternative but to use it when it seems to be called for. The methods used by the gilder may be found in a great many works but they are not suited to the average repair shop, and so what is known as transfer gold-leaf is recommended. The work is first coated as evenly as possible with gold-size and allowed to become tacky; a small area, for trial purposes, should be coated. At the proper state of dryness it will stick to the leaf, allowing the tissue paper backing to come away clean. When this has happened, the main work may be gone over placing the gold side down, rubbing the backing tissue gently with the finger and then pulling it away leaving the gold. This will probably have to be repeated as some places may have been missed while others, having been coated too thinly, dried too soon to stick to the gold. This is the common method, but for the amateur the use of spar varnish such as is sold to yachtsmen is recommended: mixed with a little yellow ochre it can be applied more evenly; it may take anything from four to eight or more hours to come to the tacky state, but it will remain in this condition for an hour or more, making a better and more leisurely job possible.

Quite often a combination of bronze and leaf is used, the bronze in the inaccessible and dirty places and the leaf on the more prominent places; both may be coated with shellac and toned with colours.

Lacquer and papier mâché

During the eighteenth century, the art of Japanning was not only the work of professionals but also a popular hobby and it still can be quite fascinating. Now known as English lacquer, it sought to match the Oriental products imported at great expense in sailing ships.

The grandfather clock in Illus 42 had little left of the original case except the waist, the back and some bits and pieces of the bonnet. The fine brass dial, however, made it seem an ideal subject for a lacquer job though the case had originally been oak. The base and bonnet were completed out of whatever old close-grained hardwood was handy and the waist was scraped and sanded.

The first step in lacquering is to make full-sized patterns of all the areas to be ornamented. A popular source book was *A New book of Chinese designs by Edwards and Darley* published in 1754, some of whose pages are included in T. A. Strange's *English Furniture, Woodwork and Decoration*, a fabulous source of really authentic information. The details in Illus 42 are from the author's scrapbook, some of which might be helpful to someone wishing to try his hand.

In preparing these designs, it is interesting to note that the practice in China was for an artist to explore and study his subject, maybe for weeks, until he had absorbed all the details he needed and then to return to his studio and paint his picture arranging the components in any way he considered satisfactory. Thus he might place a temple at the top of a hill, pilgrims ascending near the centre on a larger scale than a seashore scene below. Each feature would be equally well remembered and any one might predominate if he felt it would serve his sense of artistry. This maybe explains what is felt by the Western eye as a lack of perspective.

A feature of old English lacquer is the raised areas which include most of the prominent features; these should be traced in outline on the panels first. Gesso, a mixture of linseed oil, whitening and glue-size, was used to build up these areas, but if cellulose lacquer is to be used as the enamel, the linseed oil in it will inhibit the drying process and so a mixture of sawdust, whitening and glue was substituted, three heavy coats being applied, each being allowed to dry before proceeding. After sanding, the entire surface was covered with a filler of glue-size and pumice powder well rubbed in.

This completed the foundation for the enamel which, in this case, was red lacquer with a matt surface applied with a spray-gun.

The ornament is applied in several ways; the most important areas being gilded with transfer gold-leaf as described previously. Other details in gold such as the geometrical borders, foliage etc are worked in bronze paint with a sable pencil brush. The faces and hands of the figures are filled in with a creamy-yellow paint, while on a black ground the very restrained use of vermilion is sometimes found.

Drop black or raw umber mixed with thinned varnish is now used to add detail to the gold-leaf areas: these may be roof tiles, stonework, pavings and frets on temples, details on boats and drapery on figures; also the detail on faces, flowers and leaves. Finally, when this is dry, some areas of the gold itself may be toned with a coat of shellac tinted with red, green or brown; for instance, referring to the temple on the right-hand side of Illus 42, the tiled part of the roofs might be tinted red as indicated by the letter R while the floor could be given a checkerboard effect by using green on alternate squares as

愛好中國美術

marked by G. Brown could be used to shade the columns giving them a round appearance and also beneath eaves and in the interior.

This completes the brush work, but the effect is somewhat bright and lacks the smoothness one associates with old English lacquer and so it is French polished, a good deal of care being needed in the initial stages to avoid removing any of the decoration; when a fairly good body has been achieved it is set aside to harden before sanding down.

In the second bodying, some colouring may be added to give variety to the surface and to simulate the dirt and discolouration which would have accumulated in the hollows of the mouldings and other less accessible places; it may then be spirited-out in the usual way.

Although this covers many of the questions which might be asked regarding patching old lacquer, one or two points might be made. It is assumed of course that the woodwork has been made sound, so the next step would be to remove dirt and wax with soap and water plus the judicious use of some fine abrasive powder; this will reveal the good as well as the damaged and botched-up areas. Real Oriental lacquer, however, must be handled with the greatest care for the gold and bronze is extremely thin and easily washed away.

In addition to bumps and scratches, it is quite common for the gesso under-coat to flake off in places showing patches of light colour beneath: these in turn may have been coloured with paint or even black shoe polish. For a proper job they should all be cleaned out down to the wood; coated with glue-size and built up flush with the surrounding surface in the manner already described.

Having applied the lacquer and matched up the ornament, it is possible during the French polishing process to tone down the new work with coloured polishes applied with rubber or brush as already described in matching wood.

Victorian papier mâché

The restoration of this work is almost exactly the same as lacquer except that oil-paints such as are used by artists predominate over gold though both may be used. When the fabric of the article is damaged, quite often a piece is just broken off, but at other times the layers of paper near the bruise may have become separated giving it a spongy condition. If this is the case, thin glue should be worked between them with a thin blade before squeezing them together with spring cramps or clothes pegs. When dry, a surface can be planed flat and a piece of wood glued into place later to be faired up with the sound parts.

Coromandel screens

Of all the substances used in domestic furniture, the foundation of the ornament on Coromandel screens must be one of the most fragile and so they are not uncommonly in quite poor condition with corners chipped and quite large areas flaked off as in Illus 43.

Since this plaster-like coating is so soft, it is desirable to find something of a similar nature with which to patch it and it was by the kindness of a friendly dentist that a preparation called dental stone plaster which is used in their work was tried with satisfactory results.

Of course it is useless to build anything onto a loose or shattered foundation and so all damaged parts should be first scraped or roughened up with very coarse sandpaper or rasp to remove looseness and give key for the new material. In this case it appeared that the screen had been involved in a flood and the bottom two to three inches of the feet had had the plaster completely soaked off: the wood here was also cracked and weakened. The thickness of the sub-coating is almost one-eighth of an inch and so, in order to strengthen the feet as well as to build up a foundation for the plaster, a layer of cotton cloth was cut to fit each face and was embedded and covered with hot glue.

The following day a mixture of thin glue, coarse pumice powder and lamp black was prepared in a heated glue pot and with a small, stiff bristle brush was scrubbed into each of the places to be patched. The purpose of this was both to secure any loose bits that might have been missed and to form a link between the old and new plaster.

The plaster itself was made grey by the addition of lamp black and was applied to the large areas with a wide (3in) putty knife, levelling it out as well as possible: a palette knife is the best tool for the smaller holes. As this plaster sets up so very quickly it must of course be mixed in small quantities; a tablespoonful of water to two of plaster in a saucer being good for a start adding either as necessary while mixing: it should stand at least overnight for thorough drying.

Levelling the patches with three grades of sandpaper is a nasty, dusty job but cannot be skimped without storing up even more such work or ending up with a poor job. This having been done, a mixture of shellac, nigrosine and lamp black was prepared and two coats were given to all the patches, sealing them sufficiently well to permit washing.

At this stage the surface is likely to be grubby, not only from previous use but from finger marks and splashes of glue and plaster, and washing is indicated. First, the incised ornament should be cleaned with a clothes-brush because the colour here is water-soluble. Hot water and a cloth wrung out almost dry are used for the washing, with detergent powder used only where necessary.

Undoubtedly some small indentations will have escaped the filling process; they can now be filled with black stopping. After this, a process of repeated sanding-down and bodying-up with black polish will restore the black surface.

The penultimate job is to cut the ornamental incisions across any patches. Where they are straight they can be done with a piece of hacksaw blade using a straight-edge as guide; wider ones with the edge of a flat file in the same

43　*By permission of Michael Cotton Antiques, Victoria, BC*

manner; curved ones should be outlined with a sharp pointed knife and the area between scraped level.

The colour in the grooves can now be matched with poster colours obtainable from art dealers or with a mixture of Latex Interior household paint with dry pigments.

The usual explanation of the name for this form of Chinese lacquer screen is that it is derived from the Coromandel coast which extends north from Ceylon for over two hundred miles on the eastern shore of India (Madras). It is true that the British East India Company had a number of establishments at different times in various places here and no doubt such screens, in common with any number of other objects, were shipped home from them; what is not clear, however, is why these particular ones should have retained the name.

Mirrors and glass

Modern mirrors use a coating of pure silver on the back of the glass and, although the technique of application has advanced, there has been little change in the product since the method was introduced in 1840. Prior to that date an amalgam of tinfoil and mercury was used and although the new method was regarded at that time as being inferior, it was welcomed because of the horrible effects of the mercury vapours on the health of the workers.

The characteristic grey appearance of the mercury-silvered mirrors is prized by collectors and so should on no account be renewed without the express direction of the owner, regardless of the condition. Their backs have the appearance of a very dirty aluminium paint and the deposit is very fragile; the later silvered ones were always coated with paint, often consisting of a mixture of shellac varnish and red lead.

Early mirrors were always held in their frames with triangular wooden blocks glued in place and these also served to support the wooden back board which was commonly held by three or four brads along each side as pictured in Illus 44A. This rather crude method looks even worse when the original square iron brads have been replaced with modern finishing nails. Blued upholsterers' tracks with their heads nipped off look better.

Although silvered mirrors will take a great deal more abuse, it is still advantageous to have the back free from any contact, especially in damp conditions, and so the block method has been generally continued. Should the blocks be cut to the section as indicated in B they can be easily tacked as well as glued.

Before replacing the mirror in the frame after repairs, be sure that any new wood has received a coating of black stain because it can be very unsightly in certain lights by reflection in the thickness of the glass. A black felt 'Jiffy marker' is handy for this purpose.

One is occasionally asked to resilver or replace the glass in an old wooden elliptical hand-mirror of the kind pictured in C. Some have a bead or strip of

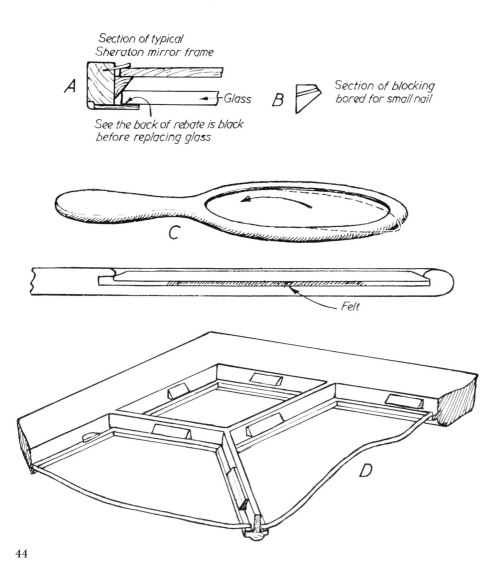

Section of typical
Sheraton mirror frame

A

Glass

See the back of rebate is black
before replacing glass

B

Section of blocking
bored for small nail

C

Felt

D

44

inlay glued in place to hold the glass, but others are very cunningly made without any joint and of the section shown below. The undercut groove is made deeper for a certain distance by the handle end; a padding of felt is placed beneath the glass to thrust it forward against the lip. It must be inserted in the approximate position indicated by the dotted line and pressed into the groove with the fingers, revolving it until it can be pressed into the recess. It is now forced outwards into the shallower part of the groove where it is centred. There is very little likelihood of its being dislodged.

Should a new glass be required and there is no broken one to provide a pattern, one should make a trial template out of cardboard or plastic which can be trimmed until its insertion is found to be possible. The new glass will of course have to be bevelled to a very thin edge.

Glazed doors

The traditional method of supporting glass in a door was to bed it into putty; that is, first to putty the rebate, then press the glass into place, securing it with pins or, later, sheet-metal triangles and then complete the puttying. The reason for this was because ordinary glass was by no means flat and it is common on old doors for the putty between glass and rebate to vary in thickness one-eighth of an inch and occasionally as much as a quarter. During the nineteenth century, however, common glass had improved sufficiently for wooden beads to supplant the putty, so that early in the twentieth century the older method was rarely used for furniture.

It should be noted, however, that old doors with puttied glass are a great deal stronger, especially in the case of barred bookcase doors, by reason of the fact that the putty fuses both glass and frame into one unit which is free from the rattle and flexibility so often found in the later ones, especially after having been shipped.

The first problem which arises for the repair man is the putty which will likely be as hard as concrete. Heat will soften it and a large electric soldering iron is perhaps the most useful tool for the purpose. Place the point of the iron in the right-hand corner of the glass and as soon as the putty smokes, draw it slowly to the left at the same time prying away the softened material with a putty knife. This may have to be repeated after the glass has been removed to get rid of the bedding putty.

The problem of holding the new glass while the putty is hardening is normally achieved with pins or triangles as already mentioned, but in the case of barred doors where the strip dividing the two glasses is normally one-eighth of an inch thick, special treatment is required. A strip of walnut of triangular section about ⅛ in by ¼ in cut into one-inch lengths is glued to the bars at strategic places as shown in D. When dry the putty is laid in the ordinary way, covering the blocks. It may be coloured by working in a little pigment ground in oil; burnt sienna for mahogany or raw umber for oak or walnut.

The side glasses in grandfather clocks are sometimes found with rebates so shallow that the new thicker glasses are almost flush. When this is the case they may be secured by cutting a half-inch strip of leather and mitring and glueing it to cover the joint.

Elliptical Sheraton mirror frames of the kind which have a cross-banded face, being fragile, are occasionally in such poor condition as to need replacement. The method of laminating the rim is very similar to the one described on page 191 for making the rail for a tray stand. For this however the outer frame would be of ¾ in material: in fact for a small one, plywood can be used and may be cut out with a bandsaw, the entering and leaving kerf being secured with a couple of corrugated fasteners (also called wiggle-nails). It is important this be accurately laid out and cleanly finished inside, for any lack of fairness will be revealed in the finished job. Four laminations are usual and the outer one, of soft mahogany, should be scarfed rather than butted, otherwise when the inner ones (usually oak) are wedged up the butt would almost certainly be opened.

A one-inch lap tapered to a feather-edge each end is about right and, after it and the other layers have been glued, a little extra pressure applied with a cramp on a curved caul at this point will ensure a tight joint.

Clear plastic with trade names such as Plexiglas can be a useful substitute, particularly in replacing a piece of bent glass. Small pieces can be heated in the oven of a domestic electric cooking range until soft enough to take the bend without losing their dimensions or surface: larger ones are best handled by industrial fabricators who have special equipment for this purpose. In either case, a form must be made to the curve required; it can be a sheet of metal or cardboard tacked to three or more cross pieces bandsawn to the necessary profile.

Convex glasses which are snapped into the groove of the bezel of clocks and barometers can be made out of this material. First prepare two discs of ¾ in plywood of the size required: turn the first to a little more convexity than required for the finished glass; remove and turn the other to a corresponding concavity. Cut the plastic to approximate size allowing for turning; hang the bezel on the tailstock so as to be in position for fitting; place plastic between the two discs, bring up tailstock and apply pressure squeezing it into shape. It can now be turned to size, the edge being bevelled so as to lock into the under-cut of the bezel, the turning tools being of the type used for brass or ivory. Once in all round, ease off the tailstock, thus allowing the bezel to receive the outward pressure retaining the curvature.

In order to clear the hands, some clocks require more curve than is possible by this method. In this case heat will be needed but this is rather a tricky job because any flaw in the two discs may be impressed on the softened plastic.

Ivory and other animal substances

These materials are akin and in many ways are similar to work.

Ivory and bone There are two problems which may arise in handling old ivory veneer. First of all it seems to become more translucent as it ages with the result that anything of a dark colour beneath it, such as common glue or dark wood, will show through like a shadow. Secondly it may have curled or warped and is liable to crack if forcibly flattened.

In order to overcome the first, it is necessary to use white glue, a form of fish glue available in flakes. This is cooked up in the ordinary way and should be further whitened by adding some zinc white. If this is not available, ordinary glue, if clean, will do if sufficient white has been added. If the veneer is not flat, however, the pressure of the cramps may force most of the glue away from some areas thus allowing some of the ground to show through. When this is the case, the only way to make a really good job is to remove all the ivory, clean the ground and replace it over a piece of linen laid in the whitened glue. Small wafers of glue-impregnated cloth are available for the purpose of laying piano keys.

If the second problem arises, the ivory will have to be softened before it can be glued down. One authority recommends phosphoric acid; this will indeed soften it, in fact, it can completely dissolve it, but its penetration is so slow that it may destroy the surface before having the desired effect. Hot water is effective, however, and may be applied in three ways. First, if the ivory can be entirely removed it may be put in the hot water for about half an hour and then cramped up between two pieces of wood. If left overnight, it will be found to stay reasonably flat. If only a corner of a fairly large piece is affected, a jet of steam directed against it for perhaps five minutes will have the desired effect (the boiler described on page 27 may be used). Lastly, a larger piece may be laid face down on a wet towel heated in a roasting pan. Here there is a danger of loosening the whole piece but it has been found useful in certain cases.

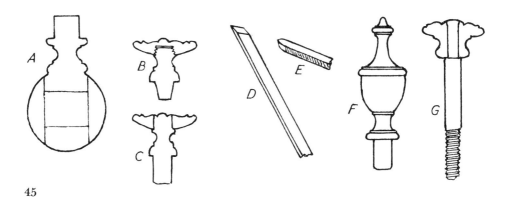

45

Probably the majority of the knobs, finials and paterae on old furniture which are described as ivory are, in reality, bone. The globular feet on old Regency toilet mirrors if examined will be found to be in three pieces cemented together, the larger diameter being made of a tubular piece with plugs fitted into each end as in Illus 45A. Another common example would be the small drawer knobs with face turning which are made in two parts screwed together, as in B. The reason for this is the difficulty of finding sound bone of suitable form to make them in one piece. The author always keeps a few bones in stock obtained from the butcher. They must of course be thoroughly cleaned first. Old piano-key ivories are useful for renewing escutcheons and patches, while walrus tusks, whales' teeth and old ivory billiard balls are also worth keeping.

Tortoiseshell and horn   Tortoiseshell is from the back of the hawks bill and other turtles. Unlike ivory or wood it can be softened and fused together with heat and forced into heated metal dies to produce sculptured effects much the

138

same as plastics are done today, a technique which was used in the production of such things as snuff boxes. The repair man will come across it mainly as veneer on tea caddies, card cases and boulle work. Like ivory it may be softened in warm water and flattened but in re-laying or patching it, the glue surface beneath it should be matched as closely as possible for it is an important element in the final colour effect.

Some kinds of horn were used as a substitute for the shell and respond in much the same way.

Working these substances usually involves first, roughing out with buttress-toothed bandsaw, hacksaw or jeweller's saw; filing to fit; glueing in place; again filing and then finishing with several grades of abrasive paper and polishing with metal polish or buff.

Turning is carried out with scraping tools such as are used for brass. A diamond-pointed tool of square steel ground as shown in Illus 45D, and held at that angle is useful for the finer details; the point as well as the cutting edges each side of it are used. C indicates how knobs similar to that in B may be made without having to cut threads. First the face pieces should be marked out on a flat piece of bone, bored right through and then cut roughly to size; next they are turned to approximate shape by mounting each one on a mandrel made out of a piece of bolt between two tube-like washers. Next turn the stems leaving a fairly heavy plug to be glued into the drawer front and the other end a tight fit into the face pieces which can now be glued on. The final step is to turn up the face as gently as possible so as to avoid breaking the stem.

E is a useful type of tool for working the hollow parts; F and G are the finial and mirror screw for the Regency toilet glass on page 226. The brass stem of G is squared where it passes through the ivory and is carefully riveted over.

It is occasionally desirable to tone down new ivory to match the older pieces. The Japanese are supposed to have darkened their netsuke by boiling them in strong tea and this certainly gives them a fine warm tone, but it is a poor match for most old ivory. An application of the iron and vinegar solution used for blackening oak will produce the colder tones. Other colours such as the black and red found on ivory chessmen can be achieved by boiling in water-soluble aniline stains. Cochineal will also match some reds. It is remarkable that stains which, applied cold, will have almost no penetration, after boiling can be handled for years without wearing off.

Mother-of-pearl   This is one of the most beautiful products of the ocean; it is particularly attractive in combination with tortoiseshell in the form of such objects as visiting-card cases and snuff boxes.

The author's main source of supply is the remains of a set of counters for an Oriental game (maybe poker); they are nice and thick and in different shapes; ideal for the odd missing keyhole or piece of inlay.

It is worked in the same way as ivory except that it is inclined to be brittle and so, when it is necessary to hold a piece in a vice or pair of pliers in order to cut or file it, a piece of leather should be folded to form a cushion between the pearl and the metal and moderate force only should be used.

139

Tambours

A tambour is a flexible door or shutter in the form of a row of moulded slats glued to a linen backing; the most common being the cover of a roll-top desk. It was first used during the eighteenth century and was popular during the Sheraton period.

When free in its groove it seldom gives trouble, but for a number of reasons it may jam or bind and the additional force required to move it may cause the backing to fail.

One of the causes of trouble is that the slats get stuck together during a repolishing job when a wet fad or varnish has been used. When opened, of course the bending will break some of the joints but groups of twos and threes may remain stuck causing rough and jerky motion. If this is not the cause, suspect dislocation of the groove due to shrinkage of the components of the carcase or perhaps pressure on the ends of the slats because of a warp in the frame. Sometimes pieces intended to guide the tambour around the back may have become unglued and displaced.

In bad cases when dismantling will be necessary, it is well to first check the closure. If it does not meet properly it may be due either to the frame or the tambour being out of square. Make a note of the degree of the fault (eg ¼in gap at top when bottom is closed). Later it will be decided how best this may be corrected.

Dismantling   Sometimes by removing the handle it will be possible to push the shutter past the closed position and feed it out through the back. With a roll-top desk, the upper part must be removed, turned upside down and the writing surface unscrewed so that the tambour, after being brought to the closed position, can be lifted out.

Now examine the grooves or guides; if dislocation has occurred, correct this and fair any sharp bends or rough spots. Clean out any dirt and give it a good wax polish. Often this is all that is needed. If the tambour is stiff, bend each joint across the edge of the bench and scrape away the gummy polish and brush it clean down to the backing.

If a new backing is indicated, a fairly light cloth should be chosen; heavy canvas or burlap is too stiff. While it may occasionally be best to wash off completely all the cloth and clean the slats, it is usually easier to do the job in two or three sections. With a narrow tambour, lay it face down on clean newspapers and cut the canvas in half across the slats with a straight-edge and knife. Now soak half with warm water and pull away the cloth; scrub and clean, giving particular attention to the edges of the slats; dry with a towel.

Before glueing the new backing, check the note regarding the closing. If correction is indicated, nail laths along each side and one at the closing end making the required correction of angle; strain and tack it as required and glue the new cloth in place. When half dry, check and clean joints where required. The following day do the other half. With a large piece, such as the fall of a roll-top desk, it may be sufficient to renew a strip, say six inches wide each side. Do this in the way described.

Renewing the leather on bellows

First remove the old leather and use it as a pattern in cutting the new piece. If it is missing, examine the bellows to see if the top and bottom boards are the same length, and when open are as in Illus 46A or, as is sometimes the case, the upper part is longer, as at B. Below are the approximate shapes of the two types, the total length being the measurement of the outline of the boards. The end flaps are to fold over the joint of the nozzle, making an airtight covering. As a matter of fact, this is usually put on as a separate piece afterwards, but it does not make quite such a tight job. The width at the handle will vary with the size of the boards but 4½ in may be suggested as an average; the remainder should be cut a little full to be trimmed off later. In cutting the nicks to accommodate the handles it is well to make them a trifle narrower and shallower than the dimensions of the handles so that there will be no air leaks at the corners. The dotted line in C indicates the section of the handle.

Now check the valve; its leather may be hard and stiff and so will need replacing. The spout may be loose or stopped up. See that the twigs which prevent the leather from being sucked inwards as the bellows are opened are in order; if necessary replace them with willow or wire. If the former, cut the ends at an angle so that, after they are tacked down, they occupy the positions seen at E. If of wire, tie them on each shoulder with string tacked to the bottom board, the other end being tacked to the upper one after the leather is in position.

The leather may now be tacked between the nicks across the handles. This may be carried out with the tacks inside as shown at D if it is done at this stage, making a neater job. Often it is turned out and tacked afterwards but this results in the leather tending to lift with the pressure.

Now place the upper board in position and tack a fairly stiff piece of leather across the joint to form a hinge. Next bring the cover round and tack the ends in place by the nozzle, leaving the heads projecting slightly so that they may be easily removed if necessary. Now prop the handles open with a suitable piece of wood; see that the twigs or wire are properly spaced and in the latter case secure the strings to the upper board. See whether the upper board is in the correct position relative to the lower one; it will sometimes be found that the leather is tending to pull it sideways or to twist it. If this is the case, remove the temporary tacks and make the necessary adjustments.

Being satisfied, the leather may be firmly tacked round the hinge, lapping the two tabs round the joint; next tack round the convex part starting each side of the handles. Having come to the concave part, it is an advantage to

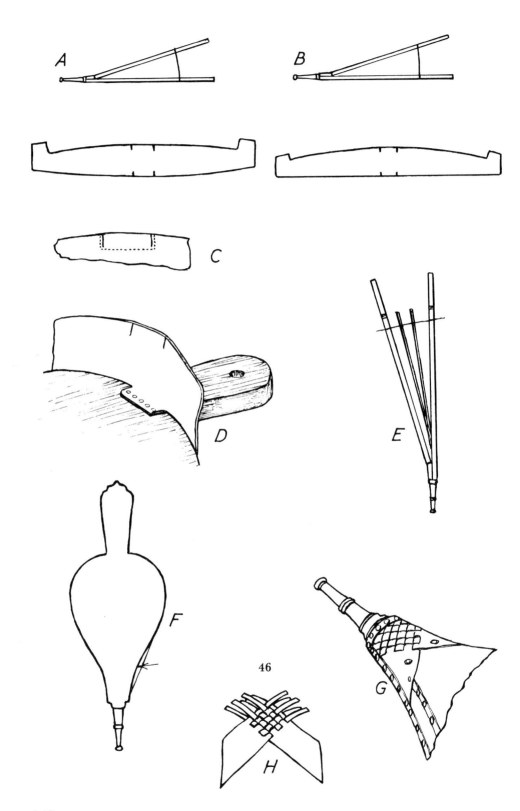

apply a little glue between leather and wood for here is a very common place for leaks unless very closely tacked (F).

The trim is usually finished with brass-headed nails starting with the strip round the upper board. The covering of the joint follows with either a plain piece or it may be cut, woven or ornamented in a number of ways. The one pictured in G and H will be found quite effective, or the brass-headed nails may be arranged to form a pattern. The band bordering the nozzle and round the lower board is usually the final finish.

Rule joints

A rule joint is a hinged joint of a drop-leaf table-top forming an ovolo moulding when the leaf is down and concealing the hinges.

The introduction of a slightly different hinge for this purpose having the centre of rotation in line with the upper surface of the flap, ie the side in contact with the wood, has somewhat complicated the work of fitting these joints.

The layout using the old hinge was as A or B (Illus 47). It will be seen that the centre of rotation was either $\frac{1}{8}$ in above the lower surface of the top if the hinge was let in flush (A) or $\frac{1}{16}$ in above if the knuckle only was let in (B). This provided the joint with either a $\frac{1}{8}$ in or $\frac{1}{16}$ in lap when the leaf was down.

The new hinge, C and D, reduced this lap by $\frac{1}{16}$ in making no lap when the hinge was not let in. It should be observed that distances O and X vary in all cases except D, thus O is $\frac{1}{8}$ in greater than X in A and $\frac{1}{16}$ in greater in B and C. These dimensions are based on hinges of $\frac{1}{16}$ in metal with $\frac{1}{8}$ in pins which appears to be the most common usage.

If a new hinge is to be fitted, it should be of the same type as the one removed. If this is not available and type A and B are wanted, the new kind may be bent to shape by placing the knuckle in the jaws of the vice with the leaves extended and the kinks hammered out. If the reverse is the case the old type will have to be raised by placing $\frac{1}{16}$ in veneer or cardboard beneath the flaps.

To correct a faulty joint it is well to check first the straightness of both moulded surfaces, the type of hinge and the distances O and X. It is assumed that the joint is in order when the leaf is up, for no one would be foolish enough to screw down the hinges unless this was satisfactory, and so there remain two faults, the cures for which are as follows.

For too much clearance, either move the hinge bodily towards the centre of the top, cutting the recess for knuckle and leaf to the left as shown in the dotted lines on E, or let the hinge in deeper as shown by dotted lines in F.

For too little clearance, either move the hinge outwards away from centre of the top, see dotted lines G, or pack up both sides of the hinge by placing cardboard or veneer beneath the leaves.

143

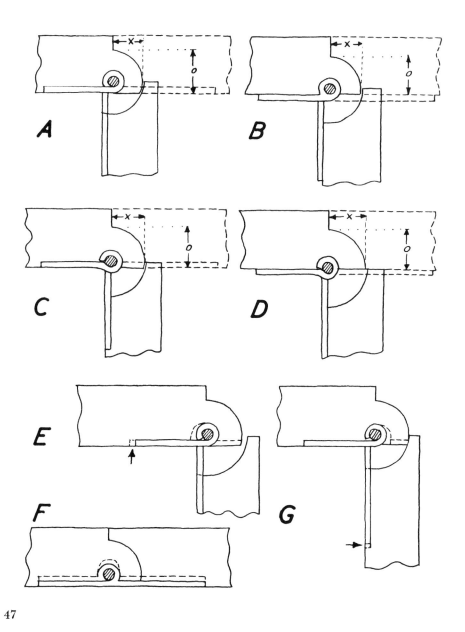

47

Fitting a steel table-leaf support

The hinged metal supports commonly used on tea waggons are easily fitted in the extended position; but should the holes be more than $\frac{1}{16}$ in out, the leaf will refuse to hang straight down.

This may be corrected by moving the screws and trying again until the right location is found; but time will be saved if the exact position is first ascertained by laying it out full size as follows (Illus 48).

Draw OX representing top and leaf extended.

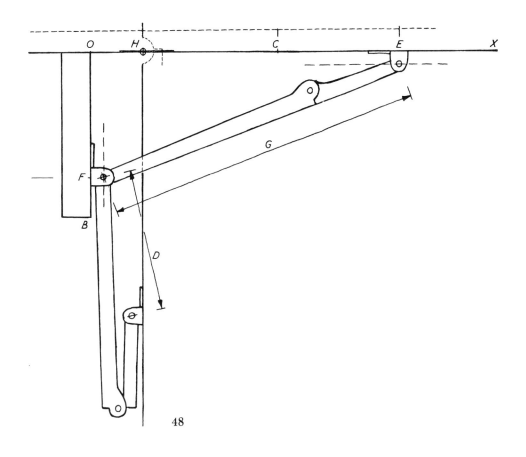

48

Draw OB representing the outer face of the rail.

Measure and mark OH equal to distance from rail to centre of hinge pin.

Draw parallels to OX and OB, represented by a series of dashes, distant from them equal to the height of the end pivots of supports.

Measure D on folded support and mark HC equal to D.

Set dividers to G and find points E and F where CE is equal to OF.

Mark F on rail and attach support with pivot level with F.

Adhesives

The question of adhesives is nearly always answered by one of three substances, glue, paste and a Bostik cement. Glue and paste for most organic substances except rubber and plastics and one of the range of Bostik cements for the rest. The strongest of these however is black in colour and makes it unsuitable for some purposes, and so as a substitute the following may be tried.

Flake shellac makes a fairly strong bond. The pieces to be joined should first be heated so that they will melt the shellac which is placed between them.

145

They are then pressed firmly together and held until cool.

Alum may be used in the same way, and has been used for repairing a broken marble column of a Viennese cabinet.

Household cement or model-aeroplane glue is quite good where a light colour is important.

A test of various cements for glueing brass to wood produced the following results strongest to weakest: a Bostik cement, household cement, liquid glue and hot glue.

To make tests, small squares of brass were glued between two pieces of wood, the two glues to be compared being on each side of the metal. After a week they were separated, thus breaking the weaker joint. In this way any number of cements for different substances may be compared, thus leather to wood is strongest with hot glue, rice paste comes next and flour paste is weakest.

To make flour paste proceed as follows: put four tablespoons of flour in a measuring cup, add a little cold water and stir into a fairly stiff paste free from lumps. Add cold water slowly until the mixture is like thick cream. Now add boiling water slowly while stirring, until the cup is two-thirds full. If the mixture assumes a translucent appearance it is in order, if not, or if in doubt, the cup should be set in a pot of hot water and heated until the mixture does become translucent. After this it is fit for use and may be thinned down with cold water as desired.

The important things are twofold: first, it is very hard to get rid of lumps if mixing flour with hot water is attempted, and so the mixture must be started with cold water; secondly, the temperature must be raised sufficiently to jellify the flour. If enough paste is mixed, the hot water will be sufficient; but when a small quantity is made, the container may absorb too much heat.

Rice paste is rather different to make: take four tablespoons of ground rice to a cup of water which should be hot, and keep hot in a double boiler for about an hour, frequently stirring, by which time it should have become of a similar nature to flour paste and may be handled in the same way. Both will keep a week, more or less, may be thinned with water and are used cold.

Where it is available, however, a proprietary brand known as Clam (which is mixed cold) is handier and quite satisfactory.

Contact Cement, a relatively recent innovation which is used mainly for cementing such materials as Formica and Arborite, seems to be the answer to many problems, including the application of veneers. The author has used it on curved surfaces but always with some misgivings although, so far, without receiving any complaints. Following the instructions, both surfaces are coated as evenly as possible and on absorbent ones, a second or even third coat may be necessary for them to dry with a glossy appearance. After the indicated elapse of time for drying, they are placed in contact and adhere immediately, the bond strengthening as time goes on, so it is claimed. The trick is to position them accurately before allowing them to touch, for sliding into position is out of the question. Since both surfaces are dry at this stage, one or more pieces of brown paper are used to cover the joint completely while the positioning is done, then each one in turn is withdrawn and the veneer rubbed down. The author cannot explain his reluctance to use this product: maybe it has to do with old dogs and new tricks.

Spinning wheels

The author can remember making a new flyer and bobbin for a spinning wheel without any knowledge of how they work. It looked quite well when finished, but it is unlikely that anyone could have spun yarn with it.

Illus 49, a drawing of a typical machine, will acquaint the reader with the names of the various parts, and a scale has been added so that anyone who wishes may make one.

In operation it has a twofold function: to twist fibre into yarn, and at the same time to wind it slowly onto the bobbin. The spinner (or spinster) feeds the wool into the eye of the revolving spindle, getting it into the proper form in her fingers. From the eye it passes over one of the hooks of the flyer and thence to the bobbin.

When ready to operate it will appear as if the wheel drives the spindle and the bobbin by means of two cords. In reality this is a single cord of double length passing twice round the pulleys. The reason for this is that it would be difficult to maintain an equal tension on two separate cords. The driving surface of the wheel is of the design shown because this double cord must cross between the mother of all, and the wheel, thus passing onto it at a slight angle.

It will be noted that the pulley diameter of the bobbin is slightly smaller than either of the grooves of the spindle pulley. The result of this is that the bobbin turns slightly faster, thus winding in the thread which has been twisted between the spinner's hands and the eye of the spindle. Her choice of the groove will result in a more or less tightly twisted thread.

The spindle with its bobbin, pulley, and flyer is perhaps the piece most commonly missing. The spindles are usually in one piece of steel, the eye being very nicely finished and polished so that it will not damage the thread as it passes through. It is threaded close to its end, usually with a left-hand two-start thread so that the pulley which is mounted on a brass nut may be removed to change the bobbin.

Owing to the high cost of such a spindle, a drawing of a less expensive one is added, using a piece of $\frac{3}{16}$in steel rod attached to a brass eye piece.

The turning of the pulley and bobbin is straightforward, but care should be taken to see that the flyer is true and in balance. In order to test this, the spindle with flyer mounted should be placed with its bearing surfaces on two blocks with hard level surfaces. It will now roll with its heavy side down. This should be lightened and the test repeated until it will remain in any position without rolling.

Originally most of the parts were intended to be demountable for ease of

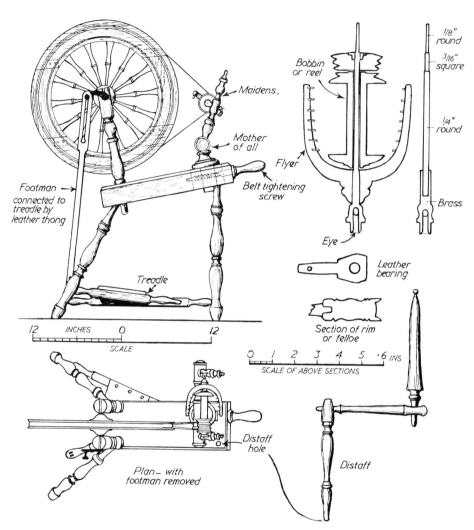

Maidens.

Mother of all

Footman connected to treadle by leather thong

Belt tightening screw

Treadle

12   INCHES   0   12

SCALE

Bobbin or reel

Flyer

Eye

1/8" round

3/16" square

1/4" round

Brass

Leather bearing

Section of rim or felloe

0 1 2 3 4 5 ·6 INS

SCALE OF ABOVE SECTIONS

Distaff hole

Plan – with footman removed

Distaff

49

storage, but owing to wear and shrinkage it may be advantageous to glue the various parts into their holes. An exception to this, however, is the maiden on the eye side which should be a friction fit in its hole so that it may be twisted to remove the spindle.

Although it is not necessary for the driving wheel to be absolutely true, it will occasionally be found so bad that the cord will no longer stay on. If it is to be used, it will have to be trued up. Proceed as follows.

A 2in × 8in disc should be screwed to the faceplate of the lathe. In this is turned a recess for the projecting part of the wheel hub and a hole into which the uncranked end of the axle will tightly fit. The wheel is now attached to the outer face of this cup-shaped block by means of three screws through wooden cross pieces each bridging two spokes.

On setting the lathe in motion, one can see whether the cranked end of the axle is running true. If not, shims will have to be placed under the appropriate spokes until this is remedied. It will usually be sufficient now to slightly reduce the diameter of the wheel and recut the groove.

If the trouble is due to the spokes being loose, they will have to be reglued. First mark one spoke, also its position on hub and rim. Now mark and drive out the pins of two tenons of the rim and take it apart. Glue spokes into hub using liquid glue and then into the rim, assembling it at the same time. Replace the pins of the tenons.

The use of liquid glue will give sufficient time to true up the wheel by manipulating it as required after watching it revolve in its bearings.

Sometimes the thread on the belt-tightening screw is worn out. If this is the case, a new one may be made out of a piece of hard maple or beech, perhaps retaining the handle part. First turn the new piece to the maximum diameter to fit into the holes in the bed. Having ascertained the pitch, mark the spiral. Now with a parting or 'V' tool, carve the spiral for a distance of an inch or so. Fit it into the nut by trial until the right depth is found when it may be continued for the required length. Aim at a fairly tight fit which can later be eased by filing away the shiny spots with a triangular file.

The leather spindle bearings can be cut out of a piece of sole leather; the narrow part passed through the slot in the maiden and secured by a wooden pin through the small hole. Such bearings last an incredibly long time if kept lubricated with olive oil.

Tip-top tripod tables

The fitting pictured in Illus 50A is drawn to scale from an eighteenth-century table with a 21in top. It forms the link between the pedestal and top permitting it to revolve, be tilted into a vertical position or dismantled by removing the wedge. It is generally known as a birdcage, but Wallace Nutting calls it a crow's nest, a name probably derived from the lookout of a Boston whaler: the tables themselves he describes as 'tip-and-turn' tables.

The Cabinet-makers' Price Book of 1823 and other older works use the term 'pillar and claw', but tripod table is more common now. If there is no birdcage the square beneath the top was called the block, and if tilting, it had pivots which fitted into holes in the clamps or cleats which were screwed to the underside of the top. The term 'claw' referred to each entire leg, regardless of its shape from its dovetail in the pillar to its toe.

Wear in the five movable joints and looseness in the four little pillars of the birdcage often combine to cause so much resilience that the table's usefulness is seriously impaired, particularly if there is also a visible slope in the top. When received for attention, it is a good idea to measure the height of the top opposite each toe; revolve it 180° and measure and note again. This will indicate the extent of the slope and also whether the fault is in the birdcage or the pillar, or perhaps both. A maximum difference of ⅜in in a 21in top is usually acceptable.

The steps which may have to be taken to make it both level and firm include the following:

Reglueing the claws, some of which may have already been badly repaired.

Adjusting the pillar so as to ensure that the upper bearing of the birdcage is centred vertically over the lower.

Reglueing the four pillars of the birdcage.

Renewing or bushing the top pin of the pillar and glueing a strip of leather within the lower hole of the birdcage to take up the wear.

Renewing or bushing the pivots.

Taking up the wear in the catch.

To test the pertinent parts of the pillar it is worth making the gadget illustrated in B, which is shown in elevation and as seen from below. The hole in the upper strip takes the pin at the top of the pillar and the V of the lower rests against the area covered by the lower part of the birdcage as indicated. By measuring from the end of the arm to the floor at each foot, the amount of error can be noted. This may be reduced in three ways: building up a foot by glueing a shim to the bottom, reducing one by planing and by changing the position of the upper pin. If it is much out of vertical, perhaps a combination of all three may be best.

If the pin is substantial, a new centre can be marked on it, a circle of smaller diameter inscribed and the surplus wood chiselled away. If it is too small for this it can be cut off and a temporary new one cut out and tacked in place; if necessary, its position can be changed as required until its exact location has been established when a proper one is turned up on the lathe with pin for glueing. If the birdcage is considered to be true the new pin should be fitted to the existing hole; if not, then make it large so that a new and true hole may be bored as will be described later.

Unless a new pin has been made as described above the upper birdcage hole will probably have to be bushed: to do this, bore it out to perhaps twice its size and then fill it with a plug turned up on the lathe and glued in place.

The only really satisfactory way to bore or true up this upper hole is to

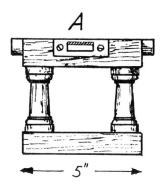

A

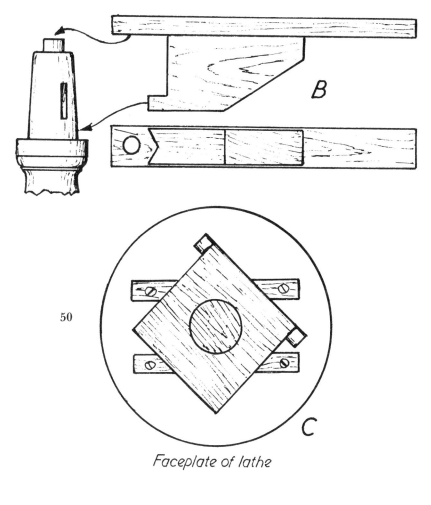

B

50

C

Faceplate of lathe

D   E

mount the birdcage on the faceplate of the lathe by means of the two bars as indicated in C. Allowance should be made for play so that it may be adjusted by tapping with a hammer until the lower hole runs perfectly true when the four screws or bolts can be tightened down.

The actual boring is a bit of a challenge because of the distance between the tool rest and the work but with due care, patience and attention all should be well. First make a centre with the point of a skew-chisel and then follow with a bit of smaller diameter than the finished hole. Now enlarge it with the chisel, frequently stopping to gauge it with inside calipers and finishing with the pin itself.

Before removing it from the lathe, clean out the lower hole so that it may be gluable, then find a piece of leather which will nicely take up the slackness and glue it in place.

It may now be necessary to fit the shoulder of the pillar to the birdcage, using a chisel at first and finishing by colouring the bottom of the birdcage with blue crayon, turning it against the shoulder and then filing off the marked areas. The upper shoulder round the pin may also need the same treatment and the slot for the wedge may need lowering.

What follows will also apply to pillars with fixed blocks which should first be tested for level by placing a straight-edge across the block and over each foot, measuring to the floor and, if necessary, trueing by planing.

Now the pivots on which the top tilts. It is sometimes possible to find suitable brass or copper tube with which to make bushes, enlarging the holes in the clamps and reducing the pivots as required. This has the advantage of retaining as much of the original as possible. It is usually more economical, however, to cut out the old pivots, including the portion of the block between them, leaving a rebate as indicated by the dotted lines on D, and then to make a new piece with larger pivots at each end, turned in the lathe and carefully fitted individually to the clamps. After glueing in place the corner is rounded and two screws should be added for extra strength. It is sometimes advantageous to make the new piece wider, as shown in E, in order to hold the top more nearly vertical when it is up.

Lastly the catch: these usually need lubricating and cleaning, but the more important thing is to take up the wear by soldering or riveting a piece of brass of the required thickness within the striking plate as indicated by the diagonal shading in A.

Barometers

Robert Boyle was credited with the first barometer fitted with a scale in England in 1663. His assistant, Robert Hooke, invented the wheel barometer in 1665 but this form did not become popular till much later. They were called barascopes till about 1700.

The aneroid barometer was patented in 1844; it is fitted with one or more sealed metal containers not unlike shoe-polish tins but with concentrically corrugated ends. These are pressed inwards as pressure increases and spring outwards as it falls, a motion which is connected to an indicator pointing to a scale graduated in inches from about twenty-eight to thirty-one. This represents the equivalent of a column of mercury which would balance a similar pressure; they are well understood by most watch-makers and little trouble is experienced in getting them repaired.

In many places, however, it is different with the older types. Obviously a multitude of experimental models have been made during the past three hundred years but the two most common kinds are illustrated diagrammatically in Illus 51. A is the stick or pillar barometer which was occasionally fitted with gimbals for use on sailing ships. In this instrument the upper end of the tube and mercury is visible and the level may be compared with the scale alongside. Usually one or two movable pointers fitted with verniers are provided so that the readings may be more precise and the former level indicated.

B was originally called a wheel barascope, later barometer, and is occasionally called a banjo barometer on account of the shape of the case. The motion of the mercury is connected to the pointer by means of a double-grooved pulley mounted on its spindle. A thread from one of the grooves is attached to a glass weight resting on the mercury and a similar thread from the other one with a lighter weight maintains the counter tension. Owing to the smallness of the force available, the hand has to be extremely light and well balanced and the spindle highly polished and free in its bearings.

If either of these instruments are laid down in a horizontal position without special preparation, there is nothing to prevent the mercury running out, rendering it useless.

Although the cup at the lower end of a stick barometer may vary from a simple cast-iron cistern (as they used to be called) to an elaborate ivory and glass one, the kind shown at C is a fairly common and representative type; it is made of a hard but porous wood, such as pear or hawthorn, and is in two parts with very nicely turned threads. Usually the joint is covered with a glued strip of leather or cloth which must be stripped off before the lower cover can be unscrewed. The upper part is bored in three diameters: the upper to receive the tube, the lower to provide space round it for the mercury, and between these two it is enlarged as indicated by the dotted area above the mercury. This is to allow air to pass through the short grain as shown by the vertical shading; a slow motion but apparently quite adequate for the purpose. The lower cover is in the form of a ring with a leather disc glued to it and further secured by being compressed against the lower edge of the upper part. The adjusting screw at the bottom of the instrument is fitted with a brass disc which comes in contact with the leather so that the mercury at X may be brought to the correct level.

As the upper end of the tube and mercury are visible, it is well to find out if

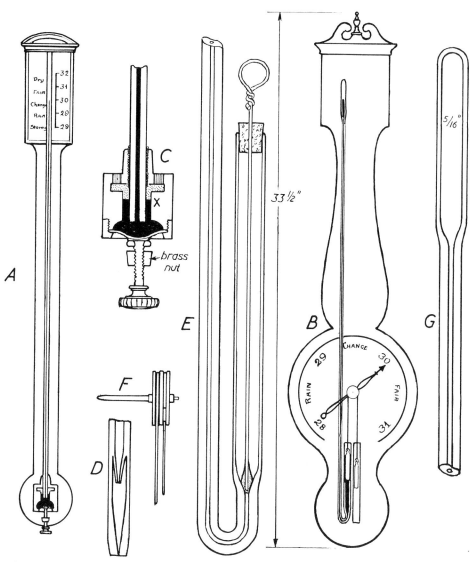

51

154

the customer insists that they be clean for in that case they may have to be replaced.

Some had the lower end of the tube restricted as at D; this was to prevent the mercury surging up and down at sea. Another device shown in the same sketch was the air trap just above, designed to catch any small air bubbles which might enter the tube.

Repairing and refilling   Although it is not always necessary to empty the tube, the work will be described in the following steps:
Emptying the tube.
Cleaning tube and mercury.
Replacing leather, cleaning spindle and fitting new tube.
Filling tube.
Setting up.
Preparation for shipment.

Emptying the tube   This is considerably facilitated by introducing a piece of steel wire. For the banjo type, a guitar E string (the thinnest) will go round the bend quite well but may buckle in the wider part unless it is first passed through a piece of thin tube about six inches long. In the straight kinds, a thicker wire may do. Holding the open end over a basin, the mercury is soon shaken out. In the unlikely case when the tube is completely full, care must be taken to avoid breaking the closed end by the column of mercury striking it. An inch of air will soon form a sufficient cushion.

It should be noted that mercury will form an amalgam with many metals, so utensils should be of enamel, pottery or glass.

Cleaning   Dilute nitric acid (everything from ten to twenty-five per cent is mentioned) is indicated by authorities both ancient and modern for both mercury and tube. It should be introduced into the tube and boiled against the stains and then removed and the process repeated until either the stain disappears or one gives up. This is followed by rinsings with distilled water and finally the purest alcohol available.

The procedure for the mercury is first to agitate it in a ten per cent solution of potassium hydroxide to dissolve the grease. This is poured off, the nitric acid solution follows and then distilled water. It is then dried and forced through wash leather repeatedly until it ceases to dirty it. Lastly any remaining moisture is removed by heating it in a pyrex measuring-cup to 110°C (or until a moistened matchstick sizzles when it touches it).

With the present wages, it is probably more practical to buy new; between 2 and 4oz being required.

Replacing leather etc   If a new tube is required it can usually be made up by one of the scientific supply houses in most large cities and in some universities.

The drawings E and G in Illus 51 are full-sized details of both ends of the type required for wheel barometers, the overall length being 33½in.

If the tube of a stick barometer is to be renewed, it will first be necessary to remove the old piece from the cistern. The only safe method is to remove the lower cover and immerse the upper part in hot water until the glue becomes sufficiently softened. This is regrettable, for moisture is the great enemy of this work and so time will be required to dry it, but forcing out the glass without moisture is very liable to crack the wood.

In fitting the new tube, the first step is to place the cistern in the case and measure from its top edge to where the sealed end of the tube fits in the upper part of the scale plate; this distance is now marked on the tube. Next insert it in place and, if necessary, cut off any excess length by nicking with a file and breaking off. If it appears that by tightening the adjusting screw it will be possible to seal the tube by contact with the leather (a very desirable feature), then remove any sharp edges or irregularities of the glass with an oilstone. Now fit a wooden peg to exclude dirt or moisture.

That part of the tube which occupies the upper bore of the cistern is now tightly wrapped with successive layers of soft cotton string laid in glue until it fits the hole snugly when it can be glued in place. Allow at least two days to dry.

It is almost always advisable to renew the leather disc in the bottom cover. Any good flexible skin will serve and it should be cut somewhat large so as to provide a reasonable amount of sag; again, allow plenty of time to dry thoroughly.

In the banjo type, the spindle and bearing should be examined; first remove the hand, it is friction tight on a taper; turn the instrument over and remove the upper bearing; it is usually secured by one screw with two positioning pins. The spindle with its pulley may now be lifted out. Clean the brass bearings with a peg of soft wood repeatedly sharpened until it comes out clean; the spindle should also be burnished at the bearings. If any doubt exists, the whole bearing and spindle assembly can be taken to a watch-maker. The threads from which the weights hang can be replaced with anything sufficiently fine and flexible; braided nylon casting line is satisfactory. Lastly check and if necessary renew the wires which secured the tube in the case. They were originally soft iron, but copper will do.

Filling tubes   Moisture is the great enemy in this task, so wear kid gloves so as to avoid leaving sweat on wire, utensils or tube. If moisture is suspected within the tube, introduce first alcohol and boil it dry in the sealed end and then do the same with a modicum of mercury, being careful to avoid inhaling the poisonous vapour.

The wire which was used for emptying should now be wiped dry with a cloth or paper towel and inserted. Now continue with the mercury shaking it down, a little at a time. With the U-tube, arrange to support it at about 45°; pour a little into the open end, cover it with the gloved finger, shake it round the bend in a horizontal position, then down to the end.

Some old instructions include boiling the mercury in the tube after filling, starting from the closed end and gradually continuing up to the other. In the author's experience, this does not work. The column of mercury should, however, be critically examined as it builds up in the tube and any flaw in the surface, indicating dirt or moisture, must be brought out either with the wire or by boiling. For this, a small wad of cotton wool stuck in the mouth of a bottle and soaked with methyl hydrate will serve as a spirit lamp with a large flame. The utmost care must be used in applying the heat so as not to crack the glass, passing it through the flame and constantly turning and moving it in the initial stages. Hopefully the boiling will drive off the moisture and after cooling, the filling can be continued. It must be admitted however that, with old mercury and tube, a perfectly flawless filling has not always been achieved either by the author or at least some others. For practical purposes, however, this is not essential, for one can make allowance for a slightly low reading in a stick barometer while with a wheel instrument it can be adjusted by altering the setting of the hand.

With the stick instrument, fill the cupped part as full as possible and replace the cap; press the leather diaphragm with the finger against the end of the tube or, if that is not possible, reduce the air pocket above it. Now reverse it and watch the tube to see if an air bubble is rising in it; if so change to the original position and try again.

The U-tube of the wheel barometer should be sloped so that it fills to the top, round the bend to just above the bottom of the part with the larger diameter.

Setting up: stick type   Quite often the lower part of the case is held with screws at the back so that it can be removed for inserting the tube and, when replaced, holds the cistern in place. In others, there is a clamp which holds it close to the bottom end of the glass. The upper end is best held in a cork collar by the lower edge of the dial; see that it fits snugly here. Having secured it, hang up the instrument and allow about five minutes for it to settle. Meanwhile, phone the nearest weather station and ask the barometer reading in inches for comparison. If it is too high, some of the mercury will have to be removed. Some cisterns have a wooden plug in the side which is designed to be at the correct level and has only to be removed and the surplus drained off. In most the cap will have to be taken off. If the reading is too low, it may be raised with the adjusting screw to some extent. If the level is excessively low, most likely air has got in; slope the instrument and see if there is a bubble at the top; if this is the case, reverse it and tap the top gently on a cork block; the bubble should gradually work its way out.

Wheel type   The spindle with pulley and weights being in place, arrange the case with the upper end on a padded block about a foot above the bench. Place the tube in place and secure it with the wires together with the short piece for the counter-balance weight. Now place the heavier weight on the mercury and the lighter in the tube alongside. See that the threads are free in the pulley grooves and that the spindle is capable of ample motion in either direction. Everything being in order, place it in a vertical position on the wall. Now fit the hand in the position which indicates the correct reading. Check it by turning it in either direction; it should return to the same reading.

Preparation for shipment: stick type   Except with those instruments which were specially designed to have their tube plugged by tightening the adjusting screw, it is difficult to suggest a practical way to solve this problem. Dismantling the cistern and plugging the tube is possible but it is not always to be expected that there is someone capable of setting it up at the other end. Whenever possible therefore it should be delivered by hand and carried at an angle of about 45°.

Wheel type   The sketch E (Illus 51) shows a satisfactory way of plugging the tube for this purpose. First remove the glass weight, find a cork to fit the tube, pass a piece of wire through it, dip the end in model aeroplane glue, then twist a piece of cotton wool round it to form a plug, repeating the process if the tube is large enough. Allow to dry, insert the cork and push home the plug. Pack cotton or paper round the weights to prevent flopping around.

A warning from experience   When the author, for convenience in repairing the case, removed a particularly heavy tube from an old instrument, he put it in an unused room on a table by the window for safety. A few days later, an almost invisible little crack was noticed; later, others developed spiralling round the surface before becoming long enough to separate the glass. Eventually there was no piece longer than a couple of inches.

Presumably this was the result of taking this old glass from a dark place where it had remained for perhaps 150 years and exposing it to the light. The reason for this is not clear, but perhaps it would have been wiser to have kept it in the dark.

Lastly, beware of the lady who complained of a poor job. The barometer said 'Set Fair' so she put out her washing and it rained. A barometer is of value only to one who has observed the relation between its behaviour and the weather in his own location; particularly as regards to whether it is rising or falling. Even then it is an unreliable prophet.

North American furniture

The indictment that the English are likely to be ignorant of American culture was largely true in the case of the author. In part at least the reason for this was due to the lack of opportunity to see and handle fine American furniture of the eighteenth and early nineteenth centuries. Because the number of surviving examples from that period when the population was small (four million in the first US census of 1790) is now shared by a large number of eager collectors, it is not surprising that a cabinet-maker on the West Coast of Canada should handle on an average no more than one such piece in five years.

With this limited experience it would be presumptuous to suggest that what follows will provide more than a glimpse of a large and interesting field.

The first such piece which was recognised by the author was a tall chest of drawers with top and drawer fronts of fiddleback or tiger maple; it had five drawers, the top one overhanging the others, and was supported on curved pilasters each side. The ends were framed up and panelled and were of plain hard maple as also were the rails, drawer sides and runners. This wood is so hard and close grained that very little wear had taken place. The dovetails were perfect and of excellent proportions; the sides were half-an-inch thick and grooved to receive the bottom without the slips common in English ones of the period.

The drawer bottoms and back of the carcase were of white pine; this wood was available in wide boards and so was normally in one piece. An old friend in describing his Ontario boyhood home mentioned that the attic room was lined with two horizontal boards on each wall; one about four feet wide from floor to rafters and a second of similar width sloping to meet the ceiling.

Another notable piece was a little Arcadian bedside table in cherry; a simple country piece with a small drawer and turned legs ornamented with spiral reeding. This is called roping when coarser, but in this case the reeds were less than one-quarter inch at their widest. No. 1, Illus 52, is a drawing from memory.

One might say that French furniture is usually more sophisticated than English: in the same way North American is less so. It would seem that they were proud of their workmanship and liked to reveal their joints, particularly their dovetails. The drawer rails in No 5, the middle rail and muntin in No 2 are fitted from the front with shoulders at the bottom of the groove for the runner. British practice would have them fitted from behind with a butt joint showing as in No 3 or, had they been entered from the front the joint would have been covered with a veneer.

The dovetails at the top of the block-front desk No 5 are housed dovetailed, beautifully fitted and showing on top. In England secret dovetails would be more likely.

No 2 is sketched from a side table converted from the stand of a chest-on-stand. Apart from the visible dovetails it will be seen that the tenons are pinned, a practice which survived longer in America. Two other details might be noted: first the downward-curving wing of the cabriole leg which is both glued to the face of the widened rail and also tenoned and pinned into the leg. Its grain is horizontal compared with the English version No 3 in which the grain is vertical and the wing normally simply glued and rubbed in place. This downward curving characteristic is found in many variations, one of which is

159

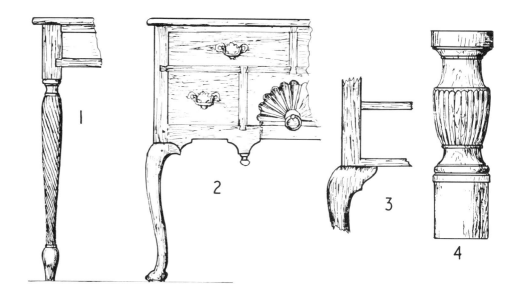

52

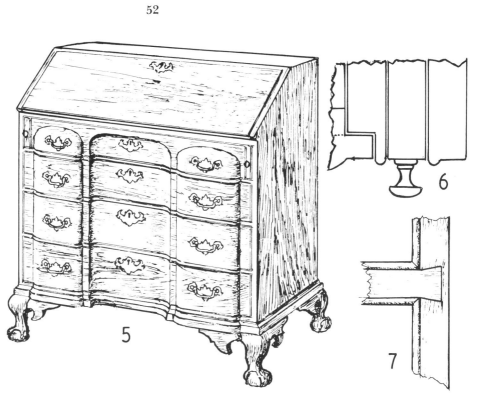

seen in No 5. The second detail is the shell on the centre drawer front which was a very popular feature. The rail below follows the line of the inward curving shell and the break lines up with the edge of the support for the turned pendant, a well contrived detail.

The mahogany block-front desk No 5 is a very desirable and important piece. The shaped front, perhaps resulting from Dutch influence, is the most striking feature: note how nicely the problem of making it conform to the straight line necessary to hinge the writing flap has been arranged. Where the side parts of the top drawer have been domed, the inside has been hollowed out but the centre part was left thick to accommodate the lock.

The next detail which might be noticed is that the beads which take the place of the British cock-beads are worked on the carcase rather than on the drawers and a good deal of thought has been given to the sliders which support the fall. The sectional plan No 6 shows how the effect of a single bead surrounding it and dividing it from the top drawer was achieved by rebating the small dividing muntin and having the drawer extend beyond its sides to correspond: an altogether satisfactory solution.

It has been said of Duncan Phyfe that he merely transplanted to New York a style which was fashionable in Britain when he left. While this may be true to some extent it was the excellence of his proportions even more than the quality of his workmanship which set him apart. The aspect of design which best exemplifies this is his turnings.

At the same time as the revival of the use of turned legs during the second half of the eighteenth century came the draughtsman designs, rather than workshop designs. This can be very misleading in laying out turnings where the lack of modelling makes the outline seem lacking in depth; to counteract this, there is a tendency to overdo the convolutions. For instance, a chair leg will probably be too deeply cut in the members immediately below the square part at the top where the greatest stress occurs and this will result in real and apparent weakness. Another point that is often overlooked is the foreshortening of the foot as most often seen; a fact which should be counteracted by making this part longer. If possible the design should be at least in part tested out on the lathe: most likely this was Duncan Phyfe's practice.

Though one rarely has a chance to examine a genuine example of this master's work, a book of measured drawings has been published and it is well worthy of study. No 4, the pillar of a dining table, is copied from it.

Chinese furniture

Early in the eighteenth century when products of the Orient first came to Europe in significant numbers, they were highly esteemed and with good reason, for in many respects they were superior to the local ones. Later, at least in Western Canada, people thought so little of them that it was rarely profitable to repair them. Now a change is again taking place with the result that such pieces as the chair in Illus 53A are fetching more reasonable prices and would no doubt be still more popular if they were not so uncomfortable to the Western human frame.

Cabinet-makers in the past were wont to excuse themselves from undertaking repairs by asserting that the Chinese teak would not bond with glue. There is no truth in this for the chair in question, in common with better class pieces of this type, is of Chinese rosewood. Padouk, billian and other substitutes were used, most of which glue quite well. In many cases most of the joints were put together dry, the wedging of the tenons being considered sufficient.

For this reason they are often somewhat loose in most of the joints and simply need dismantling and reglueing. A description of the joints and order of taking apart follows.

The back is the first piece to be removed; it is attached to each arm with two dovetailed keys morticed into the back member of the arm and locking into slots cut into the posts of the back as illustrated in B in much the same manner as a slot-screwed joint: the bottom rail is held to the seat with two loose tenons. To remove, lift the back vertically about ¾ in by inserting wedges between it and the seat on each side and alternately tapping the wedges and the arms at the back until it becomes free and can be lifted out. Next the arms, which are held in the same way to the seat; drive them back until they too are free. Now try each key and if loose remove and glue back in place.

The seat is morticed at the corners to receive tenons worked on the top ends of the four legs; pictured in Illus 53C and E so that a few taps of the hammer within the frame close to the legs will usually free it.

Now comes the frame with its complicated joint combining mortice and tenon, dovetail and mitres; it is shown in elevation at C, in plan at D and in perspective; the leg at E and the rail at F. The black area in D is cut away forming a slot occupying the position indicated by the dotted line in C. It will be seen that the rail must be removed by lifting both ends simultaneously, so use the hammer with restraint on the lower edge close to each leg alternately until it comes away.

Where we would use an ordinary mortice and tenon joint, the Chinese usually combine it with a mitre: G is the stretcher in which the face shoulder is double mitred; beneath is a thin ornamental support or apron with a bare-faced tenon. K is the joint at both ends of the bottom rails of arms and back. J is the dovetail joint on the shoulders of the back and also of the rounded front corners of the arms.

H is a section of the seat with its thin panel fitted flush and supported with one or more cross pieces dovetailed right across the thickness of the panel and tenoned into the frame. I is the mitre-tenoned corner.

Although not used in the chair, the joint L, which is drawn together by a tapered transverse wedge in the prepared notches, is commonly found in the frames of circular or polygonal tops; a stronger variation is K on Illus 11.

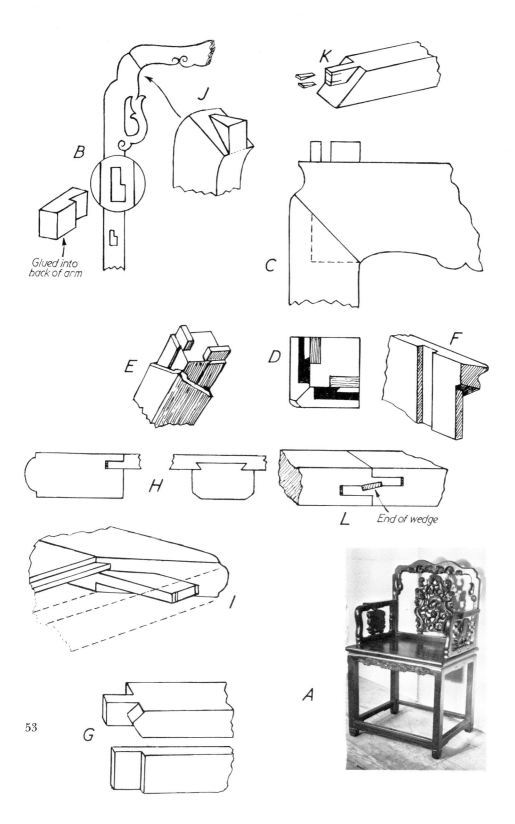

B

*Glued into
back of arm*

J

K

C

E

D

F

H

L

End of wedge

I

G

A

53

The only problem in getting seat, arms and back apart is likely to be the wedges which may have to be divided in two by drilling before removing with a suitably narrow chisel.

In most cases shrinkage will have occurred, leaving mitres open on the inside and a gap at one side of the panel. The gap can be filled with a slip of walnut glued in; after levelling and polishing it will make a reasonable match. The mitres can of course be refitted perfectly but it must be remembered that, should this be done, for instance with the seat, its dimensions will be reduced and the tenons on the legs will no longer mate with the mortices so it will be much safer to fill the gaps with sawdust and glue.

The business point of view

It is unusual for a craftsman to have the makings of a good business man and the author is no exception to this rule. The following suggestions, however, may have some value.

First of all the job should be examined in the presence of the customer before work is started. Every fault, looseness of joints, veneer raised or missing, scratches, dents and other defects of the polish, former repairs, dirty or worn upholstery, wear of drawers, condition of castors and worm-eaten parts should be pointed out, noted down and the customer's wishes concerning them ascertained.

There are two reasons for this: first, the owner is rarely conscious of all the defects, and should he want a first-class job he is much more likely to appreciate the amount of work involved in producing one; and secondly, if he only wants certain things attended to, he will not blame the repairer for the other defects. This is particularly applicable to scratches which are sometimes caused by getting the furniture in and out of the customer's car and not noticed until the work is returned.

The simplest method of keeping a record is by having a card for each job. An ordinary index card may be used, but a more elaborate printed one might be worth while. It should contain space for the following: customer's name, address and phone number; date of order; when promised; description of article when received; customer's instructions to cabinet-maker, upholsterer and polisher; price quoted; and the back might have space for workmen's time and material.

The cards may be placed in a series of pigeon holes marked:
1 Quotations
1 Orders
3 Work in hand
4 Finished but not paid for
5 Paid

As may be seen, the cards proceed from one to five whence they are periodically removed, entered in the books and filed away alphabetically. By this system one can see at a glance what work is on order, etc, and the monthly accounts can be made out from the cards in No 4. No 1 is occasionally gone over, and the cards referring to work which seems unlikely to mature are discarded.

The practice of basing the charge on time and material is the logical one, but it often happens that a job will take more time than can reasonably be accounted for and so it seems better to charge a little more for the jobs which go well so that those which prove over-cost may not go through at a loss.

Should the cost of repair seem greater than a fair market value of the article when repaired, the customer should be advised so that he may decide whether or not to have it done.

Many people recommend making a contract with the customer and insisting on a deposit. In short, in being businesslike. The author's practice, however, is to trust his customers. If they are satisfied, 99 per cent will pay and those who do not want to will not be greatly influenced by pieces of paper.

A good stock of hinges, handles, locks, castors, veneer and inlay, in addition to timber old and new is a great asset. The profit on it will be small as the turnover is very slow. The author has had some inlay and handles for twenty years. It pays one, however, in the saving of time. The cost of going out, locating and purchasing a drawer pull would probably buy a dozen. As these things are bought they should be entered in a stock book. A description of the article with a sketch should occupy the page to the left together with the date of purchase, the cost and the selling price of each. The page on the right may be divided into columns for each year in which the number and value at cost can be entered each year at stocktaking.

Example

LEFT-HAND PAGE
Drawer pulls bought of Smith Co No 1557, June 1972
30 @ 75p, sell £1.25

RIGHT-HAND PAGE
1972-1973

15 @ 75p £11.25

This combination of price list and stock book has proved most satisfactory especially at the end of the year. The cost price could, of course, be in code.

How much per hour should one charge? That is a very difficult question to answer. In working for a dealer it is obvious that, on the average, the value added to the piece of furniture being restored must be greater than the charge for the work done and dealer's work is the bread and butter part of the business. Thus the value added, divided by the number of hours worked would give a fair indication of the answer but it must be remembered that this must include the overhead expenses.

In addition to such obvious costs as rent, heat, insurance etc it should be remembered that a certain percentage of the day's work is non-productive: errands, repairs to gear, quotations and talk. Old Charlie Whitfield had a large sign on his wall which read THIS IS A WORKSHOP, NOT A TALK-SHOP; but, being human, he still lost a lot of time in this way just the same. If this loss were kept to an hour a day then eight hours' pay should be charged for seven hours' work.

By whatever means, an hourly charge should be established and stated to the customer in order to avoid later misunderstandings. It has been found, however, that many customers, even though they may be wizards at differential calculus and computer programming, may be quite unaware of simple arithmetic; the following type of conversation is not unrealistic:

Customer: I want you to do the work of course, but would like to have some idea of the probable cost.

Craftsman: Well, it looks like about three days' work spread over a couple of weeks.

Customer: That is wonderful, I thought it might take a month.

Craftsman: I charge £2 per hour.

Customer: Very moderate, why, my garageman charges far more than that.

Craftsman: Twenty-five hours at £2 is £50.

Customer: I could not possibly pay that much because I can get a similar piece at Tommy's Swap Shop for only £30.

Though there are exceptions such as insurance claims and pieces treasured for sentimental reasons, it will be seen that some jobs are just not worth doing from the point of view of economics and the sensible course is to decline to undertake them. In some cases it may be possible to purchase the wreck for the value of the materials which may be salvaged from it, especially if it is old.

The author, however, has often been foolish enough to want to do the job anyway. The reasons for this have been varied; perhaps the customer used the old gambit of mentioning that a rival had declared that the piece was beyond repair. Most likely the truth was that he had more sense than to tackle it but the challenge is hard to resist. Again, perhaps the quality of the piece and the satisfaction in the work may have been the attraction. The customer too may have been someone special, and one of the privileges of being self-employed is that of working for little or nothing if one wishes. Whatever the reason, if not over-indulged this may not be a bad thing if undertaken with the proviso that it will be carried out only when more remunerative work is not in hand, the common rationale being that it will enhance one's reputation, the loss being charged up to advertising.

9 Making Metal Fittings

Although the work of making replicas of missing handles and other fittings is not to be expected of a woodworker, yet the difficulty of getting it done by someone else, and the time wasted in going to their place of business several times, make it well worth while doing the job oneself.

The most common call is for a missing bail, that is the U-shaped part of a drawer pull, and there are three ways in which it can be made.

Cast   One of the existing parts must be removed and taken to a small brass foundry where they will make an impression in sand and cast a new one from it. This casting will be rough and will have to be filed, emery clothed and buffed to a smooth finish. It is well to specify yellow metal or common brass as some foundries cast a lot of bronze or red metal as it is called, which will not match the old brasses.

Forged   It is often practical to bend, flatten with a hammer, etc, and file a part out of wire or rod. If it is common brass, this must be done cold, and if much is to be done it must be annealed, that is heated to redness and cooled, whenever it becomes too hard to work. If any attempt is made to work it while red hot, it will simply crumble. However, Tobin bronze, which may be bought in various thicknesses as brazing rods, can be forged hot and is as easy to hammer and bend when hot as is lead when cold. It is excellent for replacing missing rings, and many other parts can be made by partly forging and leaving the final details to the file.

Cut out of sheet   When the new skip-tooth bandsaws have become too dull for wood, they are just right for brass and may be used for metal up to ⅜ in thick or more at ordinary bandsaw speeds.

With their use, all kinds of shapes can be cut out of sheet metal, after which they are easily rounded off and shaped up with files, and smoothed with emery cloth usually torn into strips about 1 in wide and used in the same way as a shoe shiner uses his polishing cloth. Polishing can be finished with metal polish and cloth or a buff.

The pummels from which the bails hang can either be cast or turned out of a piece of brass rod. This is very easy especially if the lathe has a hollow mandrel. The tools for turning may be made out of old square files, the angle of the cutting edge being very blunt, about 80°; Illus 54 (1), A, B and C are useful shapes.

Brass mouldings

As a rule the best way to replace a piece of missing brass moulding is to remove a similar piece and have another cast from it. After filing up this makes a satisfactory job, but in some cases there are quicker and better ways.

Illus 54 (2), A, B and C, shows three sections which can be made from a brass tube. The fact that they are now hollow behind is not important so long as they are well fastened, and this may be done without showing by using the tapered brass wire pins already described for brass inlay, only in this case larger sizes are usually used. The tube may be cut with a metal-cutting circular saw, if one is available, and if the mandrel can be driven slow enough, but the more common tool is the skip-tooth bandsaw. If the tube is of thin metal, it is best to insert a piece of dowel into it to prevent it becoming distorted in cutting. It must be remembered that, in the cases shown, the first cut must be at one side of the centre line of the tube, leaving one perfect semicircle and one piece reduced by the thickness of the cut. This may be facilitated by scribing a line down the top of the tube and then making a cradle as shown at (2) D and cramping it to the saw table. The hole is, of course, the size of the tube and the saw is entered clear of the centre line. An opening is gouged out so that the saw-cut can be followed. The next cut is easy as the half tube will rest on the table and so all that is needed is another scribed line.

The section shown at (3) A can be made out of a piece of sheet brass, and a piece of this section 10in long took half an hour to make. The width of this happened to be ¼in and a piece of metal of this thickness was available. The steps in filing it out are shown at D, E and F. The bevel was soon taken off with a large, coarse file but the hollow section was more difficult because the rat-tail file kept slipping off. To correct this a hole was bored through a piece of ¾in plywood about 1in square, and one corner cut away to expose the right amount of file, forming a guide, the wood moving with the file, (3) B and C.

Moulding, consisting of a series of little swellings, can be turned out of a piece of wire or rod with a tool as shown at (1) D. About ½in is left projecting from the chuck and this is turned, and then another ½in pushed out, turned and so on. If much is required, it is well to arrange a block of wood bored to receive the finished part.

A substitute for this is a piece of chain from a pull-chain light-socket cemented in position with a Bostik cement and painted with gold paint. This may be sandpapered off, the high parts showing the brass and will hardly be distinguishable from the genuine article. Other chains of larger size may be obtained from a plumber's supply store.

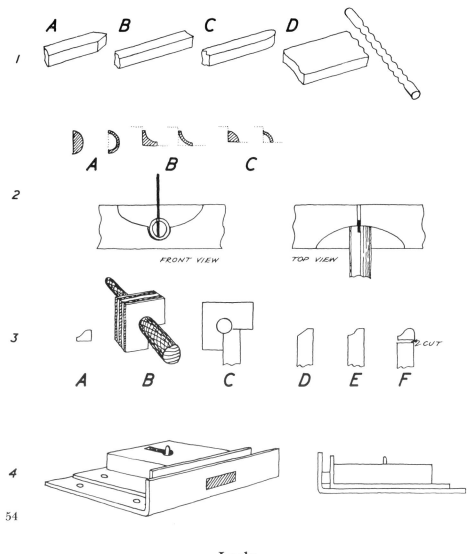

FRONT VIEW

TOP VIEW

54

Locks

While it is possible to make an entire lock if necessary, it is usually sufficient to adapt one to fill a special place. The problem, as a rule, is to get one whose keyhole is a certain distance from the top of the drawer or edge of the desk flap and also one whose back is large enough to fill the recess cut to receive it. These two requisites can be satisfied by soldering or riveting a lock inside a bent brass plate as shown in Illus 54 (4). The plate is first cut to size, bent at right angles and fitted to the recess. The position of the keyhole pin is next ascertained and marked, and a lock found which comes within the required limits. This is placed in position and either riveted or soldered there. Now the cap and bolt are removed and either a new bolt made, long enough to reach beyond the new plate, or a piece may be silver-soldered onto the old bolt to

169

give it the required length. A slot is now cut in the plate opposite the existing one by drilling holes and filing, and the lock is reassembled with the bolt sticking out. After making sure that it is in the unlocked position the face is filed off flush and the bent corner (which gives the lock a cheap appearance) slightly chamfered. All that remains is to bore and countersink screw holes.

Even when it cost a shilling to have a key fitted, it usually paid to do it one-self because it would probably take less time than two trips to a locksmith. There are of course cases when the job requires an expert, particularly when the piece is locked and no key is available, however in nine cases out of ten the lock can be removed, dismantled and a key fitted in less than half an hour provided the mechanism is understood and a suitable blank is available.

Most cupboard doors need the lock to keep them closed; particularly if they are inclined to twist. On a slope-fall desk they serve as a handle, thus saving the lip from becoming scratched with fingernails. Drawer locks used to be sold with three or four keys to the dozen and so a chest of drawers or the lower drawers of a desk can usually be served with one. Although rarely locked these days, it is a comfort when threatened by the ravages of small grandchildren to have a key available. A good place for it is in a little leather sheath tacked to the inside of one of the drawer fronts.

Prior to 1778 all ordinary locks were made on the principles of those indicated in Illus 55, the simplest being A and B. A spring is made by cutting a narrow strip along the edge of the bolt and bending it outwards so as to press the curved part against the guide, thus holding it in its locked or unlocked positions. A ward is riveted to the plate in B requiring a corresponding notch in the key as seen to the right. A is even more simple and was probably intended more as a catch to keep the door closed: they can usually be opened by inserting a knife-blade between door and frame and contriving to push the bolt back. Occasionally the spring will be found to be broken; it can be repaired by making a saw-kerf at an angle near its point of junction and soldering a new one made out of a queen-sized bobby pin in its place. Hydrochloric acid in which zinc has been dissolved is the best flux for this.

C is a little more complex having a tumbler which must be lifted by the key before the bolt may be moved. There are also three wards, two being on the back plate as indicated, while the third is on the cover secured by three projections riveted over which can be seen round the keyhole. These wards can be quite elaborate but the T-shaped one required for the key D1 can be passed by a skeleton key like D3. On the other hand, the lock which was made for D2 cannot be passed by any ordinary skeleton key. As a matter of fact, the cuts in the key were very often far more complicated than the lock required: salesmanship by deceit being not entirely new.

These locks can be picked by inserting a piece of wire through the keyhole, lifting the tumbler and then shoving down the bolt in the way already described. The early ones commonly have the bolt divided into two or more parts; but, having been in continuous production even up to the present time, it is not easy to estimate their age.

170

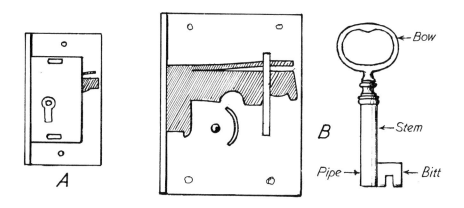

A

B

Bow

Stem

Pipe

Bitt

C

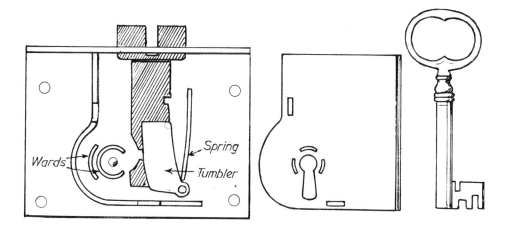

Wards

Spring

Tumbler

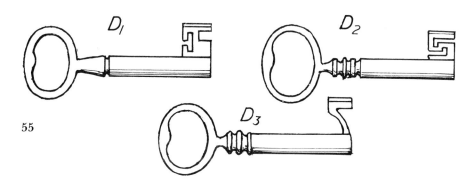

D₁

D₂

D₃

55

171

Provided they can be removed and dismantled and a blank is available, the fitting of a key is simple. The type generally suitable has a bit which is thicker near the end than at the pipe and is sold as a 'kidney bow key blank', the small one being No 1 and the larger ones up to No 6.

If it is necessary to fit one without removing the lock, proceed as follows. First see that the blank fits the keyhole with only reasonable clearance: next coat the bit with drop black or vaseline mixed with some pigment such as umber: insert it in the keyhole making sure that the sides do not touch: if it does not go right down perhaps there is a ward below, and it will show in the black on the bottom or else the hole in the pipe may have to be deepened; if the former, file a notch for it; if it does go right in but will not turn, most likely the bit will have to be narrowed as indicated by the mark of the edge of the keyhole of the lock. Once it will turn a little past the keyhole, its next stop will likely be a ward; a mark on the black will show where to file. If it is near the middle, mark with a centre punch and drill a hole: the next trial will indicate where to continue. In this way it can be fitted, the last filing perhaps being to shorten the bit to permit it to enter the notch in the bolt; this too will be indicated where the black coating has been scraped.

In 1778 Robert Barron's patent introduced a principle which was followed by most, if not all of the later developments: it was that two or more pieces of metal must each be moved a precise distance, neither more nor less, before the bolt may be moved.

In this lock (Illus 56A) there is an opening known as a gate cut through the bolt which is recessed beneath to make room for two tumblers, each having a square pin or stump projecting upwards through the gate. These are shown in black and occupy the two upper slots; in the view to the right they are shaded with diagonal lines. Now before the key can shoot the bolt it must raise the tumblers to the correct height. In this particular lock there are two wards whose function is not too important, but they do make it more difficult to see or get at the tumblers.

This is the rarest of the locks here described due to the fact that it was limited to two tumblers and the lever variation which soon took its place had no such limitation and was equally good and perhaps a little cheaper.

Ten years later, 1788, Joseph Bramah patented his lock, as illustrated in B, which achieved the greatest prestige during the nineteenth century and continued in production until at least the nineteen-sixties; it is rarely found on any but pieces of high quality. The action of the key is to turn a cylinder at the opposite end of which is an off-centre pin which moves the bolt. In the example pictured, the cylinder is locked by four thin steel sliders or guards, two of which can be seen in black in the sectional view. They are pressed forwards (towards the keyhole) by the spring in the centre and occupy the four notches in the steel locking ring which is screwed to the frame. Each slider has a notch in a different position and the key is similarly cut in such a way that when thrust forward as far as it will go, it will move each slider the amount required to bring its notch opposite to the locking ring, thus permitting the

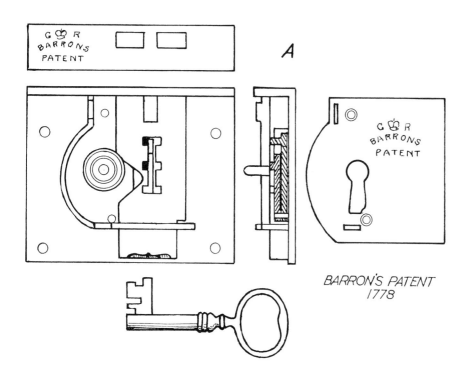

A

BARRON'S PATENT
1778

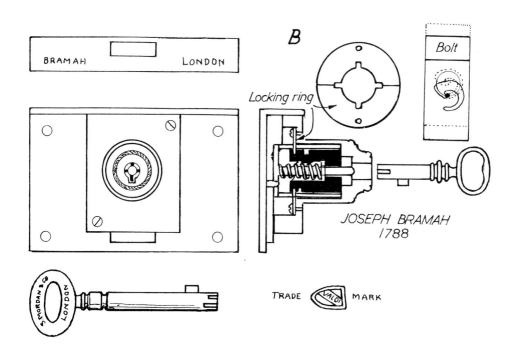

B

Locking ring

Bolt

JOSEPH BRAMAH
1788

TRADE MARK

cylinder to turn. The bit of the key is to ensure that it is inserted correctly and to hold it at the proper depth while turning.

The problem of moving the bolt and holding it in two positions by means of a complete revolution was solved by the peculiar-shaped cut in the bolt. The black dot is the pin; the circle, its path; and the dotted line indicates its position when locked.

Genuine Bramah locks always have an even number of sliders, four being common. After the patent had run out in 1816 a number of other firms started making similar ones, notably Mordan & Co who chose to use an odd number of sliders; the key below has seven.

While very few customers would be willing to pay for the time required to make one of these keys, for the amateur or even the ancient professional who no longer values his time very highly, it can be a rewarding substitute for a crossword puzzle.

If an old key which fits the hole and also has the right number of slots is available, it can usually be adapted. The lock having been removed, take out the two screws holding the box to the back plate; then two more inside holding the locking ring: the cylinder can now be lifted out, the key inserted and each slider watched while it is moved in and out. This will reveal what will be required; three options being available:

1 with key in place file new slots in the sliders;
2 file the slots in the key; and
3 remove and re-arrange the sliders.

Most likely it will be a combination; for instance one key-slot may be deepened, one slider may have a second notch cut while others are re-arranged with notches widened. To take out the sliders, remove the two screws holding the back plate while holding it down against the pressure of the spring; release carefully and lift out plate, spring and washer. The sliders may now be pushed out through the back and it will be a good time to clean everything with solvent.

If no proper blank is available, find an old key with the right sized pipe and a fairly wide bit, for there should be excess metal to file off the upper edge after all other fitting has been finished. Now cut off the excess and file it down to fit freely in the groove in the boss: next remove the lower edge, leaving about one-eighth of an inch of pipe projecting, and also cut the beginning of slots for the sliders. The remainder of the fitting starts as indicated above; with even numbers of sliders file the key to fit two opposite ones repeatedly thrusting it home as you watch its effect on the sliders; when one is deep enough, slope the file as necessary finishing the slot with the point. With odd numbers, most of the cut must be made with the file sloping. If any notch is cut too deep, file a corresponding amount off the bit and then off the other sliders: lastly, file the top of the bit flush with the cylinder.

Lever locks soon supplanted Barron's method; the levers were stacked on top of one another, each having a differing gate cut in it as seen in the four from the Hobbs lock D, Illus 57, while the stump, passing through them all,

174

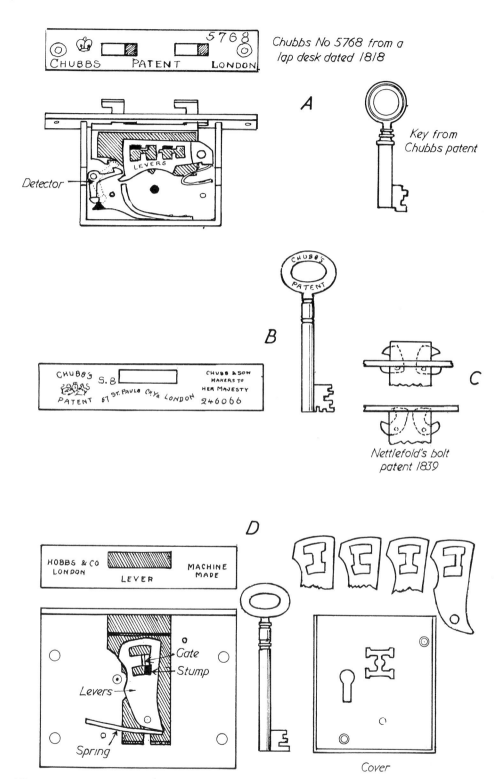

Chubbs No 5768 from a lap desk dated 1818

A

Key from Chubbs patent

B

C

Nettlefold's bolt patent 1839

D

Gate
Stump
Levers
Spring

Cover

HOBB'S FOUR LEVER from 1853

was mounted on the bolt. By 1800 most important locks were made on this principle, some having wards as well. Fitting keys after the lock has been dismantled is quite straightforward, the blanks required with parallel bits being sold as 'Cabinet blanks'. When an old key is to be adapted, it usually helps if the levers are re-arranged to conform more nearly to it. It may also be necessary to file one or more of the gates, though this, of course, reduces the security. Lastly, the smaller bobby pins will often serve to replace broken lever springs.

When Mr Hobbs returned from America for the 1851 Exhibition, he was full of enthusiasm for the machine method of production and introduced it into his workshops. His locks were excellent and were marked Hobbs & Co Machine made. Since, according to all accounts they were the first ones so marked, it would be reasonable to presume that locks marked 'Hand made' must also be later than this date.

Jeremiah Chubb's patent No 4219 is dated 3 August 1818 and it covers what he called his detector. By a coincidence the lock at A (Illus 57) is from a lap desk with a monogram and the same date engraved on a plate in the lid.

Partly by virtue of this device but even more perhaps by the excellence of workmanship, his locks held a very high reputation. The idea was that if anyone tampered with one or even attempted to open it with the wrong key, it was almost certain that they would trip the detector moving it into the position indicated by the dotted line, thus preventing the bolt from moving: then, when the proper key was used, it would fail to work, warning the owner. Between the levers and the bolt is a plate, marked with diagonal shading, capable of limited motion on the bolt. The owner, having been warned, now turns his key to the left moving this plate which now resets the detector so that he can unlock in the ordinary way.

It is amusing to compare this Victorian gentleman with a modern *pater familias*. Taking advantage of the assembly of family and servants for morning prayers he would give them a little homily on honesty and then demand that the guilty person confess his sins etc, etc. Moving on five or six generations it would be unlikely that anyone would risk offending a servant by even mentioning it.

Lastly, Nettlefold's bolt, patented 1839 (see Illus 57, C). Perhaps others as well as the author would have assumed that this had been invented at least fifty years later.

American patents

Linus Yale patented his pin-tumbler lock in America in 1865. He was soon joined by Towne, thus forming the firm of Yale & Towne of Stamford, Connecticut, which is still in existence as a branch of the Eaton Corporation; it became the leading lockmaker of the world; principally providing locks for the doors of buildings but to a limited extent for furniture.

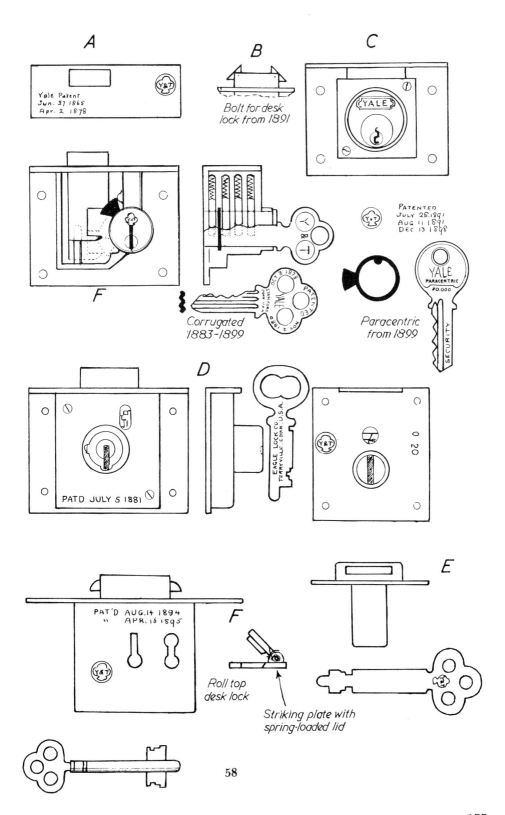

A

Yale Patent
Jun. 27 1865
Apr. 2 1878

B

Bolt for desk
lock from 1891

C

YALE

F

PATENTED
JULY 28 1891
AUG 11 1891
DEC 13 1848

Corrugated
1883-1899

Paracentric
from 1899

YALE
PARACENTRIC
#0.000

SECURITY

D

EAGLE LOCK CO.
TERRYVILLE. CONN. U.S.A.

PATD JULY 5 1881

0 20

PAT'D AUG.14 1894
" APR.16 1895

F

Roll top
desk lock

Striking plate with
spring-loaded lid

E

58

The lock illustrated in A (Illus 58) was made in about 1878 and is a wonderful piece of design and construction, being assembled without screws or rivets. It consists of a cast brass frame with a half-inch cylinder held in place by four spring-loaded wire tumblers, each of which is in two parts. When the proper key is inserted, the tumblers are raised to the point where the meeting of each pair is level with the top of the cylinder, as shown in the sectional view, when it will be free to turn. In this case the bolt is actuated by a projection on a steel ring capable of turning about 280 degrees on the cylinder; this piece is shown in black between the three keys. The small inner projection occupies a groove in the cylinder which is filled in at the bottom. By this means a complete turn of the key moves the ring about 80 degrees and it in turn shoots the bolt. It is interesting to compare this solution with Joseph Bramah's in 1788.

The principle of the pin-tumbler has remained unchanged but two advances have been made in the key, with corresponding changes in the slot into which it fits. From 1865 to 1883, the flat pattern as in A was used. The corrugated one with its section to the left was stamped out of sheet metal and lasted sixteen years till 1899. Lastly the 'Paracentric' key, which is still in production, is milled to the required section to fit the lock as shown at C. In the 1910 Yale & Towne catalogue, it is described as being of nickel-bronze with coined, gold-plated bow.

Lever locks with a cylindrical boss projecting through the door or drawer front such as at D were rarely fitted to English furniture but, since about 1875, account for maybe half those on American pieces. They take less time and skill to fit, require no escutcheon and the keys are cheaper and lighter. They work on the same principle as the older type except that a brass carrier takes the place of the pin and pipe of an ordinary key. Illus 58D shows a simple and cheaper version with symmetrical key requiring only half a turn to operate. The lock at F is especially designed for roll-top desks and dates from 1894: it uses a single-bitted, pinned key but most were double bitted such as the one below.

The Yale & Towne version of Nettlefold's bolt is shown in Illus 59B.

Castors

When a castor is worn out or broken, the simplest thing to do is throw the set away and fit either new ones or a set of glass or metal shoes in their place. This is the obvious course except when an antique is concerned, especially if it has socket or brass paw castors.

The common service required is to rebush the bowls, ie wheels. First the axles must be removed by filing off the ends which have been riveted over and then driving them out with a punch. The wheels can now be put in the chuck of the lathe and a standard size drill put through them, $5/16$in or $3/8$in are the common sizes. Short pieces of bronze rod are then soldered into these holes and

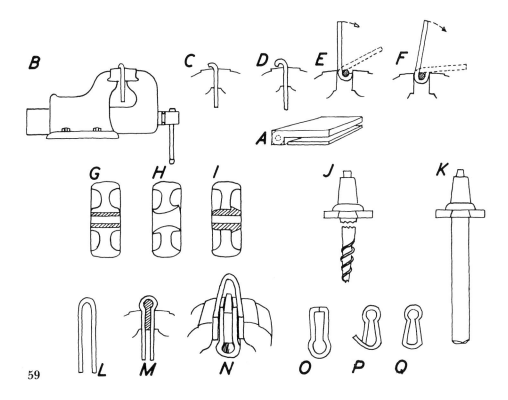

59

the bowl put back in the chuck, centred and drilled to the required size and the ends of the hub faced-up on each side (Illus 59G). All that now remains is to replace them, using new axles which may be made out of a nail of suitable size. Sometimes the bowl is so worn that a new hub is necessary and, in this case, it is best to turn it out of perhaps a piece of ½in rod with a shoulder as shown in Illus 59H and I. Occasionally the entire bowl must be replaced because it has been jammed for many years so that one side has been entirely worn away. This may be turned out of a piece of shaft or a similar bowl found in the box of old castors which the furniture repairer often has.

Illus 59J represents another common break. The job of getting out the broken screw is usually the longest part of the work. It can sometimes be done by means of a tool, sold for removing broken studs in motor-car cylinder blocks, first drilling a hole in the broken end.

In making the new part, a plain shaft 3in or 4in long will prove stronger and cheaper than a screw. It should be set in Bostik cement, see J and K.

When that part which revolves on the pin and supports the bowl between its horns get so worn that it touches the floor, there is little that can be done but replace it. This is quite a job and is rarely done, but if it is required, the part must be removed, the bowl taken out and the enlarged hole completely filled with a wooden peg fitted tightly. This should be smoothly finished above and below. From this, new parts may be cast, after which they will have to be set in the lathe and machined to fit their pins and drilled for the axles of the bowls.

179

Hinge-making

This is another job which occasionally seems well worth-while especially when one half only is needed. The author has also made them for the waist doors of grandfather clocks.

There are three ways of making them, ie from castings, out of thick sheet or by bending out of relatively thin metal. The castings can usually be made from the opposite hinge, which should be taken apart if an entire hinge is required, but may be left as it is and cast in the open or flat position if only half is missing, for it will take less time to cut away the unwanted parts than to dismantle and reassemble the pattern hinge.

Illus 59A suggests how they may be cut out of a piece of sheet brass the thickness of the knuckle of the hinge. This may be done with a hacksaw if it is large enough, but with small hinges it is easier to file the surplus metal away. As soon as the parts have been roughly filed to shape and fitted together the hole for the pin should be drilled and the pin fitted. The knuckle can now be filed up in both the open and closed positions and the screw-holes drilled and countersunk.

To bend the knuckle round the pin out of sheet is not easy but can be done. The important thing is to have only a very small amount projecting out of the vice when starting (Illus 59B). This is followed by a little more projection and again this is hammered over. This process is repeated until the sheet is sufficiently hooked to grip the pin in the hook in the vice, E. After this the finish of the job is comparatively simple.

Of course, the job may be simplified by first annealing the metal, but this will result in a weaker hinge.

Escutcheons

The type of escutcheons which are finished flush and form a lining to the keyhole are very often missing, and although a stock of various sizes may be available there are often shapes or sizes which can only be duplicated by making.

One of the reasons for these escutcheons getting lost is that they get hooked out by the key when it is withdrawn, and so the new one should be made sufficiently deep so that there is not room for the key to get behind it after leaving the lock, in fact in many cases the escutcheon may go through to the lock itself.

A strip of brass slightly thicker than the walls of the old escutcheon and as wide as the depth decided upon is first bent into a U (see Illus 59L). A key is next found that approximately fits the upper part of the escutcheon, maybe a house doorkey will do, and the strip nipped around it in the vice, M. This is then fitted into the keyhole and the position of the lower legs marked. N and O suggest the method of treating the lower end if the sides are more or less parallel. If, however, the pattern is more like Q, it is easier to make it with a soldered joint in the corner as at P since it can be manipulated until it is got to the right shape. It is then soldered, and the surplus metal is cut away. A little work with the files will soon finish the job.

Hand-finishing commercial reproductions

Although every effort should be made to retain the original handles, very often they have been replaced either with wooden knobs or with other handles of a much later design, and so a set of copies of similar style to the original should be fitted.

Reasonably accurate reproductions are available, some being quite satisfactory; others which can only be finished by hand are left as received from the tumbler except for grinding off the face surface. If the piece warrants the expense, or if an amateur is willing to do the work, they can be greatly improved by filing and polishing. The tools required are simple: a pair of

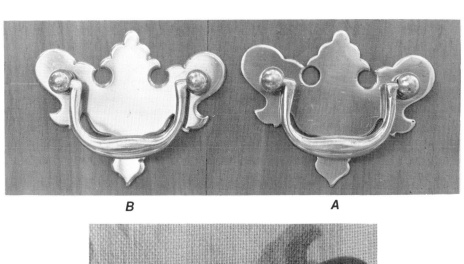

B　　　　　　　　　　　　　　　　A

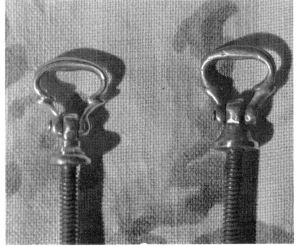

60　　　D　　　　　　　　　　　　　　　　C

vice-grip pliers, fine cut files and emery cloth; the final polish being done with Brasso or a power-driven cloth buff.

To illustrate this, the handle and mirror screw in Illus 60 have been chosen; A being an ordinary eighteenth-century style handle as received from the maker, and B the same after being filed and finished. In this case the most important part of the work was the bevelling and cleaning of the edge; note how the inner corners are treated; this emphasis gives character to the handle. No attempt has been made to make both sides identical, for small variations add to rather than detract from the appearance, as they give that human touch so desirable. Apart from removing a few rough patches and rounding the pins at each end, little has been done to the bail: looking at it critically however, perhaps it could have been improved by slimming the vertical parts each side.

Illus 60C and D are the mirror screw before and after treatment. The first step was to file the head and punch out the small pin so that the looped part could be removed. The stem was then held in the lathe chock so that the boss could be turned with a small quirk separating the concave from the rounded part; this could have been done with a file but would have taken longer. The designer's conception of the loop was an inverted C supported by two arcs whose lower ends were enlarged to receive the pin. The filing was carried out to show an appreciation of this idea by emphasizing the separation of the components by shallow grooves. In reassembling, a suitable finishing nail was used as a rivet, most of the head being filed away after fitting.

Colouring brass

For many years the author has sought the ideal method of antiquing brass. In many experiments the smells have been extremely unpleasant, but at last a solution has been found in the form of trisodium phosphate dissolved in water.

Other formulae work well only on certain kinds of brass, for it seems that a great many alloys are in use today. Again, some are not readily available and others create the unpleasant smells in the shop.

It need hardly be pointed out that any formula is effective only on metal and thus any lacquer must be removed. This is easily done by hanging the pieces in a crock or jar filled with lye and water for a few hours and then scrubbing them in hot water, or they can be boiled in soda and water for ten minutes and scrubbed clean. A wire brush will do the job if only a few are to be cleaned.

Butter of antimony gives a black colour, making a brass fitting a fairly good match for wrought iron. It works quickly by immersion and without heating. The other three formulae require boiling in an enamel saucepan or cup. The time required and the colour vary with the metal. The pieces should be strung on a piece of wire and dipped in the boiling solution; some are coloured in a few seconds while others take up to five minutes. If they are not turning colour by this time something is wrong, perhaps lacquer remains, the solution is too strong or is worn out. If none of these things is wrong, it must be an alloy which causes the trouble and the only thing is to try another formula.

Formula 1

Water	1 cup	
Trisodium phosphate	1 tablespoon	nut brown
Liver of sulphur	½ teaspoon	

Trisodium phosphate is a cleaning material similar to soda.

Formula 2

Water	1 cup	
Sugar of lead	1 teaspoon	cold brown
Photographic hypo (sodium hyposulphate)	1 teaspoon	

Formula 3

Liver of sulphur	1 tablespoon	warm brown
Water	1 cup	

Works on fewer metals than 1 and 2, moreover the smells caused are unpleasant.

Formula 4

Butter of antimony undiluted	black

Having coloured, rinsed and dried the metal, it is usual to relieve it by polishing the raised parts to give a more interesting and natural appearance. This is better done with a cloth and metal polish than a buffing wheel, for it takes but a few seconds and one has better control. Finally, it should be lacquered. First warm the metal and give a coat of thin shellac with either a brush or spray; this is more appropriate for antiques than clear cellulose lacquer as it has a pleasing orange cast. If an accurate match of colour is called for, it is, of course, possible to colour the shellac or lacquer to the shade of the metal as required.

Silvering solution

Silver nitrate	½ teaspoon
Tartaric acid (cream of tartar)	1 teaspoon
Common salt	1 teaspoon
Whiting	1 teaspoon
Water	1oz

Use rubber gloves because this material combines with the skin, blackening it for about a week.

This is used mainly for resilvering the chapter rings of grandfather clocks and other dials but it is handy for renewing the silvering on such things as copper tea-caddy handles which have become blackened. The metal must, of course, be perfectly clean; in the case of dials, the proper satin effect may be achieved by mounting the ring on the faceplate of a lathe and finishing it with worn No 180 finishing paper. The bottle must be well shaken and the solution applied in much the same way as metal polish: once the silver shows up the application should proceed gently until the coating is thick enough. At best this provides only a thin layer and so a coat of lacquer is always recommended.

Renovating ormolu

Quite often the brass mounts of a French piece are so tarnished as to be unsightly. If they are simply cleaned with metal polish, they are inclined to look brassy as they lack that matt finish with burnished highlights which gives ormolu its charm. To restore this finish proceed as follows. Remove the mounts and clean them with a stiff wire brush to remove the worst of the dirt and old lacquer. Hang them on a wire hook and immerse them in a mixture of half nitric and half sulphuric acid. After a few seconds it will start to bubble; they can now be removed and rinsed in water. If they are not clean enough the process is repeated. When clean enough, they are rinsed in water to which a little soda has been added. They are then dried.

The burnishing of the high parts is accomplished with a steel burnisher, which is simply a piece of hard and polished steel usually oval in section; the back of a small gouge will do. This is rubbed over the places to be polished and it produces a high shine in pleasing contrast to the matt surface left by the acid. All that now remains is to lacquer.

10 Composite Furniture

It is a pleasant change and good for the soul of the restorer to create something original, for it tests his skill and, if the result be satisfactory, confirms his faith in his craftsmanship. Though not so satisfactory perhaps it is still a most interesting challenge to produce a component which, when married to a genuine antique, produces a whole which is acceptable.

The three photographs in Illus 61 represent individual examples of this work. In each case a considerable amount of time was spent in measuring and drawing the original, considering the dimensions of the addition both in regard to the proportions of the whole and also to the location which it was expected to occupy. The actual details also involve research into pieces of similar vintage both from books and, if available, from museums, homes or from the showrooms of dealers.

The first piece (Illus 61A) was an old oak Bible box to which the stand was added, making it the type of desk to which is frequently added the fable that it was used by Ann Boleyn for her love letters to Henry VIII. Obviously no one would be likely to write letters on it again so the height of the slope is unimportant, good proportion being the main consideration. The pencil drawing which was submitted and from which the stand was made is included (Illus 62). Such drawings need not be elaborate but misunderstandings are avoided and time is saved if they are to scale and contain all pertinent details.

Illus 61B was a little low chest of drawers in walnut on bracket feet which had faded to an almost yellow paint colour. A thin oak top had been fitted to cover the original walnut veneer, most of which was missing. The handles had stamped brass plates ornamented with lion masks of late nineteenth-century vintage.

It was fairly evident both because of the height and the form of the cross-banded moulding beneath the top that it had either been the upper part of a chest-on-chest, or had been on a stand. Mainly because of the lack of suitable materials, the construction of a stand was chosen.

Here again a search of illustrations of similar pieces was carried out and a drawing prepared. A certain amount of old wood was incorporated, including two drawers which were originally mahogany with oak sides, backs and bottoms of similar construction though perhaps thirty years younger. They

A

B

C

61 *A: by permission of Fenwick
Lansdowne; C: photo by the owner,
Lancelot de S. Duke*

186

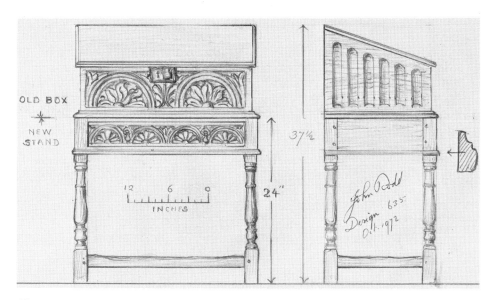

had to be cut down, and of course the fronts veneered with walnut to match the upper ones.

The handles are new but were filed and finished in the manner described on page 182 and are an important factor in tying the whole piece together.

Illus 61C was a hanging corner cabinet of the early mahogany period, sometimes called (with good reason in this case) the lion-mask period. By reason of the problems involved in attaching it to the wall every time the owner had to change his apartment, it was decided to make a lower cupboard to support it. Had modern ceilings been higher perhaps a somewhat taller stand would have given a better proportion. Luckily, old Spanish mahogany was available and so a satisfactory match was possible.

Jobs such as these three are of course very individual and do not often come one's way. It is likely, however, that a good deal of this kind of work was done in the nineteenth century, thus giving rise to some puzzlement to modern dealers and collectors.

Most of these composite antiques are the result of a demand for small, low tables to put beside one's easy chair or in front of the chesterfield. This is mainly because the easy chair is a relatively modern form and so there are practically no antique tables extant of suitable height. The next best thing is either an old tray or box to which a matching stand has been added. First the tray will be considered.

Since a good deal of work may be involved in making the stand, it is very important that the tray which is chosen shall be of good quality, reasonably flat and of the right size. If it is warped or twisted, it will not only be less satisfactory but more costly due to the time required to adjust the stand to it.

The least expensive one is pictured in Illus 63A. It is in the form of two

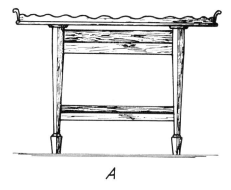

A

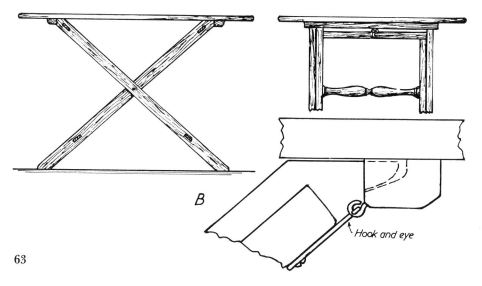

B

Hook and eye

63

frames pivoted where they cross so that it may be removed and folded. Pins are worked on the top of each leg and fit into turned discs glued and screwed to the underside of the tray. In the line drawing, the legs (which are $1 \times 1 \times 18$ inches) are tapered, and the spade feet should be worked out of the solid. The adjoining photograph is of a somewhat higher stand fitted to a kidney-shaped tray. Here the legs, for reasons of economy, are just tapered. A more elegant effect might have been achieved if the bottom six inches had been curved outward about an inch and a half in the manner often found in Sutherland tea tables.

Slightly different is Illus 63B which is derived from the original stands made for butlers' trays and indeed, if available, they may be cut down and used in this way. Since the original webbing strips will be found to be too springy in

188

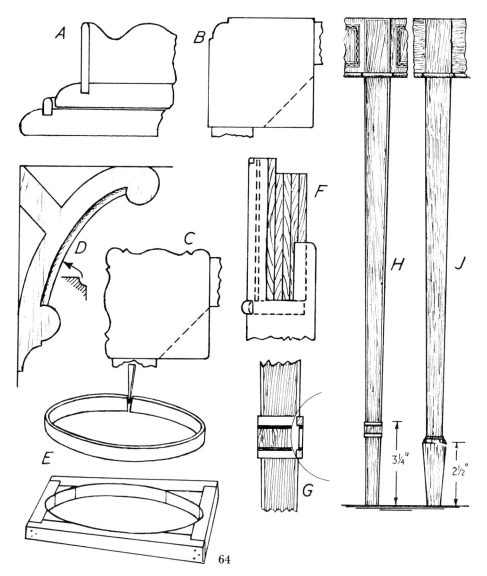

64

this low position, other means must be used to take their place. Instead therefore, two cleats are glued and screwed to the underside of the tray and a projection is worked on the upper end of each leg as indicated by the dotted line, and notches cut in the cleats to receive them. A hook and eye at each end prevents withdrawal, thus locking stand to tray. In this case the legs were ⅞ in × 1½ in and, although screws may be used as pivots where the frames cross, the author prefers the turned member as indicated which has a five-eighths pin on each end passing through the inner frame and projecting about half an inch into the outer one.

Stands in the form of a small table of suitable size and shape are quite practical with or without a little rim let into the edge to hold the tray in position as indicated in Illus 64A. They may also have the tray permanently

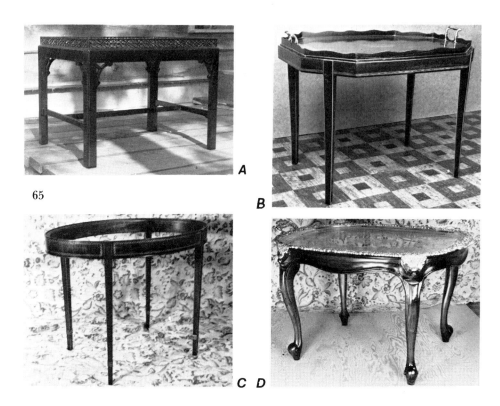

65

A

B

C D

attached to the frame by buttons, probably as indicated by Illus 38F, page 116.

For some reason, possibly to avoid any mutilation of the tray, yet have the antique comprise a significant portion of the whole, most customers prefer the open frame into which it is fitted: three fairly typical examples are shown in Illus 65 with details of construction in Illus 64.

Illus 65A is a tray with fretted gallery of the mid-eighteenth-century period and the design of the stand is based on a Chippendale chair. Details of the brackets and alternative sections of the legs are shown in Illus 64D, B and C. 1⅝ inches square is the dimension and they should be chamfered on the inner corner below the rails. Stetchers which cross, forming an X are more work but nicer because they are less likely to get in the way of one's feet.

Illus 65B and C are of the Sheraton style and, with a finely inlaid tray, make very attractive coffee tables. B is straightforward enough, though one rarely finds an eighteenth-century tray sufficiently symmetrical to fit closely both ways round: in other words if, after fitting it, one takes it out and turns it end for end, it will not go in. Maybe a little easing is all that is needed but customers are generally willing to accept the one-way fitting. Two styles of legs are shown in Illus 64H and J. They are 1 square inch at the top.

Illus 65C is a horrible stand to make and the trouble is usually compounded by finding that the tray is neither flat nor a true ellipse. In spite of this, it is the one most popular with the author's customers.

190

The main problem is the frame: there are many ways of making frames including building them up in segments of three layers and veneering and even cutting them out of the solid and dowelling through the legs, but the lamination method has been found most satisfactory.

For this it is first necessary to make a strong frame 2¼in deep whose internal dimensions give exactly ¼in clearance all round the tray; it is pictured in Illus 64E. First make the outer rectangular frame and tack it lightly together; now lay the tray on it and figure the dimensions of the corner pieces; fit and tack them. Now place the tray in position with some weight (maybe a pile of books) on it. Spend sufficient time to adjust and centre it as closely as possible. Prepare a scrap of thin wood with a hole ¼in from the edge and with a sharp pencil or scriber through it lay out the perimeter of the stand; also mark both frame and tray so that they may be accurately relocated. Before dismantling, bandsawing and reassembling, face off the bottom so that the cut may be square with all segments. In the final assembly, the outer corners must be securely nailed. If the work so far has been a nice clean job there will be no trouble in marking the position of the legs which should divide the rim into four approximately equal parts.

The face veneer can now be cut in one, two or four pieces and tacked in place with the joint or joints being within the areas to be occupied by the legs, first covering the frame with paper at these points to prevent sticking. Six laminations are next prepared out of ⅛in material either solid or plywood: the ends should be cut at a slight angle and hardwood wedges prepared as indicated in Illus 64E. Each is fitted in place dry and the wedge entered making sure there is enough reserve for driving. Now number each lamination and wedge as you remove them. You only have to glue them up now with the joints staggered.

When dry, remove it from the frame; clean it up, rebate the top edge and put it back. Now fit the tray into the rebate and mark the position of the legs. The rest is relatively straightforward.

The stand shown in Illus 65D was designed to support the largest and heaviest silver tray ever seen by the author. Both because of its weight and vintage, a fairly massive Victorian style was chosen with the legs of the stand being recessed to receive the silver feet of the tray, the carving flowing from them.

Boxes

Boxes also provide suitable table-tops and there is a great variety of them capable of harmonizing with any decor, such as small oak coffers, walnut glove boxes, jewel boxes, dressing chests and cutlery cases. It would be redundant to include photographs because such a variety is possible. Generally the stands should of course be heavier than those for a tray and may often be copied from the front part of a dining chair of the period. Another suitable treatment is the use of tapered, splayed legs such as were used to support old cellarettes.

One type of box, however, involves special treatment and, since it is readily available, is worthy of special consideration; it is the portable or lap desk.

It is not quite clear to the author why a sloping surface was considered so desirable for writing and then was abandoned at approximately the time when steel pens were introduced. Whatever the reason, these attractive little pieces became redundant and, until a few years ago, could be picked up for a few shillings.

If they are intended never to be used open, the stand could be perfectly simple. Most customers, however, seem willing to authorise the extra expense for a stand which permits their use both open and closed. Although when open it would be too low for writing, yet it is by no means as useless as might be supposed for, containing the necessary materials, it has been found very handy for the casual note while the slope served to support a book of reference perhaps. The drawer or recess will accommodate cards and scoring pads.

Two methods have been devised to achieve this; in both cases it is necessary for the box to be attached to the stand because, were it in a recess, it could not be fully opened.

For some reason, the stand pictured in Illus 66 has been by far the more popular of the two. In the manner of some old night commodes, the front legs

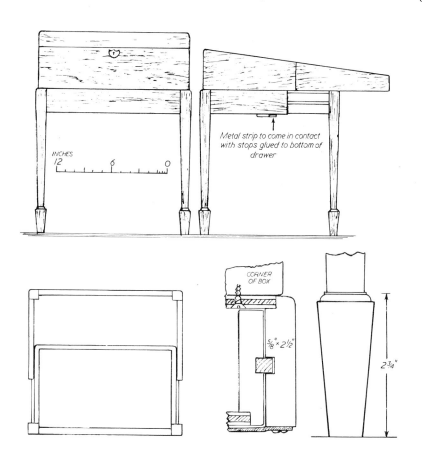

66

are attached to the drawer front and extend with it to support the opened lid. The drawing includes details of construction, and the style of leg and other ornament can be modified to harmonise with the box. In the one illustrated the box measured 15 × 24in and the legs at the top were 1⅛ square inches.

To prevent the drawer from extending too far, blocks are glued to the bottom at each end near the back. They come in contact with a strip of metal joining the two rails as shown. When it is necessary to remove the drawer entirely so as to be able to screw the stand to the bottom of the box, this strip can be unscrewed.

The second stand, Illus 67, works on the same principle as a revolving card table. While it could be made in any style, this was chosen because it has the advantage of covering a larger floor area giving greater stability; an advantage considering there is no increase when the box is open as is the case with the extending legs.

To find the centre of the pivot hole, draw a centre line across the stand; bisect it, draw a square on half and the diagonals mark the centre. The pivot itself should be as large as reasonable so as to provide the maximum area of attachment to the bottom of the box, which is usually thin. To fit the stop, centre stand on bottom of box, screw down pivot, draw a line on box bottom

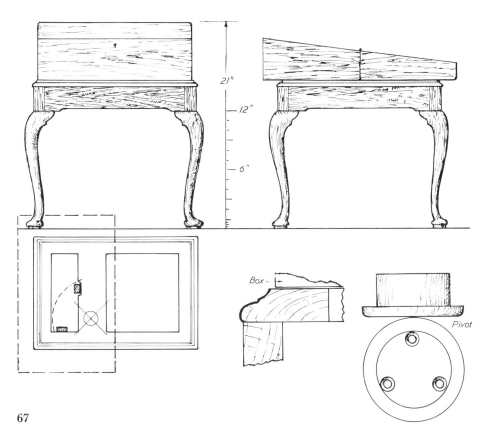

21"

12"

6"

Box —

Pivot

67

68 **A**

B

C

D

195

against cross piece of stand, turn box to open position and draw a second line against the frame. The space between lines is the width of the stop. If it is considered to be too narrow, notch the cross piece as shown. Both stop and pivot are best glued as well as screwed. As is common with card tables, a bottom and end may be fitted in the open part of the stand providing a useful receptacle.

Illus 68 shows two lap desks with stands. The leather lining seen in Illus 68B with gilt-tooled borders is modern and is available in various colours and patterns (see Sources of Supply). The inner lids of the satinwood box (Illus 68D) were missing and had been replaced with plywood covered with imitation leather. Since no old surface was involved, it was all right to add the lip to prevent papers from sliding off. When closed it occupies the opening above the pen tray.

If the purpose for which the box was made is no longer useful or the interior is in bad condition, the divisions and lining may be discarded to make place for something more attractive.

A piece of mirror may be framed within the lid or perhaps a small picture: the author's preference being a steel engraving from a nineteenth-century book. Cloth, embroidery or even hand-made lace has been used for this purpose. The remainder of the interior can be cleaned, oiled and polished or lined with paper, cloth, leather or one of the new decorative plastic materials which have their own stickiness, protected with a thin paper which must be removed before pressing the fabric in place. In some cases, notably brocade, it is preferable to cut cardboard to fit the sides and bottom allowing suitable clearance and then to cover each piece with the material, folding it around the edges before glueing them in place.

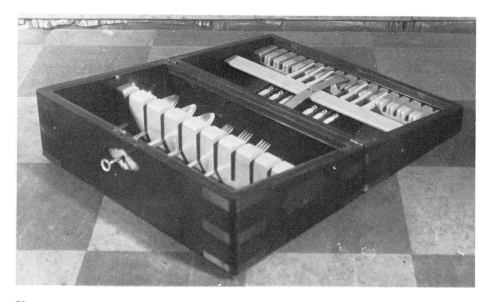

69

Divisions or trays made to accommodate small collections of coins or other objects are sometimes requested. Illus 69 shows how a box desk was fitted for a set of Georgian silver and cutlery. The slotted bar is a simple and neat way of storing the spoons and forks, up to twelve pieces being stacked in each slot. The knives are locked onto the lid by a padded bar attached to a flexible hinged strip secured with a brass turnbutton as shown. In order to gauge the width of slot for any particular set, the author uses a sample bar 1¼in wide with six slots ranging from ⅛ to ⁷⁄₁₆in wide. A sample of each spoon or fork is tried and the appropriate slot noted; also the overall width. If the box will almost but not quite take all the pieces, one of the spoons may be reversed so that its bowl is between two handles, thus gaining a little space, but this is not so handy as having them all one way. In some early silver, where minimal clearance is noted it is well to check the other pieces because of possible variations in width.

Fittings of this kind may also find a place in trays for sideboard drawers.

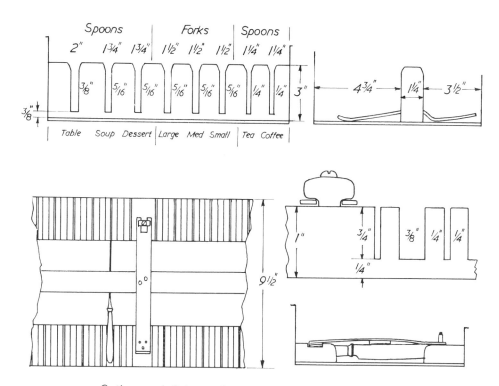

Cutlery and flatware fittings for a lap desk

11 Examples of Jobs

Repairs to a rosewood chair

The chair illustrated in Illus 70A had been broken through the twisted part as indicated by the black lines. These breaks had been glued up and further strengthened with screws and dowels put through the break. This had not held as these parts were insufficiently strong in the first place, and so something had to be done to make them stronger. It was decided to drill them and insert steel rods through them. Nine-sixteenth cold-rolled steel was the material selected.

The first thing was to cut off the broken part just above where the arms were joined on. Here was a place where the turning started. The finials were separate and already loose, but the top rail was tightly glued and had to be steamed to get it apart. Now the two broken uprights were placed on the bench and so it was easy to take apart the old repaired breaks and reglue them, binding them with rubber.

When they were dry they were set up in the lathe as shown in Illus 70B. The headstock end consisted of a piece of board with a hole cut in it to fit the upper squared end of the twist and gripping it by means of a screw through the cut side of it. This in turn was screwed to a wooden faceplate.

The tailstock was a home-made hollow one, as already described, with a wooden bush made to fit the turning. It happened that the bushing turned in the tailstock instead of the turning revolving in the bushing as planned, but this made no difference.

The wooden chuck had to be moved on its faceplate before the twist was properly centred and so it was simply held by means of two small G-cramps until the right position was obtained and then the screws put in. The drilling was now a simple matter and was continued for about three-quarters of the length of the twist, and then followed a further inch at $\frac{1}{4}$ in diameter to reduce the weakening caused by the end of the hole.

In drilling downwards the first precaution was to remove the two screws which held the arms. The guide shown in Illus 70C was then rigged up, supporting the upright with a sash cramp and a handscrew as shown. This hole was bored down to the middle of the thick part just above the seat.

Two rods were now prepared, the upper inch being reduced to $\frac{1}{4}$ in

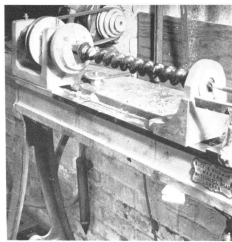

B

C

diameter. These went in very tightly indeed, for the last 6in, and so for fear of splitting the upper ends were reduced on the emery wheel until they could be got to go in by hand to within 3in of the necessary distance. They were then forced the remainder of the way in with the hammer. In spite of this the author was somewhat fearful of doing damage for the last inch or so but felt sure that they would never come loose.

The lower ends were treated in a similar way, but before forcing them home they were smeared well with Bostik cement.

The screws securing the arms were the next concern, and it was found that one could be replaced as it was, while a fresh hole had to be bored for the other.

In attempting to give further stiffness, the upholstered pad was firmly screwed to the rail, immediately below it, with two additional screws.

Grandfather clock case

Some time ago a grandfather clock case was sent in, the back of which was of horizontal boards. With the exception of a broken corner, a loose column and a few minor faults it was in perfect condition. The reason for this was the fact that the shrinkage of the back had not pulled the case out of shape as had the one to be described. The back of this one had shrunk between $\frac{1}{4}$in and $\frac{5}{16}$in and had split from end to end. Somebody had pulled it together and had nailed pieces across to hold it. This had caused the mitres of the larger mouldings to open up and the left-hand side to split away from the front frame, Illus 71.

The base panels had also shrunk and all three panels were split and had come away from the fillers between them and the waist. This had put all the weight on the moulding which had in turn given way, leaving the back holding everything. This caused the weight of the upper part to put a slight bend in it, causing the clock to bow forward, necessitating its being screwed to the wall.

The arched top of the upper door was warped as shown in the sketch, breaking the glass.

The feet were missing. This is quite common in old clocks, probably because when they went out of fashion they found their way to cottages where the ceilings were too low to accommodate them. The removal of the feet was the easiest way to shorten the case.

After removing the hood the case was laid on its back on the trestles and the door was taken off, which happened to be in good shape, replacing each screw in its proper hole so that neither they nor their positions would be lost. Now the case was turned over and the back was prised off. This released the base which came away as a unit, flimsily held together with brads. The base was next taken apart and the soft wood frame between it and the lower end of the waist was thrown away, being too rotten to retain. The large moulding with one exception came away easily.

This completed the dismantling. The next step was to remove all the nails,

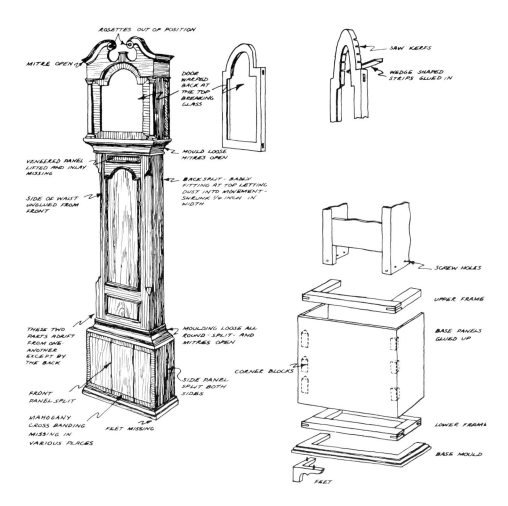

ROSETTES OUT OF POSITION

MITRE OPEN

DOOR WARPED BACK AT THE TOP BREAKING GLASS

SAW KERFS

WEDGE SHAPED STRIPS GLUED IN

MOULD LOOSE MITRES OPEN

VENEERED PANEL LIFTED AND INLAY MISSING

BACK SPLIT - BADLY FITTING AT TOP LETTING DUST INTO MOVEMENT - SHRUNK 1/4 INCH IN WIDTH

SIDE OF WAIST UNGLUED FROM FRONT

SCREW HOLES

UPPER FRAME

BASE PANELS GLUED UP

THESE TWO PARTS ADRIFT FROM ONE ANOTHER EXCEPT BY THE BACK

MOULDING LOOSE ALL ROUND - SPLIT - AND MITRES OPEN

CORNER BLOCKS

SIDE PANEL SPLIT BOTH SIDES

FRONT PANEL SPLIT

MAHOGANY CROSS BANDING MISSING IN VARIOUS PLACES

FEET MISSING

LOWER FRAME

BASE MOULD

FEET

71

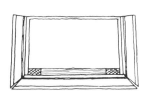

RESULT OF SHRUNK BACK EXAGGERATED.
FRONT BEING FRAMED DOES NOT SHRINK

corner blocks, cloth, etc, which had been used in an attempt to forestall the time when the case would have to be properly repaired. This was followed by a good scrubbing with soap and hot water, after which the shop was cleaned up and the rubbish burnt.

The glue being hot, the side was glued to the front frame of the waist, the two sides of the base were glued up and rejointed and the front panel, which was in three pieces, was glued. The back was also in two pieces and so it was glued up after drilling and fitting, cutting off pieces of nail in the form of dowels so as to hold the two surfaces flush while cramping. So ended the first day.

The next morning the sides of the base were fitted into the rebates in the front panel, both were sufficiently straight to go together without cramping; and so after making six corner blocks carefully squared, they were glued and rubbed together, glueing the corner blocks immediately and thus squaring the joints. The base was now a trifle smaller than it had originally been, but this did not matter. If it had, a strip of old wood between one of the front joints would have been glued in.

The inside size of the base could now be measured and the outside of the lower end of the waist so as to find out how thick the filler between them was to be. It was decided to make this in the form of a U-shaped frame and a rectangular one to go inside the bottom of the base as shown in the sketch (Illus 71). These were made of pine and bridle-jointed together. They were made to fit the base, allowing for the thickness of the back and the upper one was $1^{11}/_{16}$ in wide so as to fit over the waist.

The waist was now taken in hand; the piece of loose veneer at the top was cauled down and the missing inlay replaced. Two strips $\frac{1}{2}$ in × 1in were glued down the sides, $\frac{3}{8}$ in from the back to form a rebate for the back.

The hood was in fairly good shape except for one of the mouldings of the swan neck and both rosettes being misplaced by some former repair man; however, they came away quite easily and only had to be cleaned and reglued in their proper positions. The glass door, however, was something of a problem for the top arched rail had warped back nearly $\frac{1}{4}$ in. This was probably due to cross veneering unseasoned pine with mahogany, and of course it had broken the glass. The putty was as hard as concrete and so a large soldering iron was used to soften it. The iron must be almost red hot, and one works with the iron in one hand and a chisel in the other for the putty must be loosened while it is hot. The glass being out, four saw-kerfs were made across the warped part with a circular saw and wedge-shaped pieces were fitted and glued into them (see Illus 71).

The glue of the base was now dry enough to glue in the two frames (see photograph, Illus 71).

The back was now taken in hand. Measurements across the front of the waist less the thickness of the sides at the back showed that it needed building up $\frac{3}{8}$ in, so a strip was ripped and glued and nailed on. Similarly the base and the hood were measured and appropriate pieces were jointed on at the top and

bottom to bring the back to the correct shape, making the upper ones a little on the wide side so that they would be more closely fitted to the hood. The clearance should be left as small as is practicable here so as to keep dust away from the movement.

The base moulding was so badly split up that it was decided to replace it with another, so a piece of old moulding was mitred and it was glued together. Finally the four small feet were made.

Third day. The case was now ready to assemble. The waist was glued and screwed into the top frame of the base, being careful to line it up with a straight-edge both at the sides and in front. The back was now fitted and screwed into position. The feet were glued to the base moulding, which was attached with a couple of temporary screws. The case could now be stood up and checked with a plumb on a level floor. The mouldings at both ends of the waist had to be planed to fit and when right were glued in and secured with a small brad or two. The front of the base had an edge of mahogany cross banding and some of it was still missing, so some old mahogany was found and pieces glued in where necessary. A number of holes in the back were also plugged. The unwanted part of the strips in the upper door were cut away, and after cleaning a new piece of glass was fitted. The putty was coloured with burnt umber mixed with linseed oil. This was all that could be done until the glue had dried.

Fourth day. Little remained now but to clean and tidy. The base mould and feet were taken off, and the feet were planed flush with the mould and sandpapered up, the patches and joints levelled and the front of the base cleaned up. The feet and mould were then replaced, using six screws.

The centre door was rehung and the lock checked, the hood slid into position and the upper end of the back marked and fitted into it and the glass door was hung.

This just about finished the woodwork, but in order to minimise further changes in moisture content it was decided to coat the interior with linseed oil, and so some was poured into a cup and a couple of spoonfuls of raw umber were added to give an even colour to it. Particular attention was paid to the inside front of the base and both sides of the back.

Sheraton sofa tables

Work is apt to come in batches, and many similar examples of a piece of furniture will come into the repair shop one after the other. At one time this had been the case with sofa tables, mostly of the style of about 1800, such as the one pictured in Illus 73.

Owing to the fact that these tables have leaves at the ends they are made with the grain of the top across, and when they shrink they draw in the leaves until they touch the underframe when they are down, a little more and they will no longer hang straight down, finally the tension is released by the top

73

splitting in half. This had happened to all the tables mentioned, and one or two had had the frame planed away to make room for the leaves.

On most of them was added a strip of old stuff in the top when it was jointed up, but one which had a fine patina of a pale colour, which the owner was anxious to retain, seemed to warrant some extra work to reduce the frame.

After some thought it was decided that the division between the two drawers could be reduced from ⅞ in to ⅜ in, thus enabling the joint to be closed and also to allow a little overhang as a reserve should further shrinkage occur. This involved no special problems, the back rail was reduced ¼ in at each end, otherwise one of the false drawer fronts would have been ½ in shorter than the other which might have been noticeable.

As in the case of the other tables, the top was fastened down with buttons as described on page 117, except in the centre where the screws were put through the rails, as they had been originally.

Desk pigeonholes

In a sloping fall desk or bureau (Illus 74) the pigeonholes can come adrift owing to the sagging of the lower board. This is quite a common fault as these boards are often thin in the poorer quality pieces. Sometimes the centre can be raised by removing the back and screwing a stiff board about 4in wide across the back and onto the division between the two top drawers. This works well in

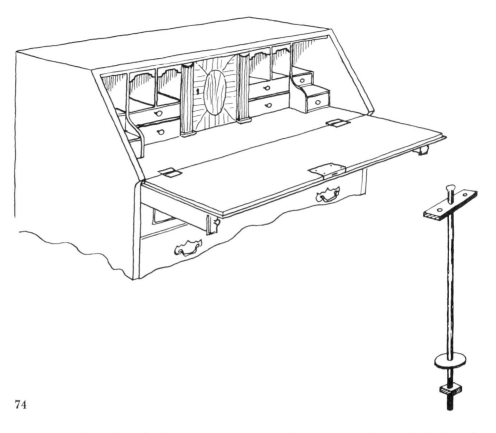

74

some cases, but there being no centre drawer in our example, and the board having sagged more in its centre than along the back, something else had to be devised.

Fortunately the centre space was fitted with a door and it occurred that a rod fitted just behind the hinges in the cupboard would not be much in the way and so a piece of $\frac{3}{16}$ in rod was riveted through a small plate as shown in the sketch and threaded the other end. The plate was screwed to the underside of the top, and the rod passed through a hole in the shelf. After the nut had been adjusted so that the upright divisions would slide nicely into their grooves from the back, these were glued into position and followed by the horizontal ones.

Sheraton tray

Parts of trays, especially rims, often need attention. These trays are quite common in inlaid mahogany with a $\frac{1}{8}$ in × 1in rim let into a groove $\frac{1}{4}$ in from the outside edge and with the top edge cut into a wavy outline.

The only practical course in this case is to replace the rim with a new one.

An example of this procedure as relating to one tray is given below.

The first thing is to remove the brass handles and the remains of the old rim, retaining a section intact as a pattern. This is achieved by cutting it off flush with the panel and later chiselling the remainder out of the groove. This requires a good deal of care, for while some sections come out whole, other parts have to be cut out in small pieces with a ⅛in chisel. If one prises up these parts one will probably split out sections of the panel, especially at the ends where the outer grain is so short. One-eighth-inch chisels are hard to get, but can be made by buying a sailmaker's needle, fitting the triangular end into a handle and grinding the round end rectangular.

The groove can still be rather messy, so it is filled with hot water and later scraped out clean.

The length and width of the rim are next measured, the width is taken from the handle which has a notch to fit over it and the depth of the groove added. A clean straight-grained piece of mahogany is obtained and cut out, finishing it rather on the slack side for it is quite hard to force a tight-fitting one into its groove. Next it is inserted, starting at the straightest part of the curve. A small handscrew is put on to prevent it jumping out and bending and pressing is continued until the two ends lap. Here the length is carefully marked and the mahogany is removed, taking care to hold the curve as it is eased out, for if it is let go a piece might split off. From the mark 2in are added and cut off. A mark is also made 2in from the other end and having cramped the strip onto a piece of 2in × 2in to support it, each end is planed from full thickness at the marks to almost nothing at the ends, thus forming a scarf.

The next thing is to make a pair of cauls to force this scarf together. These are marked from the outer edge of the tray and after cutting a few shavings brings the outer part to follow exactly the curve of the groove. The inner is padded with a piece of felt covered with wax paper.

Glueing up is simple, coating both strip and groove about a foot at a time and holding it in with handscrews. The scarf comes last, and cauls pull it up tight with a couple of G-cramps.

When dry the scarf is sandpapered level, the handles put in and their positions on the rim marked. These are removed and the wavy outline laid out in such a way that the handles rest on the high parts. It is cut with a narrow-bladed knife and rounded with glass paper.

When the panel is in good shape as regards polish it is covered with paper secured with transparent tape, following the curve of the rim, a gap about ½in wide being left to give it a surface to stick to. This enables the rim to be stained, filled and polished without disturbing the patina of the panel.

Removal of veneer from card-table top and replacement on new core

This is a piece of work rarely undertaken and involving a good deal of patient labour, eg over thirty hours, spread over several weeks.

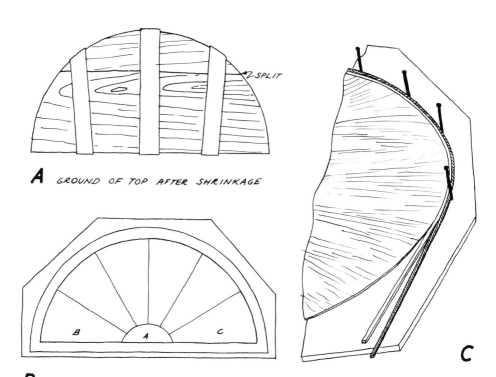

A GROUND OF TOP AFTER SHRINKAGE

SPLIT

B NEW TOP MARKED OUT

B   A   C

C

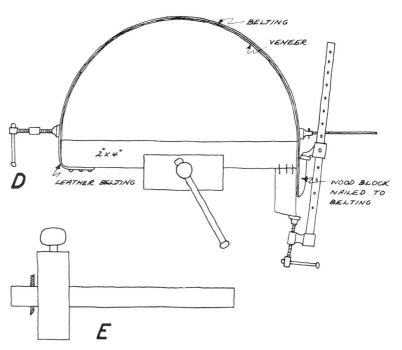

BELTING

VENEER

D

LEATHER BELTING

2"X4"

WOOD BLOCK
NAILED TO
BELTING

E

In one table the core on which the veneer had been laid consisted of a piece of deal stiffened by three clamps let in about one-third of the thickness as shown (Illus 75). This had shrunk and twisted, breaking up the veneer into a great many pieces as may be seen in Illus 72.

Many attempts had been made to repair the damage, and one of the mahogany segments had been entirely replaced; but this improvement had been only temporary, and the only way to make a permanent job seemed to be to remove the veneer completely and re-lay it on a new core.

The first consideration was to remove the veneer. In order to get moisture through it the old polish was stripped off with remover, and then the surface was covered with wet sawdust which was left overnight to soak in.

Next morning two pieces of ¾ in plywood were roughly cut to the size of the tops, for the lower one was also in poor shape, while a kettle of water and also the electric iron were heating. The old top was placed beside one of the new ones on the bench, and the new was covered with paper. Now wet cloths, hot iron and a large decorator's palette knife were used on the veneer. As each piece was removed it was carefully washed and laid out on the new top in the same position it had occupied on the old one until all had been transferred. The pieces were warped and curled in every direction and the author had some misgivings as to whether it could be put together again.

In order to flatten it as much as possible, the other top was placed on it and the two were cramped together with a number of G-cramps and set aside for two weeks so that the veneer could dry out.

On returning to the job, one of the tops was removed and the pattern of the veneer was marked out on it as shown in Illus 75B, and we prepared to lay the semicircle (Illus 75A), which happened to have broken into three pieces.

A piece of lead and a piece of wax paper were prepared, and a board large enough to cover it was procured. The lead was put on a piece of ¼in boiler plate heated on a hot plate.

Now the three pieces were glued into position and pinned with tailor's steel pins, cutting off the surplus with nippers. This pinning is necessary, otherwise the veneer is sure to slide when the pressure is applied.

Now the lead was tried by wetting the finger and touching it; it sizzled and so was hot enough. The veneer was covered with the wax paper, the board held beside the plate and the lead slipped onto it. It was carried to the veneer and the board and lead were turned over onto the wax paper and cramped down with three handscrews.

In four hours' time they were removed and everything was found in order, so the surplus glue, which was still in the form of a stiff jelly, was scraped away.

This was followed by the segment as seen in B, then C, each one being carefully fitted to A (see Illus 72B).

Illus 72C shows another segment being cramped down. Three could be done in a day: one on arrival, one after lunch and one just before leaving. On the whole it succeeded surprisingly well, considering that one segment was in fifteen pieces. However, there were some gaps into which pieces had to be inlaid.

This much being done, the edge was now fared up and some boxwood and ebony strips were obtained as a substitute for the old ones which were too much broken up to be worth putting back. The method of holding these while glueing is suggested in Illus 75C, 1in finishing nails being used. When dry they were removed and the strips planed level with the veneer so as not to prevent the cauls from pressing down the next band of boxwood, which was laid in the same way as before after being carefully fitted to the curve. Some pieces were missing but were replaced with sections cut from an old rule.

There yet remained one black and one white line and the cross banding of the edge. The white should be square to show an equal width on top and edge. Then the straight edges of both tops had to be faced with mahogany and fitted with little slots and projections, seen in Illus 72F, to hold them flush when open.

It was decided to make these strips the combined thickness of the two outer lines, and so the top was planed down to the wide boxwood band and then they were glued in position. The ebony line was fitted all round, holding it with nails as before.

The two tops were now nailed together with the straight mahogany-faced sides flush, for it was proposed to veneer the two curved edges together. The outside of the veneer had to be ⅛in from the black line to make room for the boxwood square, and so a piece of veneer was found which together with the mahogany intended for the edge made ⅛in. With this piece held against the black a line was scribed around the curve, and then the two tops were cut with the bandsaw. They were trued down to the line with a compass plane and then the edge was given a coat of thin glue.

In order to lay the veneer the jig pictured in Illus 75D was made. Two pieces of 2in × 4in were spiked together, the longer one being the length of the top and the shorter about a foot long. The author happened to have a piece of 2in leather belting one end of which was nailed to a small block to take the cramp, the other end being passed around the top and nailed to the 2in × 4in as shown. The veneer was taped together, being a band 2in × 4ft 6in. The method of laying is fairly obvious from the sketch and worked well. When dry, the edges were trimmed off and the veneer was cut in half with a cutting gauge, separating the tops.

A cross veneer had now to be laid around the inside of both tops to take the cloth lining, and then the boxwood corner lines fitted. The rebates for these were cut with the cutting gauge, with the blade having the bevel inwards so as to make a vertical cut. Two cuts took a strip clean out of the corner. The method of tying the boxwood into its rebates is pictured in Illus 72E, using a piece of board each side, into which a number of nails have been driven.

We were now able to clean up the top, obliterating a good deal of the engraving; but enough remained to form a guide, and so we were able to go over the bad parts with the finest V-tool. When filled with lampblack and Brummer stopping, this appeared as may be seen in Illus 72F.

Illus 72G shows the finished job.

Split sideboard top

An unsuccessful repair, which the author carried out, might be worth describing.

It consisted of a sideboard top which was said to be cracked from end to end. This was, however, not quite accurate, for when it arrived it was found that the crack stopped within an inch or two of each end and was about ¼in wide in the middle.

The cause of the trouble was easy enough to see, but what to do was a problem. The cause was as follows. The top had been made in this way. A piece of pine ¾in × 24in × 6ft had been built up to 1½in by glueing strips on the underside along front and back, and also several cross pieces whose grain was across that of the top board, Illus 76 (2).

Around this had been mitred and probably dowelled a 1½in mahogany moulding having a ½in piece level with the top (3). The top had now no doubt been cleaned up and veneered, the veneer covering the joint.

Now this was in order as long as the piece remained in a cool atmosphere, but after being introduced to central heating the inevitable shrinkage took place with the result shown at the top of Illus 76.

Usually, the best course when the original construction is faulty is to remake the piece as it should have been made in the first place. This might have been done as follows.

First the joint AB, in Illus 76 (3), would be cut with a saw to the corner of the mitre of the moulding in front, thus removing the mouldings across each end. Then all the cross pieces would be removed; probably these would come away easily unless they were morticed into the front and back pieces, when the tenons would have to be cut. The top would now be in two pieces. The crack would not at first go together, but probably after a month or two the ends might shrink almost as much as the middle part, allowing the crack to be well dowelled, glued and pulled up with cramps.

The end moulding would then be replaced with material cut as wide as possible and about 2¾in long across the end of a 1½in plank. This would be rebated, glued and screwed to the ends of the top with the grain in the same direction as the top, ie across the moulding, as shown in Illus 76 (4). This would produce a top capable of swelling and shrinking with changes in humidity without damage, all the wood having its grain in the same direction. It would be stiffened by replacing the cross pieces screwed dry to the underside through holes slotted at the ends as shown in Illus 76 (5).

Now this is very nice in theory, but in practice it would most likely be found that the top when released would warp to such an extent that it would be impossible to get it glued up or straightened out after glueing because this top was veneered most likely with a hammer, a process which makes the veneer very wet during the laying and causes it to pull the surface on which it is laid into a hollow as it dries.

In view of the above, and considering that no change had been noticed for

1 SPLIT IN TOP AND
NEAR FRONT EDGE

2 THE UNDER SIDE OF
THE TOP BEFORE THE
MOULDING HAD BEEN
ADDED

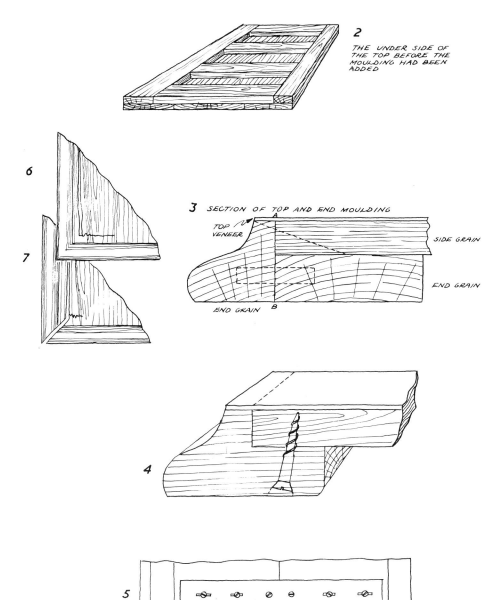

6

7

3 SECTION OF TOP AND END MOULDING

TOP
VENEER

SIDE GRAIN

END GRAIN

END GRAIN B

4

5 SPACE

76

some time, it was decided to take a chance and cut a groove down the top and fill it with a strip of mahogany.

First of all the cross pieces were bored at each side of the crack, and after glue had been inserted under them with a spatula the top was screwed down. This held the two sides level with each other and tended to strengthen the subsequent joint.

A ½in groove was now cut with a dado the whole length of the top, but sloping up at each end to the depth of the thickness of the veneer, as shown in the dotted line (Illus 76 (3)). A strip of mahogany was now carefully fitted and glued in.

Another crack close to the front edge and caused by the top shrinking away from the front moulding was easily cured by cutting about ⅛in off the mitre of the end mould, thus allowing the front mould to be glued and cramped into position (Illus 76 (6) and (7)).

After levelling and polishing this looked as good as new, but now it seems that a crack is starting again. This is due, no doubt, to further shrinkage at the end and failure of the joints which had held it up till now.

What can now be done apart from making a new top is hard to say. Perhaps it is foolish to attempt to make a silk purse out of a sow's ear, but such jobs are quite often successful.

Work on marble top and brass gallery

A French desk was dealt with, the top of which was covered with red marble and surrounded with a brass gallery. This gallery had been crushed down and the marble smashed at three of its corners, probably by having its crate turned upside down while in transit.

The first thing was to remove the gallery by pulling out the brass pins which secured it. These were driven into a wooden top beneath the marble, both wood and marble being about ⁵⁄₁₆in thick, making a total of ⅝in. This released the fragments of broken marble which were carefully saved and together with the larger pieces washed to get rid of the dirt which had accumulated on the broken edges and beneath the lip of the brass.

The gallery was now heated red hot, where it was most badly bent, in a gas flame, and when a section had been done it was cooled in water. This is not a necessary part of the annealing process but it saves time. After this it was fairly easy with pliers and hammer to straighten it out, but in the process one of the corners came apart. This was cleaned and soldered together with a small right-angled piece of sheet brass in the corner below the top of the marble where it could not be seen.

The wooden top next required attention. The corner had been broken away, and so a small triangular piece was glued and nailed in its place. The main pieces of marble were next laid in position and it was found that the joints did not come flush and level, due to irregularity in the wood. This was corrected by planing away where necessary until the marble both lay flat without rocking and also came flush where the breaks occurred. A mixture of plaster of Paris and glue was now spread over the wood and the under side of the marble, and the various pieces bedded into it. Where necessary the cracks were filled with the same mixture, and the whole thing was set aside over the weekend.

On the Monday the gallery was cleaned with Brasso so as not to show the parts which had been heated and then it was tried in position. It would not fit on. A certain amount of the cement in the numerous cracks no doubt made the marble slightly larger, and also the small piece of brass soldered in the corner of the gallery took up some space. One was somewhat at a loss to know what to do: eventually, however, a piece of coarse garnet paper was obtained and with a wooden block was used to sandpaper the marble away. It cut surprisingly fast, and in five minutes the gallery was in position.

Repair to desk fall

Illus 77A shows a desk fall which was recently repaired. It consisted of a frame with a flush panel, over which a veneer had been laid. The panel had shrunk breaking the veneer, as may be seen, and also pulling the upper member of the frame into a curve to such an extent that the bolt of the lock no longer reached into its socket.

Having removed the fall the author tried to break this top member away from the panel by inserting a large palette knife through the crack and driving it sideways. This, however, did not work so the finest saw was used for cutting

77 **A**   **B**

it away. As it had been in a curve for such a long time it did not straighten out, and so the cut had to be opened with a wedge until the outer edge was approximately straight so as to be able to measure the opening and cut out a piece of mahogany to fill it. It was slightly wider in the centre than at the ends and so it was possible to glue it in before finishing.

In order to secure the panel to the ends of the frame eight dowels were inserted as described on page 102. This finished the work on the ground, but the shattered veneer remained.

It was felt that the customer would appreciate a first-class job. The inlay around the outside was a fairly common satinwood banding, and there were in stock some strips of the same design, though slightly narrower, and so it was decided to use them to cover up the bad parts with the result seen in B.

Repairs to satinwood desk

The left-hand top of the desk seen in Illus 78D had warped and split from front to back. After having been repaired, its section would have appeared as shown in Illus 78A. The crack had been filled with a strip of wood and the top had been plastered over with stopping.

Although its appearance was not very good, it was sound and it was intended to leave it as it was since straightening would entail a great deal of work. The customer, however, pointed out that it was the most conspicuous part of the desk and asked for it to be improved if possible.

After a good deal of thought it was decided to make two saw-kerfs each side of the crack so that the top could be more easily straightened, and then to glue

78

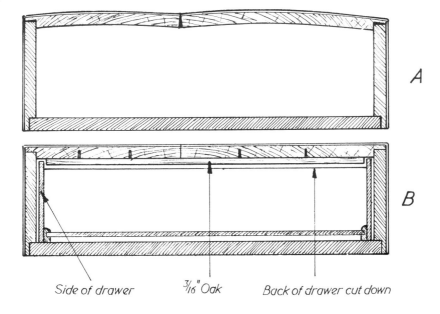

_A_

_B_

Side of drawer   _³⁄₁₆" Oak_   _Back of drawer cut down_

78

C

D

a piece of ³⁄₁₆in oak on the under side with the grain crossing that of the top as shown in section B. In order to avoid having to change the drawer any more than necessary, a ⅜in gap was left at each side to make room for the upper edges of the drawer sides, thus only having to cut down the back to clear.

Having removed the bottom of the case and the ½in clamp across the front edge of the top, work was begun on the strip which filled the crack; this was cut out in short pieces with a very narrow chisel, finishing with a thin-bladed penknife and a piece of hacksaw blade.

Saw-kerfs were now made, oak obtained and glueing up prepared for. The arrangement for this may be seen in photograph C. Two thick pieces of plywood for cauls were found, and a number of 2in × 3in cross pieces cut. After getting the handscrews in position with a slight pressure, two small sash cramps were applied to close the crack, and then tightening up was concluded.

The cramps were left on for two days so that the glue might be sufficiently set to hold the pull of the warp.

On taking it out it was found that the crack was well closed and the top almost flat, and so it was possible to go ahead and put the rest of it together.

The case was now a trifle narrower, but, as the drawer was already loose in the dovetails and some of the inlay missing, one simply had to reduce it a corresponding amount.

In polishing the top it was necessary, first, to scrape the glue joint where it showed up as a dark line, then fill the depression thus formed with yellow filler. In the final result, the crack was more apparent than would have been the case with a darker wood, but was not noticeable to one who was not aware that it had been repaired.

216

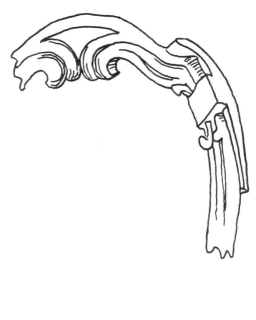

79 **A**   **B**

Three chairs

The chairs in Illus 79 were all repaired at the same time, each presenting a
different problem.

The worst was A, having been glued, nailed and screwed. It had also been
saw-kerfed and veneer-keyed. Its discrepancies had been filled with plastic
wood and stick shellac. In short it was in a bad way, and the only thing to do
was to cut away the wood on both sides of each joint and scarf in a filler.

The first thing was to make cardboard patterns of the outline at each side
and from them make one pattern having an outline as far as possible
conforming to the good parts of each. Next the bad wood was cut away leaving
as much as possible in front and planning away behind until long clean
surfaces were left.

The cut ends of legs and top rail were now marked on each side of the
pattern and the filler pieces cut out. They were made with plenty of extra
thickness behind to allow both for fitting and lining up as pictured in B.

They were first fitted to the top rail, then screwed to it from behind and
then tried in position. Of course, a good deal had to be cut away before they
finally fitted. Meanwhile, each time they were tried in position they were
studied for alignment.

For instance, if the top rail is in a plane forward of the leg, then the upper
scarf must be cut back, whereas if the reverse is the case the lower scarf must
be cut back. If the top rail is canted forward or back, then the angle of one of
the scarfs must be altered. When alignment and fit were satisfactory, the
pieces were cut to outline and most of the surplus wood cut away, and they

217

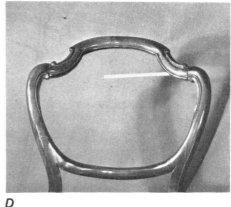

C   D

were glued and screwed together, adding a little pressure at the ends of each scarf with a handscrew. The final result after cleaning up and polishing may be seen in photograph A.

Photograph C shows how the centre splat of a chair was built up. It had evidently been cut away too much in the narrow part and had broken there. It had been repaired with a ¼ in dowel of soft mahogany and had broken again. A dowel of the hardest piece of hickory that could be found was fitted and then a piece of ¼ in mahogany was glued on the back. After it had been rounded over and polished, it was hardly visible from the front and not objectionable from behind.

Photograph D was a modern factory reproduction of a Victorian chair. The dowelled joints of the top rail were vertical as may be seen, and the glue having failed it simply pivoted on its dowels. To get it apart without disturbing the rest of the chair was a little puzzling. The author decided to prise one of the joints sufficiently open to get the dovetail saw in and cut the dowel. It was possible now to get the other end out, and after drilling out the pieces of dowel the one hole was continued through so as to be able to assemble the part by inserting the dowel as shown.

Repairs to mahogany chest of drawers

The six photographs in Illus 80 depict the progress on a bow-front chest. This piece, though of rather poor quality, was very saleable because of its small size and bow front, and so it was considered worthy of good work.

As may be seen in photograph A, it was in a very shabby condition, many pieces of veneer were loose or missing. The divisions between the drawers were loose, and the veneer was broken at their junction with the carcase ends. The top right-hand drawer had been removed revealing the inside of the carcase, the piece between the two upper drawers was missing as was the dust board, the back edge of the drawer being supported on a scrap of board tacked in.

Photograph B: the chest has now been dismantled, the veneer cut away

218

80 **A**

B

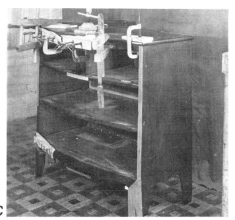

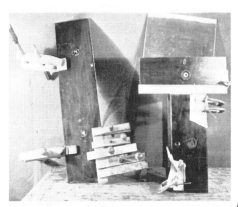

C

D

E

F

81 **A**   **B**

where it was to be replaced and the loose parts marked with chalk. A piece of old pine was found and jointed onto the front rail to replace the missing dust board. The piece dividing the upper drawers may be seen on the top dowelled to the old part and ready to be screwed to the under side of the top, its back end being supported by two dowels through the back. Also on the top is an oak bracket to stiffen the back leg, which consisted merely of an extension of the side.

Photograph C: this shows the carcase reassembled with some of the loose veneer being cauled down. Plywood was used for cauls on the curved surfaces as it bends more easily than solid wood. The front lower edge of the apron was simply planed off flat at an angle of 45° and a piece glued and rubbed in place. The straight pieces covering the front edges of the carcase sides were simply glued and rubbed. This is satisfactory only when the surface is flat, the veneer straight and the glue fairly thick. Loose veneer on the top is put down with a shore from the ceiling.

Photograph D: here some of the drawers are in cramps. The lower edge of the right-hand drawer was so badly damaged that a piece of solid mahogany was jointed onto it.

Photograph E: here is the piece ready for polishing.

Photograph F: this is the finished job. First the new wood was stained with bichromate solution about one-third full strength. The filler was coloured Vandyke brown. In colouring-up a mixture of Nigrosine and Brunswick black was used to which was added burnt umber where there was needed a strong colour, as in carrying the dark stripe across the new wood of the upper left-hand drawer.

Straightening a pair of warped doors

The author repaired a cabinet whose doors were twisted to such an extent that

220

C   D

the top corner of one projected 1¼in when they were closed.

The panels were of ½in Honduras mahogany veneered with very fine Spanish crotch. After examining them it was realised that nothing previously written in this book about warped boards would apply here, for not one of the eight sides was straight nor could either side be described as the hollow one, the curves being so irregular.

After a good deal of thought it was decided to reduce them to half their thickness and then to glue each one to a ¼in three-ply panel of similar size.

The planer being too narrow to use they were taken to a mill. In order to protect the veneered surface, a board was placed beneath them as they passed through the machine, the surplus wood being removed in three light cuts.

They were now reasonably pliable, and so they were glued to their plywood backings and placed in a veneer press where they remained from Friday till the following Tuesday when they were removed and placed in their frames.

When the job was finished the doors, though not quite perfect, required only a slight pressure of the hand to enable them to be locked.

Alterations to an old desk

The desk pictured on the left of Illus 81 was 32in from the floor to the writing surface without its feet. With feet it must have been about 38in high.

These very high desks are fairly common and were no doubt made for people who were used to those office desks pictured in Dickens's stories, with the clerk either standing or seated on a high stool.

As the feet were missing, it was suggested we might omit the bottom drawer and cut the projecting sides into feet, reducing the desk to standard height.

These out-curving feet are easily made by making a saw-kerf about ⅛in from the outer surface of the bottom end of the foot and filling it with an appropriately shaped wedge, glued in. The front part of the foot is then added together with the apron.

221

The photograph on the left shows the finished job, scraped and repolished and fitted with brass handles.

Restoring the lid of a Charles II lace-box

According to Mr Frank Davis in one of his interesting commentaries in *The Illustrated London News,* these boxes are variously called glove, lace or dressing boxes and are becoming scarce in antique shops. For this reason it is possible to devote more time to their restoration than would have been economically feasible a few years ago; Illus 82A is the lid of such a box as received for attention.

Its construction consists of a pine panel with clamps tenoned on each end. The edges were bevelled and cross banded with thick veneer and then slightly rounded: the face veneer of walnut oyster-shell pieces was then laid and then the geometric pattern of holly and ebony was inlaid.

Shrinkage of the panel resulted in the two cracks which may be seen in the photograph which also reveals the displacement of the lines of some of the inlay such as the jogs in the large circle. Various scraps of veneer and inlay were missing, some having been replaced at different times with various compositions.

As with most jobs, no permanent repair can be made without adequate attention to the foundation and so the first consideration was to widen the cracks in the panel and to cut away sufficient wood on each side to remove the layer which had become saturated with oil. An old crack such as this is always soaked with furniture polish which generations of housewives have applied to prevent the wood 'drying out' and of course no glue will stick to it.

In order to save any veneer which might be loose, the surface guck was first scraped off and then a two-inch band of masking tape was applied over each

82 **A**

B

crack. As they were fairly straight and parallel to the side it was decided to use a dado saw to clean and widen them from below. Careful measurements were taken to ensure that the cut would remove only the pine of the panel almost to the glue below the veneer and stops were fitted so that the cut would leave the end clamps intact. The first quarter-inch cut indicated oiliness on one side only and so a second finished that groove; the second groove took three cuts.

Being now roughed out, the lid was fastened face down on a flat surface and the grooves cleaned out to the clamps at each end and deepened until the back of the veneer below was exposed: this was done with a chisel, the final cleaning by using it as a scraper.

Old pine furnished the groove fillers which were fitted carefully and to the exact thickness of the panels at each end, and were clearly marked; for the panel varied somewhat. This was because it was intended to glue them in place at the same time as putting down the loose veneer: had they been proud they would have prevented the veneer from bedding properly to the panels adjacent to them.

In the shop was a heavy old letter press with a massive central screw which is quite handy for jobs like this. The arch supporting the screw had been raised by fitting longer bolts and spacers each side so as to increase its capacity and it was also mounted on a three inch deep asbestos and metal-lined box to accommodate an electric heating element. This warms the lower plate in about twenty minutes; it should be almost too hot to bear the hand.

Having set this to warm, glue was worked under all the loose veneer; next the fillers were coated and set in place and the surplus glue washed off and dried with an old towel: by now the press was warm enough to receive the lid face down on a piece of wax paper and with a stack of old newspapers on the pine side to absorb moisture. The screw was then heaved down, not forgetting to turn off the heat. It could of course have been done equally well with a heated caul and handscrews.

C

D

Having a firm foundation it was now safe to proceed to the more interesting task of patching the veneer and inlay. Some years previously the branches of a pioneer's walnut tree had been obtained. By cutting one of these at an angle and then comparing the face with one of the oyster pieces and then altering the angle by planing, a fairly good match was obtained: all that was then needed were a few cuts with a tablesaw. Various woods were compared with the white inlay: box, hawthorn, dogwood, holly and maple; of these holly seemed the best and so a scrap of veneer and a piece of stringing were prepared.

Illus 82B shows most of the patches in place and the adjustments which had been made to fair out the displacements caused by the shrinkage of the panel: before the glue has time to dry out thoroughly it is possible, by warming and pushing, to slide small pieces of veneer as required for fairing the jogged inlay. This can be done with a heated knife or, better still, with an electric burning-in tool as sold for use with stick shellac.

Arcs of the narrow strips can be bent in place but wider ones are best cut to shape, especially those of short radius: the large circle and parts of the hearts in the corner were patched in this way. The smaller cracks in the veneer were filled with walnut sawdust and glue.

Illus 82C shows the lid scraped and sanded ready for polishing, also some faking on the patches. A careful examination of the photograph will show how the adjacent grain has been carried over the patches with stain applied with a pencil brush. A filler coloured with Vandyke brown and raw sienna brought the colour so close that little toning was needed: D is the finished job after minimal French polish followed by half-a-dozen waxings.

Restoring a Regency toilet mirror

Like everything else in life, jobs can be good, bad and ordinary: the mirror in Illus 83A was good. Firstly the customer could hardly be unaware of its condition; secondly it was a genuine antique of good quality; and lastly, the work involved was straightforward and pleasant.

Here is a list of its requirements:
1 Cross banding on carcase around drawers loose and some missing
2 Some corner inlay missing
3 Mirror frame apart and chips at dovetailed corners missing, also some cross banding and corner inlay
4 Ivory drawer knobs, finials and mirror screws missing
5 Mirror supports loose
6 Glass and mirror back missing
7 Veneer on centre drawer has been replaced with plain mahogany with grain horizontal instead of vertical
8 Finish grubby

Apart from the problem of finding suitable material, this work would have

83 **A**

B

C

been an ideal and rewarding task for an amateur. Had a piece of mercury amalgam mirror in fairly good condition been available, it would have been preferred by a serious collector but it was not, so a new glass was ordered.

Old veneer for the patches was available but none thick enough for the cross banding of the frame. A table leaf of similar age had been recently shortened to fit a smaller table and so a seven-eighths piece was taken from the off-cut and then sawn into suitable strips.

Ivory for finials, knobs and mirror screws was cut from a sea-lion tusk. Since Victoria had been the home port for a fleet of sealing schooners, one was usually able, at second-hand shops, to pick up walrus and other tusks brought home by sailors for scrimshaw work; a description of the working of this material and a drawing of the items will be found on page 138.

After dismantling, the first step was to make good the two missing pieces from the dovetailed corner of the frame. Flat surfaces were planed and pieces of old mahogany fitted and glued in place. The cross banding of the missing veneer above the right-hand drawer required a caul to force it into its curve and in order to prevent it slipping to the right when cramped up, it was made long enough to hook around the top at the left: it was also later used to hold in place the corner inlay above.

The unsuitable veneer on the centre drawer was planed off and a new piece laid with a heated caul and three handscrews; as may be seen, a satisfactory replacement was available.

The following day the dovetails of the frame could be fitted and a new back cut out of an old pine drawer bottom: next the veneer on the centre drawer was trimmed and the corners cut to receive the inlay. For this a cutting gauge was used with the bevelled side of the knife facing the fence; this makes a nice clean rebate and it is well to remember to make the first cuts across the grain in case a small chip should be broken out at the end of the stroke; if this were to happen it would most likely be eliminated when the long cuts are made. The rebate for the inlay in the top above the right-hand drawer had to be finished with a chisel where the curve meets the corner post.

Next, the mirror posts were cleaned in their joint: they were slack enough to need a veneer glued to the back of the tenon (p 29, Illus 8).

The second glueing now followed: it included the veneer fillers on the posts which were held in place with masking tape which also covered the rest of the tenons for it is much easier to polish posts and top before glueing them in place. The frame was glued with the back in place to square it up; the cross banding was also mitred and glued and then it was put in an old letter press; lastly, the corner inlay of the drawer, using string where necessary to pull it home, and the curved piece above the drawer using the caul as already mentioned.

The last glueing was the inlay round the mirror frame: before doing this it is wise to examine the rebate for the glass and carefully clean any lumps of glue so as to be sure that the glass will bed down nicely; also paint or stain it black. If this is done now the final clean up will remove any splashes of stain.

The ivory was now prepared and, after the frame had been cleaned up, the polishing was commenced. The centre drawer needed a little darkening and a weak solution of potassium permanganate was used; bichromate would have produced too warm a colour. This was followed by a filler coloured with Vandyke brown and then a minimum body of French polish. Illus 83B is the piece before polishing and C the finished job.

Perhaps the centre drawer would have been a better match had it been darker; this brings to mind the polisher's explanation which is: 'should the customer complain that the match is too light, the answer would be that it will darken with age; whereas if the contrary criticism is made, one must allow for fading'. This was from John Hayhurst who was, in his day, Victoria's most skilful polisher.

Mulberry

Some years ago an exceptionally fine bureau-bookcase in mulberry and rosewood inlaid with pewter with its original Coxed & Wooster label was received for restoration.

Because of its quality and value, the instructions were to obtain genuine mulberry at any cost for the replacement of the missing pieces. Accordingly a letter was posted to the Victoria and Albert Museum asking for advice in obtaining it. Mr N. S. Brommelle, keeper of the Department of Conservation, very kindly replied with a list of possible sources but warning of the difficulty in obtaining this wood. His list was sent to an old friend, the late H. R. Hayward, retired maker of *Military Pickles*. Except for a few years pioneering in a log cabin in British Columbia, Bert's working life had been spent in London and he anticipated no trouble at all in producing the necessary veneer. Just as a matter of interest another letter was sent to a Chinese architect in Hong Kong; surely in the land of silk, mulberry must be readily available.

More than six months later a strip of mulberry veneer was taken from the carcase beneath the lower edge of the bookcase doors; it was nearly 1in wide by 3ft long and provided material for the most conspicuous patches; its place was filled with old rosewood cross banding. Birds-eye maple was used for the other but quite a bit of faking was necessary to achieve a satisfactory match.

It is probable that, had English or Vancouver Island maple been used it would, being softer, have absorbed the stain more readily and have made a better match. Quebec and Vermont maple, by reason of the very cold winters, is so hard that it resists staining which was essential to the effect achieved in eighteenth-century work. In spite of this, at least in this case, the author is unable to accept the hypothesis, lately advanced, that so-called mulberry was in reality figured maple.

Water, tropics and mildew

Damage to a container followed by a shower of rain on a dock in England was probably the initial cause of the damage seen in Illus 84: the tropical heat of the Panama Canal also made its contribution, to the dismay of the Canadian collector when he unpacked his purchase.

It was of course impractical to start work on it until it had had time to dry out. In the meantime, the owner and his wife undertook, as far as possible, to tape together and mark as much of the loosened veneer as could be located and to continue the process as more fell away: this eventually included nearly all of the cross banding and the moulding above the foot on the lower left side. Masking tape was used for this purpose and nearly all was saved.

Since the purchase price in sterling was well into the four figure bracket, it was essential to use every effort to make the restoration as complete as possible: it was started after a drying period of about four months.

The first step was to finish the removal and marking of any loose pieces remaining, take out the drawers and writing slide and then to make a thorough check of any damage to the ground work. The top was of pine with cross clamps at each end; the one at the left was projecting a little beyond the centre part which had shrunk and was more or less as pictured in Illus 84B and the joint there was loose. Two of the feet also required reglueing, but apart from that the framework was sound.

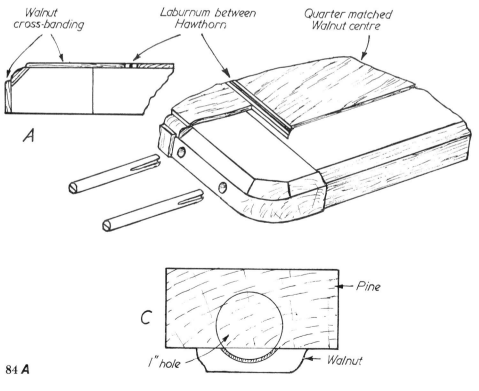

84 **A**

228

Since the veneer was off the edge at the end near the corner, it was a simple matter to secure the clamp by dowelling. Two quarter-inch holes were drilled and dowels prepared as indicated at B with short grooves cut with a fluter on opposite sides and a line marked on the other end to indicate their positions. The carcase was then placed with its right-hand end on a pad, the dowel holes now being vertical. Hot thin glue was then poured into one hole, about half filling it: the glued dowel, now inserted with the line on its butt end being in line with the edge of the top, was driven home thus forcing the glue along the joint by way of the two grooves. This was repeated with the second and the joint closed with a sash cramp. When dry, the front edge was trimmed flush.

Sketches A and B show the construction; the ground had been first chamfered as shown and then a thick cross banding laid on the bevel; later, it was planed flush with the top and edges and then rounded. The finish cross banding was later trimmed to the edge of the curve thus completing the job. The replacement of the loose pieces followed in the same order; first the rounded pieces were cauled down with a warmed piece of aluminium angle iron held down with G-cramps and a sash cramp across the top. The re-laying of the veneer was mostly a matter of patiently finding the correct places for the untaped pieces and taking extra care that the heated cauls should have perfectly smooth faces so that practically no cleaning up would be necessary. Due to shrinkage, some gaps occurred but a piece of a worm-eaten leg from a Queen Anne chair provided walnut of a similar age: perhaps a total of one square inch was required, also a piece for a gap in the moulding above the foot and for the curved cross banding of the rounded corner. This was cut out of the solid in the manner indicated in C. A scrap of the old walnut was held in a drill-press vice against a piece of matching pine, both with the grain vertical. A one-inch hole was then drilled with a forstener bit to a depth of half an inch; after cutting off, the outer radius was cut with a bandsaw making a nice, clean corner.

Between the cross banding and the centre veneer of both top and drawer fronts is a white-black-white band, the black having been most likely dyed. As happens quite frequently, some of this had become worm-eaten. In places the insects will follow along the grain leaving a paper-thin strip on top; in others, it will have caved in and become filled with wax, dirt and polishes. Where this had happened it had of course to be renewed, and so three veneers were cut and worked to the correct thicknesses and glued together to provide stock from which the necessary strips were to be cut. Hawthorn was chosen as the best match for the white, and laburnum for the black, which had become so faded that ebony would have been altogether too dark.

When all the veneer was down and cleaned up, the question of finish arose; the faded colour being one of the piece's greatest assets. Heavy-handed scraping or sanding would have uncovered the darker wood beneath but the mildew had caused blackish stains in some places. This was a bit of a problem but they were eventually sufficiently reduced by a combination of judicious sanding alternating with the application of oxalic acid solution. Next, the filler; any form of oil filler would have been too dark and so a mixture of glue-size, silica and a very little yellow ochre was prepared and rubbed in hot; the surplus being wiped off with an almost dry, hot cloth. The result was most fortunate; all that now remained to be done was the application of minimal French polish followed by half-a-dozen waxings. The last photograph is the finished job, the right-hand side being untouched since leaving England.

A gilt Regency mirror

Illus 85A shows quite clearly the new central part of the ornamental cresting: what was originally there is of course unknown, the only indication being the 1½ inch mortice in the centre of the frame and the side swags.

No 2913 of Wallace Nutting's *Furniture Treasury* (The Macmillan Co 1954) provided the source for the design. This book, though mostly of American pieces, is very useful for this sort of thing, for it has 5,000 photographs grouped according to article. The one in question being English Hepplewhite was a good deal earlier and so the details had to be modified and made heavier to harmonise with the remainder of the frame.

A full-sized pattern of the new part was first made and placed in position to check the alignment of the side pieces which were to be notched into the ends of the centre part and screwed in place from the back. Everything being satisfactory, the three members were cut out of old pine, and morticed and tenoned together, the centre piece with horizontal grain being 1½in thick, the supporting section 1¼in and the finial 1in. They were shaped up with spokeshaves, files and carving tools and glued in place as seen in Illus 85A.

In Ernest Spon's *Workshop Receipts* dated 1888 the instructions for gilding picture mouldings include the following: '7 coats hot-size and whiting various with between-coat smoothings also various. Further smoothings with pumice stones and water, the stones made to fit the various members. 4 to 8 coats gold size followed by further smoothings. Gold leaf laid on whetted size, and, at a critical period of the drying process, partly burnished with polished flint or agate burnishers and the matt areas coated with thin gold size'. This is a bare bones outline of instructions taking a couple of pages, but is sufficient to suggest that, even if tools and materials were to hand, such a job is rarely practicable at a modern wage.

Because of the unyielding nature of the white coating it is not uncommon for the wooden foundation in shrinking to pull away, leaving a shell which can easily be crushed and flake off. This had happened in a number of places, notably the most prominent member of the moulding on the right-hand side. The first step was to scrape these areas, removing the gold paint which had been applied in an attempt to make them less noticeable: next, hot glue-size was brushed into them especially where looseness seemed probable.

The following day a dry mixture of one part whiting to two of fine sawdust was made; glue was heated and thinned and the procedure was as follows.

85 **A** *By permission of The Connoisseurs Shop, Victoria, B.C.* **B**

Place a brushful of glue in the palm of the left hand; add a modicum of the sawdust, mix with a palette knife which is also used to fill and smooth over the cavities leaving them a trifle proud. The success of this operation depends on good vision and finishing each section before it cools: the process is then repeated till all are filled up. At this stage, further smoothing may be achieved with a knife dipped in hot water which will momentarily soften the mixture as it passes. When thoroughly dry, the straight patches were levelled with a plane, others with carving tools and then medium-grade sandpaper.

Following this, a mixture of whiting and glue-size coloured with ochre and a pinch of lamp black was prepared and heated in an old glue pot: it should have the consistency of thick cream. The new part and the patches were given two fairly heavy coats with a six hour interval for drying, and then left for two or three days.

Now came a very thorough sandpapering, taking care to level any lumps, particularly in grooves and hollows, by folding the paper and using the fingers and fingernails: ending up with 150 garnet paper.

As the original gilding had deteriorated so much, a coating of banana oil with bronze powder was considered sufficient for the new and repaired areas. A tube marked 'Pale rich gold lining' seemed the best match and so a mixture was made and flowed on with a sable brush in a fairly heavy coat. This dried very well but appeared a little too bright against the old, and so a coat of very thin shellac tinted with raw umber was applied to tone it down at the same time using an old fad to wipe it off the high places so as to give the effect of dirt in the hollows. This resulted in a very good match which, for a purist, might well have been left; however, the author considered it rather dull and lifeless, and so a modicum of bronze powder was placed in a saucer; a scrap of cotton batt was moistened with banana oil; rubbed in the bronze and then passed lightly over the surface touching only the highlights of the carving and mouldings.

One of the nice things about this piece is the glass with its very flat and irregular bevel. The mercury silvering is in exceptionally good condition, suggesting that it had been 'new quick-silvered' during the dying years of this process which appears to have lasted till the eighteen-eighties. Illus 85B is the finished job.

Rope handles (or beckets) for sea-chests

The rope handles which formed such an important feature of a seaman's chest in the days of sail have very often become rotten and have been replaced in lubberly fashion with a piece of sash cord. Illus 86 shows the various stages of construction and a photograph of a reasonably satisfactory replacement.

The handle itself is made of a piece of $\frac{5}{16}$in diameter hemp signal halliard 30in long. First put a whipping of thin string 7in from each end and then fold back and tie again, forming eyes as shown in Illus 86A. Unlay the strands to this point and make eye splices in the ordinary way, tucking each strand five times: as may be seen in Illus 86B the strands overlap and each, after having been pulled very tight, has the last half inch tucked under a strand.

The object is now to thicken the centre four or five inches and to produce a smooth bulge tapered at each end on which a winding of string may be laid; in sailors' parlance this was known as serving and the material used was called spun yarn. To achieve this, take a piece of $\frac{3}{8}$in rope about 4in long, separate the strands and then tease out each end with a knife as seen in Illus 86C. Space these around the centre and tie with a piece of soft string or knitting wool, add bits of caulking cotton or cotton wool to fill up any hollows and then marl it down each side as seen to the right of C; hammer down any lumps and fill up any hollows. Now tightly bandage with a 1in strip cut from the leg of an old pair of pyjamas, continually checking for smoothness, and unwinding and restuffing where necessary.

The serving starts where the splice ends, the first ten turns being laid in the ordinary way; from here, each turn was hitched in the manner shown at D thus producing a spiral effect for the central portion; the method of finishing off is shown at E: simply take about a yard of string from the ball, lay it back holding it in the left hand, continue the serving for at least half-a-dozen turns

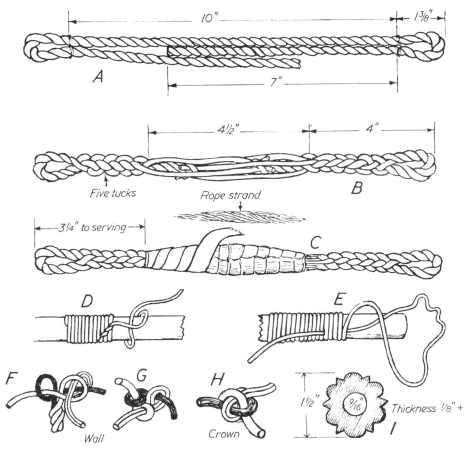

86 A

and then pull the surplus through and cut off. This finishes the handle itself except for bending into shape.

It is secured to the wooden block on the box by means of what might be called a rivet made of rope with a leather washer and a knob at each end. The washers, see Illus 86, are often spur-shaped and can be circular, octagonal or any other pattern. The knobs in this case are what is called a wall and crown knot and, hemp not being available, half-inch cotton rope was chosen; 15in being needed; 3in to pass through the eyes, washers and the 2in wood block and 6in for each knot.

First put a whipping of either string or masking tape 6in from the end of your rope: now whip each strand separately, for cotton is bad for unravelling (this is not necessary if it is hemp). Unlay to the whipping and work the wall, as in F, starting with the white strand which may be looped round a finger of the left hand. Follow with the black around the white, then the striped round the black and through the loop from which the finger is now removed. Pull each strand in turn, round and round, a little tighter each time until it is all snug, when the end should look like G. The crown (see H) is done in like fashion; the white over the finger and down to the left of the black, the black over it and

234

B

the striped over the black and through the loop in the white. Again snug up as before, ending as tightly as possible.

Next measure 9in from the wall, whip each side of the mark and cut. First thread on a washer, then one of the eyes, through the block, the other eye and washer; pull tight and work the other wall and crown. This is easier if the block can be removed from the chest, but the screws from inside are usually so rusted that it is quicker to do it in place.

Lastly the whole thing is given a heavy coat of canvas preservative or a thin mixture of varnish and turpentine; this will cement it together and prevent any unravelling. When dry, the ends are cut off short and you are ready to run away to sea.

There are, of course, infinite variations and embellishments found on old handles: some are served all over including the eyes, etc. In place of the wall and crown, a manrope or star knot may be used but the foundation is nearly always the same.

For further information on this subject, see *The Ashley Book of Knots* by Clifford W. Ashley, Doubleday & Co; or *Knots, Splices & Fancy Work* by C. L. Spencer.

Sources of Supply

Materials and services available, with key to suppliers

Adhesives and glues	A, B, L, M
Barometer tubes	H
Brass castings from sample or pattern	F
Carvings from sample or pattern	K
Clock parts and ornaments	E, G, H
Glass, mirrors, resilvering and bent glass	P
Glass domes and convex glasses	G
Identification of woods	Y
Inlay and marquetry	Q, A, B
Inlay, metal strips	T
Ivory and mother-of-pearl	R, S
Leather, tooled in blind or gilt for desk linings	I, J
Metal fittings, handles, locks, hinges etc	C, D, E, F, A, B
Music box and automata repairs	U, V
Polishing and wood-finishing supplies	L, M, N, A, B
Timber	A, B
Tools, hand	W, X
Upholsterers' supplies	O
Veneers	Q, A, B
Wrought-ironwork	C, E
General information and help	Z

The first two firms supply a great variety of products for the amateur and small shop and publish catalogues.

A   Albert Constantine & Son Inc, 2050 East Chester Road, Bronx, NY 10461

B   Craftsman Wood Service Co, 2727 South Murray Street, Chicago, Ill 60608 (A minimum charge is made for handling and postage.)

Metal fittings, handles, hinges, locks, etc

C   J. D. Beardmore & Co Ltd, 2-5 Percy Street, London W1P 0EJ. (Also ivory knobs Nos GC160 and 161 in various sizes.)

D   H. E. Savill, Sunwood, Weaponess, Scarborough, Yorkshire

E   Horton Brasses, Box 95, Nooks Hill Road, Cromwell, Conn 06416, USA

F   William F. Tillman Brassfounders Ltd, Crouch Lane, Borough Green, Kent TN15 8LT. (Also restorers and reproducers of antique furniture.)

Clock ornaments and parts

G   Southern Watch & Clock Supplies Ltd, 48 High Street, Orpington, Kent BR6 0JH

H   Garner & Manley, 41 Southgate Street, London N1

Makers of tooled leather desk linings

I   J. Crisp & Sons, Crispin Works, Hawley Street, Chalk Farm Road, London NW1 8BY. (Also upholsterers and antique leather restorers and craftsmen.)

J   Clements Linings, 6 Fullers Road, Woodford, London E18

Wood carvers

K   Frank Hudson & Son, Rosebery Avenue, Pinions, High Wycombe, Bucks HP13 7AH. (Also furniture reproductions.)

Polishing and finishing products

L   W. S. Jenkins & Co Ltd, Jeco Works, Tariff Road, Tottenham, Middlesex N17 0EN

M   Henry Flack Ltd, Borough Works, Croydon Road, Elmers End, Beckenham, Kent BR3 4BL

N   Mohawk Finishing Products Inc, Amsterdam, New York 12010 *or* 1121 Isabel Street, Burbank, California 91506 *or* 10130 Garon Street, Montreal-North, Quebec, Canada

Upholstery supplies

O   Biggs & Co, Worcester House, Worcester Park, Surrey

Glass

P   Sussex Glass Bevelling Co, 24 Castle Street, Brighton, Sussex

Veneers

Q J. Crispin & Sons, 92-96 Curtain Road, Shoreditch, London EC2A 3AA. (Also double knife-cut veneers in some species.)

Ivory and mother-of-pearl

R F. Friedlein & Co Ltd, 718 Old Ford Road, London E3 2TA. (Wholesale only.)

S Erica Banjos, 14731 Lull Street, Unit 3 Van Nuys, California 91405. (Minimum order $10.)

Since conservation measures have prohibited trade in these two products in a number of countries, the only practical source of supply may be salvage from old pieces.

Non-ferrous metals

T J. Smith & Sons (Clerkenwell) Ltd, 42-54 St John's Square, Clerkenwell, London EC1P 1ER

Music box and automata repairs

U Keith Harding, 96 Hornsey Road, London N7 6DJ. (Also musical and antique clock restorers.)

V George A. Bidden, Barrington, Rhode Island 02806, USA

Hand tools

W Parry & Sons, 325 Old Street, London EC1

X Woodcraft Supply Corp, 313 Montvale Avenue, Woburn, Mass 01801, USA

Identification of woods

Y The Director, Forest Products Research Laboratory, Princes Risborough, Aylesbury, Bucks

The Center for Wood Anatomy Research, Forest Products Laboratory, PO Box 5130, Madison, Wisconsin 53705, USA

General information and help

Z J. S. Learoyd, The Council for Small Industries in Rural Areas, Camp Road, Wimbledon Common, London SW19. (A government-sponsored organisation.)

Index